THE EUROPEAN PERSPECTIVE

The European Perspective

Transnational Party Groups in the 1989-1994
European Parliament

TAPIO RAUNIO
University of Turku

Ashgate

Aldershot • Brookfield USA • Singapore • Sydney

Published by
Ashgate Publishing Limited
Gower House
Croft Road
Aldershot
Hants GU11 3HR
England

Ashgate Publishing Company
Old Post Road
Brookfield
Vermont 05036
USA

British Library Cataloguing in Publication Data
Raunio, Tapio
 The European perspective : transnational party groups in
 the 1989-1994 European parliament
 1.European Parliament 2.Law - European Union countries
 I.Title
 341.2'424

Library of Congress Cataloging in Publication Data
Raunio, Tapio.
    The European perspective : transnational party groups in the
  1989-1994 European Parliament / Tapio Raunio.
      p.   cm.
    Includes bibliographical references.
    ISBN 1-85521-988-3
    1. European Parliament. 2. Political parties–European Union
  countries. I. Title.
  JN36.R33   1997
  324.2'094–dc21   97-19090
                                                              CIP

ISBN 1 85521 988 3

Printed in Great Britain by The Ipswich Book Company, Suffolk.

Contents

List of Figures and Tables

Figures

Tables

Preface

This book is a revised version of my doctoral thesis *Party Group Behaviour in the European Parliament*. The book is organised as follows.

The first chapter begins with a brief discussion on the role of the European Parliament and Europarties in the governance of the European Union. The literature review presents the state of scholarly research on the internal workings of the Strasbourg Parliament.

The theoretical framework is introduced in chapter 2. Intra-parliamentary decision-making is explained and the roles of the respective actors (individual members, committees, party groups) are analysed. Section 2.4. contains the main research question that will be subjected to empirical investigation in later chapters. The final section concludes the chapter with a brief discussion on the balance between endogenous and exogenous preferences.

Chapter 3 examines the evolution and institutionalisation of EP political groups, concentrating on the directly elected Parliament. The formal status, leadership structure, and the internal organisation of the party groups are analysed. The powers, composition, and role of the committees are also discussed. In section 3.5. the evolution of the EP party system, the institutional imperative of achieving legislative majorities, fractionalisation of the Parliament, and the voting power of the party groups in the 1979-1994 Parliament are investigated.

Voting behaviour analysis of the 1989-94 Parliament is in chapter 4. The mainly negative factors which have been argued to affect party group cohesion and coalition behaviour in the Strasbourg chamber are presented. Technical aspects of voting in the EP are explained. In section 4.5. the cohesion of party groups is analysed, focusing in particular on the relationship between party group heterogeneity and party cohesion. Section 4.6. introduces a comparative perspective into the study by comparing the unity of EP party groups with the cohesion of parliamentary parties in selected national legislatures. The nature of the EP party system is analysed in section 4.7 by measuring the voting similarity of the groups. In section 4.8. the effect of legislative majority requirements on party cohesion and coalition behaviour is examined. The voting behaviour of the party groups on foreign affairs issues is investigated. The final section summarises the results, and ends with a brief discussion on the relevance of the findings to the party structure of the current Parliament.

Chapter 5 contains a content analysis of parliamentary questions. The importance of questions in the context of national legislatures is discussed. Section 5.5. analyses in detail the evolution, processing, and function of parliamentary questions in the European Parliament. Turning to the presentation of results, the next section measures the questioning activity of party groups and national delegations. Section 5.7. examines the political profiles of the party groups, national delegations, and individual MEPs by categorising the written questions according to their subject dimension. In the next section (5.8.) the concept of representation is in turn discussed by analysing the questions on the basis of their territorial dimension. Section 5.9. examines the level of MEPs' questioning activity, and the variation between individual representatives. In the final section (5.10.) the findings are summarised, together with a brief discussion on the role and importance of parliamentary questions.

The first part of the concluding chapter serves as a summary of the arguments and results, with the second and final section analysing the future problems and prospects of Europarties.

Acknowledgements

Can we democratise international relations? Does transnational, or supranational, democracy work also in practice and not only in the minds of some political scientists? Interested in doing research on the democratisation of state-to-state relations, Professor Olavi Borg suggested to me in 1993 that I did postgraduate studies on the democratisation of the European Union and in particular on the European Parliament. I noticed that while there was an abundance of texts on the Parliament, surprisingly little research had been done on the individual members or the party groups in the Parliament. I thought that my contribution would not reduce the democratic deficit of the Union, but at least I could help reduce the existing deficit in our understanding of the way the Parliament works.

Several individuals deserve recognition for their valuable assistance during the past three years. I am greatly indebted to my two supervisors, Professor Olavi Borg and Associate Professor Matti Wiberg. Olavi Borg has supervised my work with much appreciated professionalism. His active interest in students' progress is a delight for persons who need positive and open encouragement. Olavi's experience in organisational matters made things much easier for me since I did not have to worry about the technical aspects or about arranging the necessary finances.

Without the help of Matti Wiberg the thesis would still be far from finished. His expertise, frank and insightful criticism, and always constructive comments were crucial factors in helping me to clarify and reconsider my own thoughts. We have discussed this work, among other things, in universities and bars in Turku and elsewhere in Europe. Finally, Matti put much effort into patiently reading various drafts of this work.

I am grateful to both external examiners, Professor Fulvio Attinà and Dr David M. Farrell, who read the text carefully and made several suggestions for improvements. Their insightful comments have been duly incorporated into the work. Both have also at an earlier stage read parts of the text and kindly offered their assistance when I needed advice. My sincere thanks to both of them.

Various colleagues have discussed the project with me over the years. I would like to mention in particular David S. Bell, Karl Magnus Johansson,

Robert Ladrech and Christopher Lord. The development of my ideas has benefited significantly from these conversations. Most of what is printed between these covers has been presented in numerous international conferences and national seminars. The comments I received during these meetings have substantially helped me in clarifying my arguments. Finally, Virpi Johansson at the Eurooppa-Instituutti in Turku assisted me in compiling the data and in tracing the right documents.

The research was facilitated by scholarships from the University of Tampere as part of the VAKAVA Graduate School programme and from Suomen Kulttuurirahasto.

This book is dedicated to my mother and father. Both have in their own special way contributed to my work. Their love, material support, and experience from academic life has been of immeasurable help throughout the often rather lonely and tiresome process of writing the thesis.

Tapio Raunio
Turku, 30 January 1997

List of Abbreviations

CAP	Common Agricultural Policy
CDI	Technical Group of Co-ordination and Defence of Independent MEPs
CFSP	Common Foreign and Security Policy
COM	Communist and Allies Group
COREPER	Committee of the Permanent Representatives of the Member States
CSPEC	Confederation of Socialist Parties of the European Community
EB	Eurobarometer
EC	European Community
ECSC	European Coal and Steel Community
ECU	European Currency Unit
EDA	European Democratic Alliance
EDG	European Democratic Group
EE	European elections
EEC	European Economic Community
EFA	European Free Alliance
EFGP	European Federation of Green Parties
ELD	Federation of Liberal and Democratic Parties of the European Community
ELDR	European Liberal, Democrat and Reformist Party
EMU	Economic and Monetary Union
EN	Europe of the Nations
EP	European Parliament
EPC	European Political Co-operation
EPP	European People's Party
ER	European Right
ERA	European Radical Alliance
EU	European Union
EUI	European University Institute
EUL	Group of the United European Left
FE	Forza Europa

GRAEL	Green Alternative European Link
IGC	Intergovernmental Conference
LU	The Left Unity Group
MEP	Member of the European Parliament
MP	Member of Parliament
NA	Non-Attached
PES	Party of the European Socialists
PQ	Parliamentary Question
RB	Rainbow Group
SEA	Single European Act
STD	Standard deviation
UPE	Union for Europe
V	The Greens

1 European Parliament and the Governance of the European Union

1.1. Democracy, Federalism and the Development of Europarties

What is the relationship between the internal organisation of the European Parliament (EP) and the behaviour of its party groups and the individual members of the Parliament (MEPs)? How do the structural properties of the Parliament facilitate the cohesion of the party groups? How cohesive are the transnational party groups inside the Parliament? Whom do the elected representatives see themselves as representing? How are the various partisan and territorial interests accommodated inside the chamber? How does co-operation work inside the Parliament between and within transnational party groups?

When thumbing through recent literature on democracy and political participation in nation-states, it is obvious that one of the main concerns is the distance between the decision-making system and the average citizens. Various contributors have emphasised the need to narrow that distance, to bring politics closer to the people. However, far less attention has been paid to another parallel problem, that of involving people in the governance of international relations.

No interested observer can deny that international governance is assuming new forms. International, or inter-state, relations used to be the private playground of governments and diplomats. But this is no longer the case. A whole range of supra/transnational non-governmental organisations and movements share the international public space together with more traditional forms of international co-operation. The proliferation of various multinational corporations, environmental and human rights organisations, sectoral associations, and other movements bring together citizens across the established borders of nation-states. This co-operation is obviously still limited to a rather thin layer of people, and most likely this will remain the case. But most people are in one way or another aware of, or at least feel the effects of, the developments occurring outside their nation-states. Therefore questions concerning alternative forms of international governance are ones that deserve the attention of scholars.

The European Union (EU) constitutes one, and arguably the most developed, example of a new form of international governance. The term European Union is used throughout this work to refer to (i) the various forms of European-level decision-making taking place in the context of the current three-pillar structure of the EU (internal matters, common security and foreign policy, and co-operation in justice and home affairs), and (ii) the citizens and territory belonging to the Union.

The evolution of European integration has mainly been the result of intergovernmental negotiation, with bargaining, compromise-seeking and mutual adjustment providing the key phrases for understanding EU's development over the past four decades. Integration has proceeded through various phases: from its early stages as the European Coal and Steel Community (ECSC); to the signing of the Treaty of Rome in 1957 establishing the European Economic Community (EEC); through the drawbacks and partial stagnation of integration in the 1960s and 1970s; to the Single European Act (SEA) in 1987 and the Maastricht Treaty on European Union which came into force in November 1993.

What is significant is that even though amendments to the EU 'constitution', the Treaty of Rome, have always required the signatures of member state heads of state or government, non-governmental actors have been instrumental in bringing the whole project about and in keeping it going. Determined and influential individuals, powerful economic lobbies, political parties, economic and political changes taking place in third countries, and the supranational agencies in Brussels and Strasbourg, mainly the Commission and the European Parliament, have all been important factors in shaping the continent's future. The process of integration has evolved as an interplay of all these factors, with the ascendancy of a particular explanatory factor depending on the time period and/or the policy sector being investigated.

During recent years, in particular since the adoption of the SEA and the Maastricht Treaty on European Union, a number of academic works have recognised the originality and multi-level nature of political organisation in Europe of the 1990s. Scholars working in the fields of international relations and political science have too often perceived the integration

2

process as having a certain determinism about it or a particular blueprint to follow. To quote Sbragia:

"perhaps most important, the possibility of exercising originality in designing future Community institutions is not fully acknowledged. Ironically, the debate over future institutional development does not live up to the originality of institutional design manifested at the time of the Community's founding." (Sbragia, 1992: 260-261)

With the completion of the internal market and the passing of the Maastricht Treaty, the EU can now be characterised as a federalist system, no matter how unique or peculiar it may be in comparison with other federal-type structures. Federalism is here understood more than anything else as a process or as a political ideology.

"Federalism has been examined as political ideology in the precise sense that it reflects values and beliefs which recommend specific forms of federation. The particular type of federation prescribed is determined by the particular configuration of interests which seek actively and purposively to benefit from state-building and institutional reconstruction. Federations vary widely because federalisms are similarly diverse. There is, however, no simple causal relationship between these two distinct phenomena. We can understand them only by constant reference to their continuous interaction." (Burgess, 1993b: 112)

Treating the EU as a federal system does not, however, imply that there would necessarily be some rigid and permanent model of division of authority between the central organs at the European level and the member state institutions. While precise and understandable constitutional rules are definitely needed to clarify the powers of the respective institutions, the history of federations and federalist systems has shown that rigid separation of powers is often unworkable in real life situations requiring adjustment and procedural flexibility (Chapman, 1993). The experience so far has shown that the implementation of, and adjustment to, directives and regulations pouring out of Brussels is often a slow and cumbersome process. Furthermore, decisions taken at European level need to be balanced against local needs and national traditions. Simple references to federal decision-making can prove to be a bad tactic of selling EU to the public if people feel their vital interests are threatened or continuously ignored.

This problem has become more important during recent years as the government representatives in the Council of Ministers have been forced to recognise that support for decisions taken by them has not necessarily been forthcoming from the electorate. Referenda held on Maastricht in Denmark and France sent warning signals throughout the Union, while *Eurobarometers*[1] have shown that while in general supportive of the broad goal of European integration, the citizens in EU member states are ambivalent and sceptical about further moves to deepen integration.

The European Union is still very much alive, with the direction of its future evolution uncertain. The current intergovernmental conference (IGC) that began in March 1996 has revealed the lack of consensus between member states on the nature of the EU polity. However, the EU does constitute a specific territorially defined political system, where decisions at the central level are taken concerning both *internal* policies and *external* relations with third countries or organisations. The EU does therefore possess a 'domestic' arena of its own. As Simon Hix argues in his discussion on academic works on European integration:

> "the political questions in the EC system are no longer simply issues of faster or slower, or more or less, 'integration'. The launch of the Single Market programme inherently introduced an 'internal' arena of conflict in the Community. The acquis communitaire now involves decision-making on questions of 'domestic' rather than 'international' politics; such as the regulation of the market place, the implementation of environment and industrial policies, and the reallocation of substantial economic resources under the regional and social funds (beyond the level of simple 'side-payments')." (Hix, 1994b: 11)

Discussions on democratisation and political participation *inside* the EU have in recent years focused on rather vague albeit very important concepts such as federalism, subsidiarity, and transparency of decision-making. While nation-states are still recognised as important factors in the political organisation of Europe, various authors have pointed out the increasing relevance of both sub-national levels of democracy and decision-making and various supranational agencies such as the European Parliament. Given these simultaneous tendencies or aspirations towards decentralisation and supra/transnational co-operation, academics and politicians have entered a lively debate concerning the institutional solutions required to meet the demands of Europe's future political organisation.[2]

The debate consists primarily of two dimensions: *where* matters are decided, and *what* gets decided. Especially since the 'relaunch' of the integration process in the mid-1980s, "we have seen considerable political battles concerning fora rather than outcome" (Weiler, Haltern, and Mayer, 1995: 27). At the European level discussion has tended to focus on power-relations between the member states and/or the various EU-institutions. Voting power analyses, for example, have shown the significant effect the choice between various majority rules and seat distributions can have on the influence of member states in the Council and in the Parliament.[3] Research on decision-making under the various legislative procedures (consultation, assent, co-operation, co-decision) has, on the other hand, examined the respective powers of the Commission, the Council, and the Parliament.[4]

As a part of that institutional build-up the EP has been fighting hard in order not to lose out when the formal powers of the respective EU institutions are decided upon. As the only directly-elected European-level institution, it has usually based its claims on the twin pillars of legitimacy and representativeness, highlighting the existing 'democratic deficit' prevailing in the context of EU decision-making system.[5] With gradually more competences being shifted to the European level, and national parliaments in a weak position to control the deliberations in the Council of Ministers, especially since the substantial increase of qualified majority voting in the Council following the SEA, there is a need to balance this national-level deficit by making the intergovernmental negotiations accountable to the EP. While the continued role of national parliaments in the governance and democratisation of the EU is widely recognised, the EP is arguably better placed (both informationally and by virtue of the Parliament being an EU institution) to subject the passage of EU-level legislation to parliamentary scrutiny than national parliaments that are already suffering from heavy workload.

But what has been the contribution of political parties? In an oft-quoted passage, Ernst Haas argued in the late 1950s that since they

> "appeal to an overlapping and diffuse group constituency political parties are far more crucial carriers of political integration or disintegration than even supranationally organised interest groups." (Haas, 1958: 437)

Political parties are, and indeed have been, "crucial carriers of political integration", with national parties (elites, activists, and electorates) endorsing and even initiating the moves made to unify Europe. But transnational party co-operation has so far been slow to develop.

With the prospect of direct elections to the EP - held eventually in June 1979 - looming in the distance, EC national parties, or at least party elites, had from the mid-1970s onwards an electoral incentive to pay more attention to European politics, and the forthcoming first ever transnational election led to the intensification of party co-operation at the European level. The three main ideological families in Europe - the Socialists, the Christian Democrats, and the Liberals - established party federations in anticipation of the direct elections. The Confederation of Socialist Parties of the European Community (CSPEC) was created first in 1974, and the Federation of Liberal and Democratic Parties of the European Community (ELD) was created two years later. Christian Democrats were the only party family to directly form a European party, The European Popular Party. Established in 1976, the party later changed its name to European People's Party (EPP).

The party federations lost little time in responding to the 'party article' (article 138a) in the Treaty on European Union. This article recognised for the first time officially the role political parties were meant to play in the integration process. The article reads:

"Political parties at European level are important as a factor for integration within the Union. They contribute to forming a European awareness and to expressing the political will of the citizens of the Union."

The Party of European Socialists (PES) was established in November 1992, and the European Liberal, Democrat and Reformist Party (ELDR) was created in December 1993. Also the Greens and regionalist parties have established transnational links. Building on already existing, but rather weakly developed, co-operation, the Federation of Green Parties (EFGP) was established in June 1993, and regionalist parties created the European Free Alliance (EFA) as their umbrella organisation in 1981 (Lynch, 1994).

Despite naming themselves European-level parties, these transnational parties have remained rather weak outside the European Parliament. This has been clearly evident in the resources of transnational parties and federations: according to Simon Hix (1995: 535) they "have been nothing more than clearing houses; providing information, campaign materials, and organising (poorly attended) conferences and candidate exchanges." Even though these parties have recently become more important by providing forums of policy co-ordination for national party leaders, some of whom are member state heads of government, prior to the EU Summits (Hix, 1993, 1994a, 1995), the transnational party organisations are still financially dependent on their respective EP party groups, with little staff and resources of their own (Bardi, 1992, 1994). Alas, the main arena for transnational party co-operation is found inside the European Parliament.

According to Philip Norton (1995: 192) "the EP has increased its powers enormously, but could be described as still only on the edge of constituting a legislature." The Parliament is clearly behind the legislatures of the EU member states as far as its formal powers are concerned: there is no EU government nominated by the Parliament as found in the member states, and despite the introduction of the various legislative procedures, in many areas falling under Union's competences it has no formal powers at all, being reduced to the role of a mere outsider eager to criticise the lack of democracy at European level. Furthermore, it has to be kept in mind that several important policy areas - such as co-operation under the second (Common Foreign and Security Policy (CFSP)) and third pillars (Justice and Home Affairs (JHA) - are still primarily governed by intergovernmental co-operation and remain thus formally outside the EP's framework.

The first meeting of the ECSC Common Assembly, EP's predecessor, was held in September 1952. The first Assembly had 78 members. Following the establishment of the EEC in 1957, the enlarged (142 members) Assembly was renamed the Parliamentary Assembly. In March 1962 the Assembly unilaterally decided to call itself the European Parliament. The size of the Parliament was further extended to 198 MEPs after the accession of Denmark, Ireland, and the UK to the EC in 1973. First direct elections to the Parliament were held in June 1979, and the number of members was further increased to 410. Following the successive enlargements of EC/EU to include Greece (1981), Portugal and Spain (1986), the former East Germany, and Austria, Finland, and Sweden (1995), the Parliament currently consists of 626 directly elected representatives.

Reduced originally to an assembly with mere consultative functions, the legislative role of the Parliament has been considerably strengthened over the last three decades. A significant break was made in 1970 and 1975 when the EP was given budgetary powers. The SEA introduced two new legislative procedures, the assent and co-operation procedures, with the former applying to accession and association agreements with third countries, and the latter used mainly in connection with legislation required for the completion of the internal market. The SEA was also the first time the title European Parliament was officially recognised in the Treaty. The Maastricht Treaty increased EP's powers by introducing the co-decision procedure (which applies roughly to the items previously covered by the co-

7

operation procedure), and by extending the use of assent and co-operation procedures, and by giving the Parliament a formal role in the appointment of the Commission.

The Parliament has also significant advantages when compared to national legislatures: in control of its own agenda it is free to debate any issue it chooses; the lack of an EU government means that it takes decisions independent of the executive branch; and with its transnational composition the MEPs are exposed to a diversity of information arguably not found in any other European-level decision-making forum.[6]

The European Parliament is a part of a federalist political system, the European Union. EU itself is built on, and draws its legitimacy from, the citizens and national political elites of its member states. While its members are elected from constituencies inside the individual member states, the Parliament has from the very beginning chosen to base its internal organisation on the principle of trans/supranationalism, with MEPs sitting in transnational party groups. Such a decision was based on the need to avoid the consolidation and dominance of national voting blocs inside the Parliament. Therefore the work of the representatives in Strasbourg consists of both territorial and ideological representation. These two aspects of representation are naturally present also in other parliaments, but the nature of the EU together with the transnational composition of the Parliament gives this duality a stronger role than in national legislatures. This duality - with representatives elected from member states but sitting in trans/supranational political groups - indeed distinguishes the EP and other transnational parliaments from more traditional forms of international governance (Kuper, 1991; Kuper and Jun eds., 1997).

Obviously members' priorities will vary. However, if the Parliament, and decisions taken by it, are to be perceived as legitimate throughout the Union, these two dimensions of representation must be accommodated. This does not imply that both dimensions of representation could or should be accommodated in every policy choice, but that MEPs from, and electorates in, a particular member state may come to re-evaluate the EP and the whole integration process were they given reason to feel that their interests are neglected inside the Parliament. "A central feature of federalism has been its capability of establishing varying balances between centripetal and centrifugal forces. Difficulties emerge only when a sense of unfair treatment, perceived or real, is being felt by communities." (Gagnon, 1993: 26) It is therefore a matter of 'getting the balance right'.

8

But how much do we in fact know about the Parliament in Strasbourg? How well does it fulfil its representative function? Whom do the elected representatives see themselves as representing? What is the relationship between the citizens and the Parliament? How are the various partisan and territorial interests accommodated inside the chamber? How does co-operation work inside the Parliament between and within transnational party groups? Do parliamentarians develop broader interests as a result of their work in the Strasbourg chamber?

1.2. Academic Importance and Practical Relevance

Regardless of what the future holds for the Parliament, and more specifically what the outcome of the on-going IGC will be, it is important to identify and analyse the special features of the EP as a legislature. *Research on the EP has both practical relevance and academic importance: former is explained by the Parliament's increased powers, and latter justified by lack of scholarly knowledge on the EP.* Despite the growing amount of works on the Strasbourg Parliament, both the membership and the internal organisation of EP have remained under-researched, as argued by Shaun Bowler and David Farrell:

"so far little attention has been given to the membership of the EP. ...At the heart of many of these debates lies an implicit (and unanswered) question: How prepared is the EP to take on a more powerful role as a representative institution? One reason why this question remains unanswered is that not much is known of how the EP functions as a representative body under current conditions. A fundamental question thus becomes how do MEPs function as representatives in the current situation?" (Bowler and Farrell, 1992a: 1-2)

Elsewhere the same authors argue in similar fashion:

"Despite the fact that the EP represents an intriguing example of an institution under construction, and of a parliament seeking to assert itself in an age of 'parliamentary decline', its internal workings are still largely unexplored. Moreover, how that institution is constructed will have consequences for the future path of European Union development, particularly for addressing such issues as the resolution of the 'democratic deficit', and the implementation of the (still vague) process of 'subsidiarity'." (Bowler and Farrell, 1995: 240-241)

9

This work seeks to redress this deficit by increasing our understanding of the EP, specifically of the important relationship between Parliament's internal organisation and the behaviour of its transnational party groups and individual representatives. Analysing the way in which intra-parliamentary organisational attributes influence the behaviour of parliamentarians and political groups is crucial for understanding the work and input of the whole legislature in the EU inter-institutional system.

Political science must also be forward-looking. Since political institutions are directly concerned with questions such as the representation and allocation of values, the design of political institutions needs and deserves to be taken seriously. As Michael Th. Greven has commented:

"most of our thoughts are post facto; they have no practical perspective, they do not aspire to change reality, and they do not contribute to political debate. But today this reality is changing rapidly, and perhaps we cannot afford to face these changes without inventing new institutions based on theoretical and empirical knowledge provided by political science. Some of the problems just mentioned clearly indicate that the path of developing our democratic institutions must go beyond the political form and the accepted restrictions of nation-states, not merely in any utopian sense of a 'one world scenario', but with the tendency to overcome the merely intergovernmental character of international politics and political regimes which is still dominant in the process of European unification." (Greven, 1995: 472-473)

Whether one wishes to see the EU develop towards a fully-fledged federal political union or not, the gradual transfer of competences from the national to the EU level has created a practical need for discussion on present, new and alternative forms of political organisation required at the European level. Since European integration and its further evolution is primarily based on the voluntary co-operation of its member states, each with its own separate national identity, history, culture, language(s), aims, and preferences, the construction of such political institutions is an exercise worthy of special attention. As Michael Burgess argues:

"Political science itself should contemplate new models of federal union. Political scientists have the responsibility to engage the contemporary debate about new federal structures and institutions from the standpoint of practical relevance." (Burgess, 1993a: 10-11)

The aim of this work is far less ambitious. Instead of suggesting or designing alternative political institutions, *the research contributes to debate by providing new information on the way the existing institutions work.* Without such knowledge, based on empirical analysis that can be replicated, it would be impossible to identify the features of current institutions, and to compare them with the performance of alternative forms of political organisation. More specifically, since the European Parliament is the only transnational assembly vested with legislative powers, we can examine its modes of operation vis-à-vis other more traditional forms of international governance.

Students of both international relations and political science have written extensively on globalisation and interdependence and their consequences. Europe is the continent where regional co-operation is by far at the most advanced stage, but other regions are also forced to consider similar solutions to problems of policy co-ordination, economic development, and peaceful coexistence.

Regional parliaments are already functioning in Central and South America, and calls for a stronger role of such institutions, as part of a more democratic international order, have been made (Held, 1995: 108). Obviously regional parliaments are only one of many available institutional solutions to meet the demands of future political organisation. Regional assemblies could perhaps be viewed as "sharing a transnational public space" with nation-states and transnationally organised societal movements (Peterson, 1992: 376). However, for such a process to become reality, this would require a steady and long-lasting commitment from member state governments to invest in the development of regional co-operation, a commitment which may well not be forthcoming (Kuper and Jun eds., 1997; Sabic, 1994).

1.3. Literature Review: Probable But Not Proven - Lack of Empirical Research

Reflecting the overall situation regarding literature on the European Union, there is definitely no shortage of works on the EP. An overwhelming majority of the publications deal with direct elections, the so-called 'democratic deficit' prevailing in the Union, the systemic inter-institutional functions of the Parliament, and the history and emergence of transnational political parties. This section introduces the current state of scholarly

11

research on the Parliament's party groups. The literature review shows that the existing works are primarily historical and descriptive: little empirical research has so far been done on the internal organisation of the EP, its party groups, and the MEPs. The hypotheses, predictions, and arguments put forth still lack empirical testing.

The majority of the publications deal with the directly elected EP, but the most important works from the days of the nominated Parliament are also introduced. An overwhelming majority of the publications listed below are in English, with some also in German, French, Dutch, and Italian. There are obviously general texts and brief articles on the Parliament in almost all EU languages. These have also been omitted from the review as they normally contain no additional data to the sources mentioned below. The review discusses the contents of the publications together with their main findings, and the aspects of the Parliament that still remain under-studied.[7]

In order to analyse the role and function of party groups, it is essential to understand the inter-institutional context in which the Parliament operates. There are a number of textbook accounts available in most main EU languages on the Parliament, describing its evolution as an institution, its legislative role, and its internal modes of operation. The standard work in English is *The European Parliament* by Francis Jacobs, Richard Corbett, and Michael Shackleton (1992, 1995). Now in its third edition, the book is very comprehensive and benefits from inside information to complement its overall descriptive approach. Another recent and largely similar textbook is *A Modern Guide to the European Parliament* by Martin Westlake (1994c). While these sources have been labelled as 'textbooks', these works are in fact the only sources of information regarding many aspects of EP's organisation, and similarly their descriptions of EP's legislative role and evolution as an institution are better than many sources with a more narrow research focus. An excellent, and very readable, introduction to the evolution of the Parliament from its early days in the 1950s to its current role is found in *The European Community in the Historical Context of its Parliament* (EP, 1992), which contains the proceedings of a symposium arranged by the Parliament to celebrate its 40th anniversary. The book is a collection of brief papers given by people who have themselves been influential members of the institution or otherwise closely involved in its work. There are also several briefer general introductions to the work of EP, describing its internal organisation and inter-institutional position. Information on the MEPs and on European elections is found in *The Times Guide to the European Parliament* which is published every five years after the EP elections (Wood ed., 1989; Morgan ed., 1994). The book introduces the members of the Parliament (age, background, contacts with extra-parliamentary organisations, occupation), the results of the elections in each member state, and offers a brief overview of the outgoing Parliament and the main challenges facing the newly elected representatives.

The Parliament's position vis-à-vis the Commission and the Council of Ministers has undergone significant changes throughout the decades as EP has acquired more influence. These changes in EP's formal powers have been well documented in the general texts mentioned above, but a number of works have also studied the inter-institutional dynamics in more detail. Perhaps the best and most comprehensive work on EP's various functions is that by Eberhard Grabitz et al. (1988), *Direktwahl und Demokratisierung - Eine Funktionenbilanz des Europäischen Parlaments nach der ersten Wahlperiode*. The volume contains much data on the Parliament's output (legislative acts, reports, questions, debate topics etc.), and through a number of chapters on case studies illustrates EP's influence in the EU decision-making process. The period under analysis covers mainly the first elected Parliament of 1979-84, and therefore EP's role has since then changed and become more important. Data from the same project is also presented in the article by Bourguignon-Wittke et al. (1985). Also of German origin is another closely related study, *Das Europäische Parlament im dynamischen Integrationsprozeß: Auf der Suche nach einem zeitgemäßen Leitbild*, edited by Otto Schmuck and Wolfgang Wessels (1989), which analyses Parliament's performance in fulfilling three functions: policy-shaping, system-shaping, and interaction with the electorate (see also EP 1989a; Wessels, 1992). Martin Westlake's *The Commission and the Parliament: Partners and Rivals in the European Policy-making Process* (1994b) gives a thorough analysis of the relationship between the Commission and the Parliament. The book covers both the formal and informal contacts between the two institutions. The relationship between national legislatures and the EP has recently attracted scholarly attention. The country reports in *Parliaments and Parties: The European Parliament in the Political Life of Europe*, edited by Roger Morgan and Clare Tame (1996), trace the intensity and quality of co-operation between the legislatures, and analyse the way the work of the Strasbourg Parliament is perceived in the member state capitals. A useful summary of the four Euroelections is in turn provided in *Voice of the People: The European Parliament in the 1990s* by Julie Smith (1995) which also includes a chapter on the internal organisation and powers of the Parliament.

Publications on transnationalisation or europeanisation of parties *outside* the Parliament have on the whole been few and far between, excluding the books and articles focusing on the European elections and making passing mention of the role of transnational parties in them. This is only natural, considering the limited scope of party co-operation between the elections.

National parties in member states have in general been fairly supportive of the integration process. Familiarity with research on national parties' European policies is essential in order to understand the evolution of transnational party co-operation in the context of European integration. After all, transnational political groups in the EP consist of national party delegations to these groups. Research on the national parties' policies towards European integration has been dominated by publications looking at individual parties' adaptation to the integration process. There have been hardly any comparative cross-national surveys on parties' relationship with the EU. Even the recent volume edited by John Gaffney (1996), titled *Political Parties and the European Union*, suffers from this shortcoming. The volume includes however useful summaries on the EU-policies of the communist (Bell, 1996), the extreme right-wing (Fieschi, Shields, and Woods, 1996), and the green (Rüdig, 1996) party families, and individual chapters on party politics at the European level. European Parliament's (1988) own study contains a comparative analysis of the European policies of the national parties of the then twelve EC member states. Kevin Featherstone (1986, 1988) has traced the evolution of socialist parties' policies towards integration.

The approaching direct elections of 1979 gave a further stimulus to co-operation among European national parties. This institutionalisation of transnational party co-operation also received the attention of a number of scholars. The two main works from this era are *Transnational Party Co-operation and European Integration. The Process Towards Direct Elections* by Geoffrey Pridham and Pippa Pridham (1981) and *Europäische Parteien? Zur grenzüberschreitenden Interaktion politischer Parteien im Rahmen der Europäischen Gemeinschaft* by Oskar Niedermayer (1983). Both of these books are data-rich and include also lengthy references to party co-operation inside the European Parliament. Other works from the same period include Hrbek (1976), Claeys and Loeb-Mayer (1979), and Pridham and Pridham (1979a,c). These early contributions all identified several obstacles that stood in the way of transnationalisation of party politics. The diversity of national political cultures, the ideological discrepancies between parties belonging to the same federation, the lack of progress in European integration, the primacy of national over European politics, and the weak powers accorded to the EP were hypothesised to influence the degree or quality of co-operation achieved between the parties both outside and within the Parliament.

During the 1980s scholarly interest in transnational parties declined, but the relaunch of the integration process during the last decade has led to a renewed interest in the role of transnational party co-operation. These publications naturally focus exclusively on Europe, with the exception being the recent study by Ernst Kuper (1995), *Transnationale Parteienbünde zwischen Partei- und Weltpolitik*, in which the author, utilising party programmes and interviews, also extends his comparative analysis of the development of transnational party co-operation outside Europe.

The organisational aspects (staff, funding, formal rules) of transnational party federations have been analysed by Luciano Bardi (1992, 1994). Simon Hix (1993, 1994a, 1995) has undertaken content analyses of the transnational parties' programmes and examined their participation and input in the framework of the wider EU decision-making system, especially in connection with the EU Summits. A recent chapter by the same author (Hix, 1996) offers a very useful outline on the emergence, membership, and role of the transnational parties. Chapters by Ladrech and Brown-Pappamikail (1995), Lécureuil (1996), and Pedersen (1996) discuss the nature of transnational parties and the inter-institutional environment in which they operate.

Other scholars have mainly focused on individual transnational parties or on a particular aspect of transnational party co-operation. The work by Karl Magnus Johansson (1993, 1996) on the rapprochement between the EPP and the Conservatives provides an interesting insight into the formal and informal aspects of international party co-operation. Hanley's (1994) chapter looks also at the EPP, explaining its functions and evolution towards 'a new party form'.

Comparative analyses of party groups are mainly from the days of the nominated Parliament. The early stages have been well covered in *The Political Parties in the European Parliament: The First Ten Years (September 1952 - September 1962)* by Guy Van Oudenhove (1965). The article by Zellentin (1967) examines the various divisions found in the chamber: roll-call analysis of the cohesion of the groups and national delegations, attitudinal differences on major issues between the party groups, and the use of parliamentary questions by groups. The chapter by Henig and Pinder (1969) offers an excellent discussion on the party groups in the 1950s and 1960s, and compares the role of EP party groups with party groups in other international assemblies. *The Party Groups in the European Parliament* by John Fitzmaurice (1975) provides a clear and informative account of party groups, including chapters on individual groups, an analysis of their cohesion and the influence of external factors on the behaviour of party groups and the EP. Utilising primarily interviews, Geoffrey Pridham and Pippa Pridham (1979b, 1981) throw light on the evolution and practices of intra-party co-operation and organisation within party groups.

Transnational party groups have not been equally well covered in the directly elected Parliament. What literature there is on party groups relies far too often on hasty judgements that are not backed up by sufficient evidence. More positive assessments of the party groups have so far been in the minority. But while most contributions amount to little more than general discussions, a number of scholars have undertaken research to analyse the cohesion and behaviour of EP parties.

The work of Fulvio Attinà is significant in this respect. He has measured party group cohesion by roll-call analysis in the first and second terms of the directly elected Parliament (1990, 1992a), and his results enable me to introduce a longitudinal element into this research. In subsequent publications and papers Attinà (1992a,b, 1993, 1994a,b, 1997) has examined the nature of the EP party system (based mainly on coalition behaviour at national level), the various factors enhancing and impeding party cohesion and co-operation in the Parliament, the impact of the electoral formulas used, and the question of seat distribution between the member states.

The roll-call analysis of Leon Hurwitz (1983, 1987) is much more limited, based on a very small sample and covering only a short time-span right after the first direct elections to the EP. Menno Wolters and Marcel Quanjel have in their roll-call analyses measured voting likeness between the political groups, the cohesion of the groups, and voting in committees (Wolters, 1982, 1988; Quanjel and Wolters, 1992, 1993). The data set consists of a sample of votes taken in the first three elected Parliaments. Joanne Bay Brzinski (1995) measures party group cohesion in the 1989-1994 EP by a roll-call analysis and by examining the members' level of absenteeism during voting periods. However, the reliability of the cohesion indices computed by Bay Brzinski is very debatable considering the small number of votes included in her sample. The previous works by the present author (Raunio, 1995, 1996b,c, 1997a,b) analyse the voting behaviour of party groups in the 1989-94 EP by a roll-call analysis based on a sample of 159 votes. These studies are partly reproduced here in chapters 3 and 4.

Simon Hix and Christopher Lord (1996) have in turn examined the interaction between domestic and EP party politics by analysing the MEPs' voting behaviour in the vote on the nomination of Jacques Santer as the President of the Commission.

Several authors have undertaken case studies of individual party groups. The work of Sweeney (1984) looks at the ideological problems facing the left, the Socialists and the Communists, in the Parliament. Chapters by Bomberg (1993) and Buck (1989) focus on the problems, organisational and ideological, that faced the Rainbow Group - and in particular the Green contingent in it - in the second elected EP, while the study by Bowler and Farrell (1992b) charts the profile of the Green group in the 1989-94 Parliament. Ewing (1989) gives an informal insider's account of the discipline and hierarchy of the smaller groups. Thomas (1992) has used a combination of party programmes and interviews to assess British MEPs' influence on, and co-operation with, their national parties back home. Vallance and Davies (1986) have studied the influence and activity of women members in the Parliament.

Turning to studies focusing primarily on the EP party system, Rattinger (1982) examined the distances between party groups by a survey asking the MEPs to place the groups in rank order according to the proximity of the groups from their own group, and was thus on the basis of the replies able to compute the various possible coalitions and their voting strengths. Five studies have measured voting power in the Parliament by using the well-known Shapley-Shubik and Banzhaf power indices. Research by Fowler, Polhuis, and Paine (1983) covers the period from 1952 to 1981 and analyses the voting power of national delegations, party groups, and also national delegations within party groups. In their article on voting power in the EU institutions, Herne and Nurmi (1993) analyse the voting power of the political groups in the directly elected Parliament. Unfortunately, however, the seat distribution between party groups is erroneous in their work, thus largely invalidating the results. Similarly in the study by Lane, Maeland and Berg (1996), analysing voting power in the Council and in the Parliament, the authors measure the voting power of imagined 'party families' instead of actual party groups as they exist in the Parliament, and therefore the results are of somewhat dubious value. The recent manuscript by Peters (1996b) includes data on the voting power of national delegations, the party groups, and the national delegations within the Socialist and EPP groups in the 1994 and 1995 Parliaments. The most comprehensive work dealing with the voting power of the party groups is Wiberg and Raunio (1997), which offers a detailed analysis of the groups' voting power under different majority requirements in the directly elected Parliament (see section 3.5.).

The insider's account in Arndt (1992) contains valuable information on the institutionalisation of the process of inter-party bargaining in the chamber. In his recent article Luciano Bardi (1996) has examined the effect of European elections on the EP party system, arguing that while institutionalisation of party groups occurs during the legislative term, the elections can be very disruptive especially on the smaller groups, thus causing realignments at the start of each five-year legislative term. Delwit and De Waele (1995) also analyse the impact of European elections on the EP party system. The chapter by Robert Ladrech (1996) includes a discussion on the current role of EP party groups, on the problems facing them, as well as on the prospects of a more politicised (left-right) nature of EU party politics. Johansson's (1997) illustrative chapter analyses the nature of intra- and inter-group dynamics in the Parliament, and uses two individual votes, the Santer vote and the vote on the latest EU enlargement, to highlight the interaction between EP party politics and domestic politics.

Surveys of MEPs and candidates in EP elections have tapped their attitudes to several items relating to European integration and transnational parties. The attitudinal socialisation of representatives in the nominated Parliament was studied by Kerr (1973). Based on a survey carried out in 1967-68, Kerr compared the 'europeanisation' of French and German MEPs and national MPs, and found that work in the Strasbourg chamber led to members becoming better informed and more interested in European matters. However, these cognitive changes were not accompanied by MEPs becoming more supportive of European integration. The study by Hagger and Wing (1979), based on a survey carried out in 1977, focused on the role concepts of the nominated members.

Bardi's *Il parlamento della Comunita Europea. Legittimita e riforma* (1989) contains the results of a large-scale survey of MEPs carried out in 1983 by the European University Institute (EUI) under the direction of the late Rudolf Wildenmann, probing members' attitudes to a wide range of European issues and the congruence of opinion between MEPs and their electorates. The set of questions included items such as the powers of the Parliament and other EC institutions, the way MEPs understand their role as representatives, the desirability of intensifying transnational party co-operation, and the future of European security and defence policy. Parts of the findings appear also in subsequent work by Bardi (1993, 1994) and others (Sørensen, 1989). The responsiveness of MEPs was also the subject of an article by Edward L. Scholl (1986) who examined the difference in constituency-oriented activity between British (single-member majority rule electoral districts) and French (proportional representation, one electoral district) members. Scholl's data consisted mainly of interviews and his conclusion was that British MEPs were more constituency-oriented than the French representatives in their behaviour. However, his final sample was far too small to enable us to draw any reliable conclusions.

MEPs, Voters and Interest Groups: Representation at the European Level by Shaun Bowler and David M. Farrell (1992a) is the most recent work dealing with the concept of representation within the Parliament. This work has benefited greatly from the results of that study. Utilising the results of a survey of MEPs carried out in 1990, they analysed the following aspects of members and their work: the background of MEPs, the length of their tenure in the chamber, MEPs' level of contacts with individual voters and pressure groups, their understanding of their representative role, the responsiveness of MEPs to various demands placed on them, time spent on matters concerning constituency issues, and the impact of electoral systems on constituency-oriented activity (Bowler and Farrell, 1993a, 1992a). Based mainly on the results of the same survey, Bowler and Farrell (1993b) have in a subsequent paper traced the (non)existence of norms and rules of parliamentary behaviour in the chamber. The same paper includes also an analysis of MEPs' oral questions.

The 1994 European Elections Study focused on questions on MEPs' role orientations. Unfortunately, however, the overall response rate was just under 20%, and with two member states excluded from the survey, the sample cannot be considered as representative of the Parliament (see Katz, 1996). Finally, the chapter by Ionescu (1996), based on interviews, discusses the 'European' orientation of the elected representatives.

The most under-studied features of the Strasbourg Parliament are its internal organisation and the behaviour of individual MEPs and party groups. Probably the most comprehensive work on MEPs, party groups, and their activity in the chamber is Emil Kirchner's *The European Parliament: Performance and Prospects* (1984). The temporal scope of the research is the first three years of the directly elected Parliament (1979-82), and the book analyses the political profile (sex, age, occupation, political experience) of the members, their activity in the chamber (reports, questions etc.), and the relationship between background and behaviour in a very data-rich fashion.

In *Britain's Emerging Euro-Elite? The British in the Directly-Elected European Parliament, 1979-1992*, Westlake (1994a) has analysed the career patterns among the British contingent in the directly-elected EP.

Based on data on committee assignments and voting records, and on interviews, Westlake studies the existence of career pathways in the Parliament, and the attitudinal changes of British MEPs towards EC's constitutional reform. Focusing on the British Conservative and Labour delegations, Westlake's book contains also much valuable information on the internal organisation of committees, party groups, and national party delegations.

The use of question-time, especially by British members, has been analysed by two authors. The study by Lionel Cohen (1979) focuses on the institution of question-time in the nominated Parliament, while the paper by Westlake (1990) concentrates mainly on the 1980s. The recent article by Bowler and Farrell (1995) analyses the composition of EP committees by looking whether the committees reflect the ideological and national balance of the whole chamber, and if members' occupational backgrounds explain committee assignments. The article also traces the development of committee-based specialisation by a content analysis of oral questions asked by MEPs of three committees, and in the final section looks at the formation of an internal hierarchy structure in the chamber. Results of a content analysis of MEPs' written questions (reproduced here in part in chapter 5) by the author are found in Raunio (1996a,b, 1997c). The works analyse the questioning activity of the MEPs, party groups, and national delegations. The chapter by Mark Williams (1995) contains a longitudinal description of the evolution of EP's Rules of Procedure, focusing on the growth in political group domination at the expense of individual MEPs' rights.

When analysing the state of scholarly research on the European Parliament and transnational party co-operation, two inter-related shortcomings stand out: *lack of research on activity inside the Parliament, and lack of comparative perspective*. Addressing the latter question first, it appears that, apart from cross/transnational research projects focusing on European elections, far too few studies include a comparative perspective. The existing information comes in bits and pieces, with articles too often focusing on one party group, one national delegation, or on one policy area. The projects conducted in connection with European elections have usually compared the elections in the various member states, and have then pooled the results in order to analyse the existence of 'European' trends. The large-scale surveys of MEPs' preferences have used a similar method to investigate differences between national delegations or party groups. Other important topics that would benefit from such an approach include: the performance of the Parliament vis-à-vis the Council and/or the Commission (differences between policy areas and/or legislative procedures), the attendance and activity of MEPs inside the chamber (differences between party groups and national delegations and individual members), the internal functioning of party groups and committees, the relationship between MEPs and their national parties back home, and the adaptation of national parties or party families to the integration process.

The grey area of scholarly knowledge lies definitely in activity *inside* the Parliament. Direct elections to the Parliament have received much attention, a fact largely explained by their uniqueness as the first ever set of transnational elections. Parliament's legislative role and position in the EU decision-making system has likewise been fairly well covered, excluding, however, the latest developments which have bolstered EP's position. Considering the limited scope of transnational party co-operation outside the European Parliament, it is not surprising that scholarly interest in the topic has remained small.

While various surveys have been carried out over the years, offering us valuable information on MEPs' and euro-candidates' preferences on a wide range of issues, the actual *behaviour* of individual representatives and/or party groups has so far received too little attention. This is probably at least partly explained by the laborious nature of such research. In particular the important relationship between EP's internal organisation and the behaviour of its members has been under-studied. *The value of this work lies primarily in presenting a data-rich analysis of the behaviour of EP party groups and individual MEPs, and therefore in substantially increasing our understanding of what goes on inside the Parliament.*

Notes

[1] Public opinion surveys carried out by the Commission in all EU member states since 1973. For recent contributions on research on public opinion on the EU utilising *Eurobarometer*-reports, see for example Bréchon, Cautrès, and Denni (1995), Laursen (1994), and the individual chapters in *Public Opinion and Internationalized Governance*, edited by Oskar Niedermayer and Richard Sinnott (1995b).

[2] See for example the volume edited by Mario Telò (1995), *Democratie et Construction Europeenne*, which includes contributions in English and French from leading scholars in the field.

[3] Recent years have witnessed the proliferation of such voting power analyses. See for example Herne and Nurmi (1993), Hosli (1995, 1996), Lane, Maeland, and Berg (1996), and Peters (1996a,b).

[4] See for example Crombez (1996), Garrett and Tsebelis (1996), and Schneider (1995).

[5] The term 'democratic deficit' usually covers a variety of shortcomings identified in the present EU governance. Here the term is understood as the weak role of the directly elected representative institutions (national legislatures and the EP) in the EU decision-making system.

[6] For those interested in the increase in EP's powers, the reader is referred to Jacobs, Corbett, and Shackleton (1995), and Westlake (1994c), which both include detailed descriptions of Parliament's evolution as a legislature. Both sources also explain in detail the working of the various EU legislative procedures.

[7] The European Parliament has also periodically compiled lists of publications dealing with the institution. For a thorough and detailed overview of research on the Parliament, see the literature review in Raunio (1996b).

2 The Framework for Analysis: Legislative Organisation and Preference Formation

2.1. Introduction: Why Focus on Institutional Features?

Drawing on recent renewed interest in the study of political institutions - labelled often as 'new institutionalism' - this work examines the European Parliament from the perspective of a transnational parliament, concentrating on the formal and informal processes of decision-making, specialisation and representation *inside* the Parliament. Institutionalist approach to political science and international relations examines decision-making and preference formation by focusing on the institutional environment in which the various actors perform their activities and functions. As March and Olsen explain:

> "without denying the importance of both the social context of politics and the motives of individual actors, therefore, institutional analysis posits a more independent role for political institutions." (March and Olsen, 1989: 17)

But why focus on institutions? Institutions may appear to outside observers simply as organisational structures and rules created out of sheer practical necessity to regulate and organise the activities of a group of individuals in any given situation. While this undoubtedly is often the case, institutions themselves are the result of conscious human design. Within decision-making bodies choices over alternative internal institutional arrangements reflect particular preferences and values and have a direct effect on the decisions and policy choices of that body. While the importance of informal aspects of political bodies should not be neglected, we must not "dispense with a concept that pinpoints regular processes or mechanisms for channelling certain activities, meeting certain recurrent challenges and contingencies and settling disagreements on and about the allocation of values - or indeed determining what the values are which will be allocated in a given territory in a specific era." (Bogdanor, 1987, cf. Rhodes, 1995: 50)

Considering the application of institutionalist approach to a wide range of social sciences - sociology, organisation theory, economics, political science etc. - it is not surprising that there is an equally wide range of definitions for the word 'institution'. According to the broad definition of Kiser and Ostrom

"institutional arrangements are the rules used by individuals for determining who and what are the included in decision situations, how information is structured, what actions can be taken and in what sequence, and how individual actions will be aggregated into collective decisions." (Kiser and Ostrom, 1982: 179)

In the case of legislatures the institutionalist approach has mainly explained political processes inside parliaments by focusing on legislatures' formal rules. Formal rules matter because they

(a) influence the strategies of the intra-parliamentary actors by setting limits (or by offering opportunities) to behaviour;
(b) provide continuity and clarity to proceedings by spelling the rules of the game;
(c) determine the composition of intra-parliamentary decision-making bodies;
(d) regulate conflict-resolution and forms of collective action inside the parliament; and
(e) because of (a-d), have an impact on intra-parliamentary preference formation and therefore also on the outcomes.

What these institutionalist approaches to the study of legislatures have in common is the explanatory value consigned to institutions. Majority of the recent contributions on institutional features of parliamentary politics have been in the rational choice framework. While "sociologists have focused on *relationships* among individuals, rational choice theorists have turned to *institutions*. Like relationships, institutions may be thought of as part of what embeds people in social situations. They are the social glue missing from the behaviouralist's more atomistic account." (Shepsle, 1989: 134)

However, institutionalism in political science and in the study of legislatures is not restricted to rational actor models, with alternative theoretical approaches complementing the picture. In the case of parliaments, to arrive at a better and more purposeful understanding of their work, the scholar benefits from going beyond simple reductionist formal models often characteristic of rational choice approaches (see Patterson, 1995). According to this perspective, the way actors pursue their goals and the way their information and preferences are fashioned into social outcomes is the result of an interplay between individual's goals and the constraints set by institutional design:

> "Individual action is assumed to be an optimal adaptation to an institutional environment...Prevailing institutions (the rules of the game) determine the behaviour of the actors, which in turn produces political or social outcomes."(Tsebelis, 1990: 40)

Legislatures are complex organisations, and one general feature characteristic of most parliaments is the ascendancy of parties, the dominance of parliamentary parties over individual representatives. The role of the individual member has changed as legislatures have become more party-dominated. Usually this has meant curtailing the rights of the backbenchers. While such loss of procedural rights may have been compensated by alternative channels of influence within parliamentary parties and committees, the average individual MP is nowadays dependent on his or her parliamentary party:

> "Parliamentary politics is usually more complicated. Obviously, Members of Parliament are not just reacting individually to stimuli at the macro level of a political system. Their choices are, in addition, constrained by the institutional rules of the legislature, decisions of their parties, rules of their parliamentary parties and other factors." (Saalfeld, 1995: 40-41)

In short, individual representatives have different goals, belong to parliamentary parties, understand their roles differently, but yet they all operate within the limits set, or opportunities offered by, the formal rules of their workplace. These formal rules are of course complemented by various informal processes:

"The formal structure of an organisation is found in its constitutional code which defines lines of authority and divisions of work by specifying the organisation's principal offices and their principal duties and responsibilities...the formal rules set boundaries for the informal rules and thereby guide informal relationships along lines that are appropriate for pursuing the organisation's goals." (Searing, 1991: 1241)

In this work the focus is on the legislature's structural properties. These can be divided into two levels of organisation:

(a) the formal organisation of the whole European Parliament; and
(b) the internal organisation of the Parliament's most important sub-units, its transnational party groups and committees.

Institutions are therefore defined here as *the formal rules or otherwise established forms of collective action according to which the whole parliament and its parliamentary parties choose to organise their work.* The 'formal rules' refer to the EP Rules of Procedure, which regulate the intra-parliamentary division of labour, and the powers, rights, and duties of the various actors inside the Parliament. The 'otherwise established forms of collective action' refer to forms of collective action not specified in the EP Rules of Procedure but which are regular procedures in the Parliament and at the party group level. By collective action is simply meant the set of actions in which more than one individual representative takes part.

The approach chosen in this work combines features of both institutionalism and behaviouralism. Since the main purpose of this work is to analyse the relationship between the institutional framework in the European Parliament and the behaviour of the EP party groups, the activity of the transnational party groups and the individual MEPs must be carefully examined. The theoretical statements and hypotheses presented in the work are subjected to empirical investigation in order to validate or to falsify them. It is important to note that behaviouralism and institutionalism are complementary: while formal rules and institutions are emphasised, rigorous empirical testing is needed to establish their effect on actors' behaviour (Sanders, 1995; Rhodes, 1995).

2.2. Delegating Authority Without Losing Control: Party Groups inside Parliaments

While elections to parliaments, the role of individual representatives, and parliaments in general have been studied fairly extensively, parliamentary party groups have so far received much less attention among scholars interested in legislatures and/or party organisations (Heidar and Koole, 1996; Strøm, 1995). Parliamentary parties are naturally mentioned and included in various studies on parties and parliaments, but there is definitely a shortage of works that focus on party groups inside legislatures as their primary unit of analysis. This is all the more surprising considering the strengthened position of parliamentary party groups.[1]

The existing theoretical literature focuses mainly on the U.S. Congress, which in the words of Shepsle and Weingast (1994a: 147) is "the most studied" but "also surely the most untypical example of the legislative institution." The theoretical models referred to below were also developed in the context of Congressional politics. However, despite the inevitable differences between the 'individualistic' Congress and the more 'party-oriented' European legislatures, the main features of these models are not context-specific and can thus be applied to other legislatures, including the EP. Here I will focus on two complementary aspects of parliamentary party group behaviour that are crucial in facilitating their internal cohesion:

(i) their overall dominant role inside the Parliament, and
(ii) their control over the committees and individual representatives.

These two points both emphasise the ascendancy of party groups inside a legislature vis-à-vis other intra-parliamentary actors (committees, individual representatives). The first point underlines the importance of the party groups' ability to choose the way the parliament conducts its business. This dominant position inside a legislature increases the power and status of the party groups, thereby creating incentives for cohesive action by them. The second point looks at the internal structure of parliamentary party groups. By controlling nominations to committees and other intra-parliamentary posts, the party groups are able to develop collective specialisation that will facilitate their unity and give them organisational and functional coherence.

According to Cox and McCubbins (1993: 86) parliamentary parties face the problem of overcoming "collective dilemmas." A collective dilemma is defined as "a situation in which rational behaviour on the part of individuals can lead to unanimously dispreferred outcomes." In order to avoid free-rider problems, and since purely voluntary co-operation is unreliable and cannot be trusted to last long in to the future, self-interested re-election-seeking legislators develop a system of intra-party hierarchy in which the central authority (party leadership) monitors the behaviour of its members.

Criticising alternative approaches for their excessive focus on the role and autonomy of the committees, Cox and McCubbins view the role of parliamentary parties as critical in understanding legislative organisation. In *Legislative Leviathan* they argue that legislative parties - especially the majority party - behave like cartels, using a variety of institutional solutions to increase their power. Primarily by controlling intra-parliamentary assignments (committee membership, legislature's leadership posts), the majority party is able to control much of the legislative agenda. The tactic used is straightforward: by having their own men in positions of influence, the policies adopted will automatically reflect the views of the majority party.[2] The former feature, institutionalised intra-party co-operation, thus facilitates the latter, that of agenda control.

Obviously the Congressional two-party system differs from the EP party system, with the main difference being that no single party group currently controls or indeed has at any point controlled the majority of the seats in the Parliament (see section 3.5.). Also noteworthy is the fact that the Strasbourg parliamentary parties have no government to defend or to bring down. This is indeed the main structural difference between the EP and the EU national legislatures. Fulvio Attinà has termed this a "liberating element" for the whole chamber:

"The absence of a majority-opposition arrangement and of loyalty ties between the Community government institutions (Commission and Council of Ministers) and the representative institution (Parliament) is not a limitation to the EP because the absence of this requisite renders it free from the binding condition of having a majority subordinate to the political executive branch. The absence of this requisite is rather a liberating element for European Parliament Members who can attempt to influence the European integration process in full autonomy." (Attinà, 1990: 557-558)

We should expect to find evidence of similar tendencies of parliamentary party dominance in the EP as well. The development of EP party groups into cohesive parliamentary parties is argued to be facilitated by concentration of intra-parliamentary power in the hands of party groups. The internal organisation of the Parliament should show signs of increasing party group dominance over agenda control, intra-parliamentary appointments, and the growing formal role of party groups at the expense of individual MEPs' rights. Such intra-parliamentary power is a prerequisite for the cohesion of the EP party groups: it provides incentives for the individual members and national party delegations to seek membership in a party group, to co-operate with fellow-MEPs in the group, and to stick to deals within the groups as these party groups are in control of appointments and organise the work of the legislature. However, the cohesion of EP party groups is also dependent on their ability to accommodate partisan and territorial interests.

Division of labour and informational efficiency

Here it is necessary to draw the distinction between distributive ('gains from exchange') and informational perspectives on legislative organisation. Distributive theories have treated legislatures primarily as marketplaces for bargaining processes, focusing on aggregating (previously fixed) preferences. The main emphasis is on legislators pursuing goals originating in the extra-parliamentary arena, with MPs reaping benefits for their respective clienteles. Two basic premises are that "policy preferences are heterogeneous and policy choices are multidimensional." (Shepsle and Weingast, 1994b: 167) The solution lies in institutional design that facilitates gains from exchange (or gains from trade). The committee system is seen as providing the answer. Entering the legislature with heterogeneous tastes, the representatives seek influence over their priority interest areas, and this happens through appointment procedure which accommodates legislators' wishes. Thus gains from exchange "entails swapping influence across jurisdictions", with committees consisting mainly of preference outliers (Ibid.: 156).

However, it is questionable whether such distributive theories actually produce net increases in aggregate welfare. Considering that most situations are characterised by scarcity of resources and thus unavoidable conflict over them, such trade-offs between legislators seeking particularistic benefits run the risk of leading to inefficient outcomes (see Gilligan and Krehbiel, 1994).

In his book *Information and Legislative Organisation*, Keith Krehbiel differentiates between distributive and informational theories of legislative organisation, arguing that

> "informational theories, like distributive theories, are individualistic in their axiomatic foundations, but informational theories uniquely embrace the notion of policy expertise as a potential collective good. If obtained and shared, individuals' policy expertise rebounds to the whole, that is, to all legislators. As in the distributive perspective, informational theories view legislatures as arenas of individual distributive conflict. But unlike the distributive perspective, informational theories also view legislatures as organisations that may reap collective benefits from specialisation....the focus in informational approaches is on choosing rules and procedures that provide incentives for individuals to develop policy expertise and to share policy-relevant information with fellow legislators, including legislators with competing distributive interests." (Krehbiel, 1991: 5)

Individual goals thus need to be reconciled with collective ones. Formal rules are significant in this process. The goal is

> "an informationally efficient legislative organisation ... one in which collective benefits are reaped from individuals' policy-specific expertise and in which distributive benefits - rather than accruing disproportionately to high-demanders - are carefully kept in check by legislative majorities." (Krehbiel, 1991: 6)

Krehbiel's theory is based on two postulates:

(1) The Majoritarian Postulate: Objects of legislative choice, such as its rules and intra-parliamentary assignments, are chosen by a majority of the legislature.
(2) The Uncertainty Postulate: Legislators are uncertain about the relationship between policies and their outcomes. Thus members have an incentive to encourage specialisation and sharing of policy expertise in order to reduce such uncertainty (Ibid.: 16-20).

Thus informational theory takes the distributive model one step further. Krehbiel suggests that we should "abandon the view of legislatures as institutions that are overwhelmingly preoccupied with distributive politics." We should "instead adopt the view of legislatures as institutions of issue-by-issue majoritarian policy-making under uncertainty. In this new, informational view, both the objectives and the achievements of legislative decision-making extend well beyond the classical pork barrel." (Ibid.: 258)

Informational advantages do not necessarily lead to better policy-making. "Informational theories are careful not to take for granted that meaningful deliberation and discussion occur (or, equivalently, that uncertainty is reduced via specialisation and information sharing). They only characterise choice processes in a manner such that the political game has a common-good component that, by definition, political actors all value." (Ibid.: 73)

Institutional features are thus important in the reduction of uncertainty over outcomes and in the development of specialisation among representatives. The key problem is in how the whole legislature can benefit from the members' asymmetric information - "a condition in which some legislators have better knowledge than others about the relationship between policies and outcomes." (Ibid.: 68)

The European Parliament, like its national counterparts, suffers from heavy workload, and therefore the delegation of responsibility inside the legislature is a practical necessity. Time is an even more scarce resource in the European Parliament than in the EU member state legislatures. The Parliament's work schedule is rather chaotic, involving much travelling. The 626 MEPs travel regularly between their constituencies, Brussels, and Strasbourg. A full plenary is normally held only once a month (excluding August), with each plenary lasting only four-five days. Additional 'mini-plenaries' are nowadays held in Brussels during the committee weeks, lasting normally two days. Two weeks are reserved for committee meetings, with the one remaining week of the month reserved for group meetings (see section 3.2.).

Decision-making inside the Parliament is largely based on an interplay between committees and party groups. Most of the preparatory work is done in Parliament's committees, where a rapporteur is charged with the task of producing a report on the issue (see section 3.3). The party groups usually have their spokesperson(s) or working groups on various issues, and these persons inform the rest of the group (those not sitting on that particular committee) on the proceedings in the committee. Without such a process of 'cue-taking' based on intra-group division of labour, the individual members and party groups would not be able to cope with the large number of legislative and own-initiative resolutions handled simultaneously by the Parliament (Van Schendelen, 1976). Thus it is a problem of how to delegate authority within the legislature without surrendering control over outcomes (Lupia and McCubbins, 1994).

Considering the influence of committees inside the EP, the legislative majority has an incentive to control the nomination process. As argued by David Baron (1994: 292): "if institutional features provide individualistic incentives for preference outliers to seek membership on committees to obtain programs that diverge from the central preferences of the parent legislature, the legislature might be expected to exercise a degree of collective control of the committee assignment process rather than allowing it to be governed by self-selection."

For the European Parliament to be called informationally efficient, and for the party groups to be able to achieve and especially maintain cohesion, two points are of particular importance: transnationality of committee membership, and specialisation within the party groups.

The appointment process to committees and other intra-parliamentary positions should reflect both the partisan balance and transnationality of the Parliament's membership. This would in turn facilitate the development and sharing of expertise within the committees (and thus in the Parliament as a whole). This would help the Parliament in 'striking a balance' between ideological and territorial representation. Since in the Parliament the committees are vested with significant powers (see section 3.3.), an assignment process based on the twin pillars of majority control and transnationality of the chamber's membership would thus also reduce external risks associated with outcomes. We should see evidence of individual-level specialisation within party groups along policy lines (based on committee membership), with neither party groups nor national delegations specialising in any particular issue area (there are, nor have been, any 'one-issue' party groups in the chamber[3]). Such intra-group division of labour would facilitate co-operation inside the groups.

2.3. Decision-making and Preference Formation in the European Parliament

The way a legislature chooses to organise itself may therefore be regarded as involving a choice as how to best meet the demands of its everyday work. "We should expect all rules adopted by a majority of the legislators themselves to serve some anticipated, past or present, collective purpose." (Strøm, 1995: 64) This choice itself is based on a set of preferences concerning the way intra-parliamentary decision-making should be performed. This section introduces the features of internal organisation that affect preference formation and party behaviour inside the Parliament. The role and importance of the various factors are explained in more detail in chapter 3.

While the legislative powers of the European Parliament are largely determined by actors outside the Strasbourg chamber, mainly by the heads of state and government meeting as the EU Council, the EP has the right to arrange its own internal organisation, a right specifically recognised in the EU's 'constitution'. Article 142 of the Treaty on European Union reads:

> "The European Parliament shall adopt its Rules of Procedure, acting by a majority of its Members."

That the internal organisation of a parliament matters is impossible to deny (Polsby, 1968). However, in a situation where a decision-making body is the master of its own rules, as the EP is, the very choice of its Rules of Procedure acquires special importance. The Rules of Procedure determine the structural properties (internal organisation) of the legislature, and therefore the formal rules have a direct effect on agenda formation, transmission of information within the chamber, and on the final outcomes (Shepsle and Weingast, 1984).

Obviously legislatures may choose to find ways to circumvent the routine procedures codified in its formal rules (and are sometimes forced to do so in a situation putting special demands on the legislature), but the formal rules provide the guidelines for conducting business within the chamber. Formal rules and other established, regularised forms of collective action can be considered particularly important in the EP where the turnover of members is unusually high both at elections and during the legislative term itself.

The internal organisation of the Strasbourg Parliament - the way the 'Voice of the People' is organised - has also important repercussions outside the Parliament. Considering that the SEA and the Maastricht Treaty have strengthened the Parliament's position in the European Union's inter-institutional decision-making system, the voice of the EP has acquired added weight: its own-initiative resolutions receive more regular coverage in the media than before, lobbying has increased greatly in the Parliament, and it participates in drafting legislation which is subsequently implemented throughout the whole European Union.[4]

Figure 2.1. Preference formation and internal organisation in the Parliament

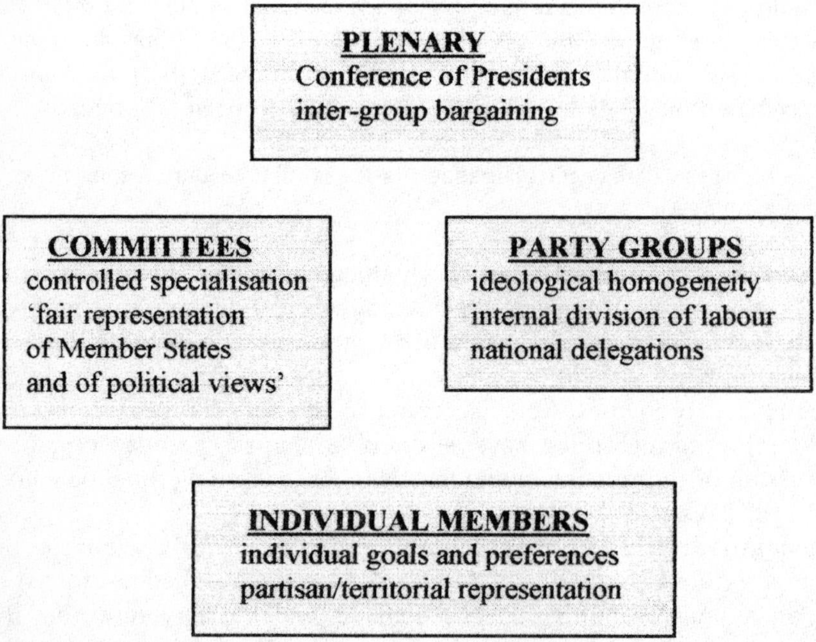

```
┌─────────────────────────────────────┐
│           PLENARY                    │
│      Conference of Presidents        │
│      inter-group bargaining          │
└─────────────────────────────────────┘

┌────────────────────────┐   ┌────────────────────────┐
│      COMMITTEES         │   │     PARTY GROUPS        │
│ controlled specialisation│   │ ideological homogeneity │
│ 'fair representation    │   │ internal division of labour│
│ of Member States        │   │ national delegations    │
│ and of political views' │   │                         │
└────────────────────────┘   └────────────────────────┘

┌─────────────────────────────────┐
│      INDIVIDUAL MEMBERS          │
│  individual goals and preferences│
│  partisan/territorial representation│
└─────────────────────────────────┘
```

The Parliament is uniquely positioned in the EU decision-making system to capture information flows from both the member states and from the other European-level institutions.[5] Its 626 directly elected members offer a potentially vast repository of knowledge and expertise. With direct links to their respective national parties and constituencies, the MEPs are in regular contact with events at the local level. Within the Parliament the individual representatives transmit and exchange information, formulate it into policy proposals, and develop expertise within particular policy areas. Informational efficiency is crucial for the Parliament in its relations with the Commission, the Council of Ministers, the various national-level bodies, and the general public.

Figure 2.1. depicts the principal actors involved in preference formation inside the Parliament, and introduces the key explanatory factors that facilitate the cohesion of the party groups.

Since this work focuses on the relationship between the internal organisation of the Parliament and the behaviour of its party groups, two important types of actors have been omitted from Figure 2.1.: the various informal actors operating inside the Parliament and the extra-parliamentary actors. The informal actors within the EP refer to actors whose role is not specifically mentioned in the Parliament's Rules of Procedure. To this category belong first and foremost the various intergroups - bringing together MEPs with common interests on a cross-group basis - functioning in the chamber, together with other means of informal communication taking place between the representatives. Extra-parliamentary actors refer to the various actors outside the Parliament that influence the preference formation process inside the chamber. The most significant among them are public opinion, national parties, interest groups, and the other EU institutions.

Below are descriptions and definitions of the various actors shown in Figure 2.1.

Individual members (MEPs)

The Parliament's Rules of Procedure recognise the independent mandate of the MEP:

> "Members of the European Parliament shall exercise their mandate independently. They shall not be bound by any instructions and shall not receive a binding mandate." (Rule 2)

As in other legislatures, this principle of the independent mandate is in practice heavily curtailed by the representatives' work environment. *Representatives are elected to the Parliament from the EU member states, but sit in transnational political groups.* Constituencies often coincide, and in no case cross national borders. Members represent national parties that control nominations to the party lists in the European elections. Depending on the MEPs' electoral district, his or her personal interests, and the ideological profile of the member and his national party, the MEP brings to the Parliament his *individual goals and preferences*. Inside the Parliament the overwhelming majority of members sit in party groups and committees, and must respect the formal and informal rules of their workplace. A small minority of MEPs have over the years chosen to remain as non-aligned members.

Members form transnational political groups inside the chamber. Alternatively, members could sit as individual representatives without being affiliated to any group, or they could have decided to form national delegations. The organisational choice to establish ideological groupings was based on the desire to avoid the dominance of national viewpoints. A parliamentary party group in the Parliament is defined here as *'a set of individual representatives who have formed a party group inside the Parliament in accordance with the rules laid down in Parliament's Rules of Procedure'* (Rule 29).

These party groups are mainly based on the traditional party families found in Western European societies and recognised in the political science literature. Therefore it is expected that a certain degree of *ideological homogeneity* prevails within the groups. A minimal definition of ideological homogeneity is used here: it is simply assumed that the set of members forming a party group have ideologically more in common with each other than they have with the sets of members belonging to the other EP party groups.

National party delegations are important players within the party groups, and group decisions are often compromises between the respective national party delegations. Party groups control appointments to all intra-parliamentary posts, including nominations to committees. Party groups have developed institutional means (intra-group meetings and hierarchy, committee-based division of labour) to foster the cohesion of the groups. Intra-group *internal division of labour* (bureaux, group meetings, national party delegations, spokespersons, working groups) is significant in increasing the cohesion and functional efficiency of the group.

Committees

The committees are the arenas where the Parliament's legislative and own-initiative reports are drafted and much of the EP's oversight functions also take place in the committees. *The composition of the committees is based on a rule of proportionality, reflecting (i) the partisan balance in the chamber and (ii) the seat distribution between the national delegations.* MEPs have the opportunity to specialise in the framework of the EP's committee structure, but such committee-based specialisation occurs under the scrutiny of party groups who control appointments to committees (*'controlled specialisation'*). The composition of the committees, accommodating both partisan and territorial interests, is important since it facilitates informational efficiency in the chamber.

Plenary

The Conference of Presidents, consisting of the EP President and the chairmen of the political groups, is the body responsible for organising the work of the Parliament. When consensus is not reached in the Conference, decisions are taken by a vote with votes weighted according to the size of the groups. This arrangement has consolidated the dominant role of party groups in intra-parliamentary proceedings.

Inter-group bargaining often precedes the final vote taken in the plenary, with the leaderships of the groups building mutually acceptable compromises. Such inter-group negotiations are usually motivated either by the need to achieve the required legislative majorities or by the concern with increasing the Parliament's influence by showing the wide support the resolution enjoys among the MEPs (representatives of the people).

To conclude this section, the behaviour of the EP party groups is constrained and influenced by the factors introduced in Figure 2.1. At the plenary level, the party groups organise the work of the Parliament through the Conference of Presidents. Inside the party groups there is ideological homogeneity as the groups are in the majority of cases based on the traditional party families recognised in the political science literature. National party delegations are important sub-units within the transnational party groups, with intra-group decision-making often consisting of negotiations between the various party delegations. Party groups control appointments to the EP's standing committees, and therefore MEPs' committee-based specialisation happens under the scrutiny of party groups. EP party groups have also developed internal institutional mechanisms to foster intra-group co-operation. Internal group hierarchy, group meetings, and the system of committee-based division of labour all contribute to intra-group cohesion.

2.4. The Research Question

What is the relationship between Parliament's internal organisation and the behaviour of its party groups and individual Members of the European

Parliament? How do the structural properties of the Parliament (internal organisation) facilitate cohesion inside the party groups and in the whole Parliament? How cohesive are the transnational party groups? Whom do the elected representatives see themselves as representing? Are there any differences between the various party groups and national delegations? Do members specialise in their questions? How are the various partisan and territorial interests accommodated inside the chamber? How does co-operation work inside the Parliament between and within transnational party groups?

By 'party cohesion' is meant "the extent to which, in a given situation, group members can be observed to work together for the group's goals in one and the same way." (Ozbudun, 1970: 305) This *cohesion is important since it provides stability to the party groups and the Parliament's proceedings, it reflects the ideological homogeneity prevailing within the groups, and it prevents the establishment and consolidation of national voting blocs in the chamber.*

The main argument is that *the choice over Parliament's internal organisation is crucial in explaining the behaviour and cohesion of the party groups.* Intra-parliamentary organisation influences behaviour inside the Parliament and its party groups by structuring the division of labour in the chamber and inside the party groups and by creating institutional mechanisms to facilitate co-operation.

Altogether 16 hypotheses are subjected to empirical testing in the voting behaviour analysis in chapter 4 (cohesion of the EP party groups) and in the content analysis of parliamentary questions in chapter 5 (division of labour, specialisation, and representation).

Hypotheses 1 to 7 (chapter 4) are tested by a roll-call analysis.[6] The data covers a sample (N = 159) of votes from the third directly elected Parliament of 1989-1994. Following dimensions are investigated:

(a) the voting cohesion of the EP political groups;
(b) the relationship between party group heterogeneity (degree of fractionalisation and transnationality) and party group cohesion;
(c) coalition behaviour inside the chamber (voting likeness);
(d) the relationship between legislative majority requirements and party group voting behaviour; and
(e) cohesion on foreign policy issues.

Obviously roll-call analysis is not the only way to measure party group unity, nor does the author consider it sufficient to give a comprehensive picture of party group unity. However, voting is the time when MEPs must decide whether to support the group position or not, and therefore roll-call analysis is arguably a better method for measuring party cohesion inside the legislature than alternative methods (for example, questionnaires probing members' opinions on various issues).

Hypotheses 8 to 16 in chapter 5 are tested by a content analysis of MEPs' written questions (questions for written answer) to the Commission, the Council and the Foreign Ministers meeting in the context of European Political Co-operation (EPC). The data consists of all written questions submitted during 1992 to which an answer had been given by the time of conducting the research. The sample includes 4077 questions. The questions were categorised according to their subject category and territorial dimension. Following dimensions are analysed:

(a) the questioning activity of individual members, party groups, and national delegations;
(b) the specialisation of individual MEPs, party groups, and national delegations; and
(c) the territorial dimension of the written questions.

The first dimension was studied in order to analyse behavioural differences inside the chamber, and to measure the activity of party groups, national delegations, and individual members. The second (subject category) dimension was analysed in order to investigate the political profiles of the party groups and the national delegations, and in order to study the relationship between committee assignments and use of parliamentary questions. The territorial dimension was introduced in order to analyse the representational foci of the party groups and the national delegations.

But is a content analysis of parliamentary questions an appropriate method for testing the hypotheses put forward? The main limitation of parliamentary questions is that it is only one of the many channels MEPs have available to pursue their goals. Members often prefer to use other formal and informal strategies such as contacting the Commission directly, or concentrating on work and contacts made inside the committees and the party groups. However, submitting a question costs relatively little in terms of time and resources, presents an opportunity for the MEP to make the matter public, and in their written questions representatives can raise any issue they want. Analysing parliamentary questions gives therefore an excellent idea of the way members understand their role as representatives.

In order to acquire a deeper understanding of the institution of parliamentary questions, and the usage of it by the representatives, interviews were carried out with MEPs, their assistants, and the staff of the Parliament in February 1996 in Brussels and in Strasbourg. A full list of the interviews is included in the bibliography.

2.5. Conclusion: Endogenous Preferences and Legislative Behaviour

The main argument as introduced in the previous section is that the internal organisation of the whole Parliament and of the EP party groups facilitates the cohesion of party groups.

While most theories of legislative organisation and collective action are mainly concerned with finding efficient institutional solutions to aggregating heterogeneous (and fixed) preferences, the legislature's institutional design also has a direct effect on preference formation inside the chamber. As March and Olsen argue:

> "In particular, it should be noted that the values and preferences of political actors are not exogenous to political institutions but develop within those institutions. The endogeneity of preferences is a major problem for theories of politics that picture action as stemming from prior preferences." (March and Olsen, 1989: 40-41)

Actors, parliamentary parties and representatives in the case of parliaments, usually have prior preferences of their own, but work and contacts within the legislature often changes or modifies their preferences. Thus prior preferences do and indeed should matter, but they are also formed by social interaction within the institution. According to Wendt (1994: 390) "if we treat identities and interests as always in process during interaction, then we can see how an evolution of co-operation might lead to an evolution of community." What Wendt calls "the production or reproduction of identities and interests" is much the same as what March and Olsen (1989: 165) have in mind when they argue that "if we see politics as building community and a sense of common identity within which decisions are made, we welcome the role of political institutions as agents in the construction of political interests and beliefs." However, since the diversity and intensity of preferences vary, and since there seldom is time for unlimited discussion, the "transformation of preferences can never do more than supplement the aggregation of preferences, never replace it altogether." (Elster, 1986: 115)

When discussing the importance of exogenous and endogenous preferences in the context of the European Parliament, the reader is reminded of the enormous variety of interests that are represented in the Strasbourg chamber. Exchanging and transmitting information is of particular significance in a legislature which brings together representatives from 15 member states and from over a hundred national parties. If the sheer complexity of issues often seems bewildering in national legislatures, the party groups and MEPs in the Parliament face the even more demanding task of taking into account the opinions of extra-parliamentary actors found in the EU. This obviously does not mean that each interest is accommodated in EP resolutions. Moreover, it is important to acknowledge that while representatives may have the interests of the whole community (here the EU) at heart, each member still has his or her own preferred version of what the future should hold for that community (Maass, 1983).

In the European Parliament in some instances vote-maximising elements will dominate, in others partisan cleavages are relevant, and in some concern over informational efficiency is crucial. As David W. Rohde points out:

> "the main point is that the interaction of the partisan, distributive, and informational considerations produces a complex legislative environment, one which cannot be captured adequately by a single-motivation, universal perspective." (Rohde, 1994: 357)

Treating legislatures primarily as marketplaces where electorally-motivated politicians seek to maximise benefits for their clienteles is misleading. To quote Krehbiel:

> "...while distributive concerns are undeniably a part of legislative politics ... informational concerns - in the sense of how politicians can be provided with incentives to study public problems and formulate public policy - are at the heart of legislative organisation." (Krehbiel, 1991: 265)

Notes

[1] The forthcoming volume edited by Knut Heidar and Ruud Koole (1997) is a welcome exception. The project focuses exclusively on the role of parliamentary

parties, with chapters on parliamentary party groups (PPGs) in various European legislatures. Also included is a chapter on the EP party groups.

[2] Cox and McCubbins (1993: 258) name this strategy "automatic pilot" control. However, such automatic control works only in situations in which the parliamentary party has collective interests to promote. This is obviously not always the case. See Aldrich (1994).

[3] This holds true also for those party groups opposed to the current form of European integration, for example the Left Unity (LU) and Europe of Nations (EN).

[4] Since the Parliament does not keep a register of lobbyists, it is impossible to measure the exact increase in lobbying activity. However, it is beyond doubt that lobbying "has increased greatly". The parallel rise in media coverage is shown by the upward trend in journalists and TV reporters attending the plenaries, and in the footage shown on TV of the sessions. (Jacobs, Corbett, and Shackleton, 1995: 280-281, 297-298)

[5] As Kerr (1973: 50) argued: "...one might expect that as members of the parliament are exposed to a welter of new and often challenging information within the assembly, they *may* broaden their outlook on integration, appreciate more easily the complexity of the issues, and entertain and tolerate opposing views more readily...their cognitions of European integration *may* become more complex and differentiated as a result of this experience." (emphasis added) See also the interviews in Ionescu (1996).

[6] For more detailed information on methodology and the samples used in voting behaviour analysis and the content analysis of written questions, the reader is referred to sections 4.4. and 5.4.

3 The Ascendancy of Political Groups in Strasbourg

3.1. Introduction[1]

Parliamentary parties are important players within national legislatures. They come under different labels, some are called 'clubs', others 'fractions' or 'party groups'. Their relationship to the extra-parliamentary party organisation varies both within the same political system and between different national systems. Their minimum size varies depending on the numerical criterion a party group must meet in order to gain official recognition.

No realistic analysis of modern party democracy can describe parliamentary parties as mere subordinate branches of the national party organisation. While definitely more or less accountable to both the central party executive and to the local party branches, parliamentary parties are during the legislative term often relatively independent from the extra-parliamentary parts of their parties.

While recent accounts on national governance have stressed the dominance of the executive over the legislature, the impact of parliamentary parties on governmental policy choices should not be underestimated. After all, the survival of governments is dependent on commanding the support of the parliamentary majority. Parliamentary parties are also in control of the proceedings inside the parliaments. They are responsible for setting the agenda, draft the internal rules of the legislatures, and determine the composition and powers of various intra-parliamentary sub-units, including the committees.

Transnational political groups were officially recognised in the standing orders of the ECSC Common Assembly in June 1953, only less than a year after its inaugural meeting. Already before that in January 1953 the members agreed that the composition of the Assembly's committees should reflect political tendencies as well as the balance between nationalities. Party groups were organised by March that year, and when given formal status in June they were allotted a financial allowance from the budget of the Assembly to cover their administrative expenses.[2]

The decision to form transnational groups was taken by the members themselves. While this choice may in hindsight seem self-evident to us as the oldest party groups have existed now for over four decades, forming transnational party groups was by no means the only organisational alternative. Stanley Henig and John Pinder list four possible variations:

> "National delegations can either group themselves together in permanent blocs or they can align together as the issue demands. Alternatively, individuals within different national delegations can band together to promote specific sectional interests; one can talk here loosely of an international pressure group. Or, finally, transnational party groups can be formed cutting across the national delegations." (Henig and Pinder, 1969: 476-477)

The establishment of co-operation based on ideological groups instead of on nationality was seen as necessary by the members in order to avoid the dominance of national viewpoints.

> "Accordingly, the work of the Assembly was to be influenced by the existence of ideological groupings, which were to discuss the general problems of European integration to a much greater extent than the practical arrangements for implementing the ECSC Treaty or the interests of a particular country. Naturally, national interests were not forgotten; but the Members were concerned to set them in an overall context." (Gerbet, 1992: 13)

The nominated members sat originally in alphabetical order, but when the ECSC Common Assembly was replaced by the Parliamentary Assembly in 1958, the seating order was rearranged so that the members sat with their own party groups. The three groups formed back in 1953 - Christian Democrats, Liberals, and Socialists - are still present in the current Parliament and have been joined by other party groups. Throughout the years these political groups - in particular the larger and more established ones - have developed their internal organisation and have consolidated their position inside the Parliament. Yet these groups differ from their counterparts in national parliaments in terms of their composition, internal division of labour, and their role in the decision-making system.

3.2. The Formal Status and Internal Structure of EP Party Groups

Life inside the European Parliament revolves around its party groups. The political groups are the backbone of EP's internal organisation. They provide stability, consistency, and functional efficiency to the Parliament. Without them intra-parliamentary decision-making would be much more difficult and unpredictable. Their existence is officially recognised in Rule 29 of the Parliament's Rules of Procedure:

1. Members may form themselves into groups according to their political affinities.
2. The minimum number of Members required to form a political group shall be 29 if they come from one Member State, 23 if they come from two Member States, 17 if they come from three Member States and 14 if they come from four or more Member States.[3]
3. A Member may not belong to more than one group.
4. The President shall be notified in a statement when a political group is set up. This statement shall specify the name of the group, its members and its Bureau.
5. The statement shall be published in the Official Journal.

Funding and staff

Political groups enjoy considerable rights. They receive financial allocations from the Parliament's internal budget. This sum amounted to about 20 million ECU in 1994. Money allocated to the party groups accounts for over 10 % of the EP's budget. The sum each group receives is dependent on the number of members in the group. Groups receive money for hiring staff, for various information activities, and for acquiring technical facilities. The funds provided by the Parliament may not be used for European election campaigns. Party groups are also given office space and rooms where they can hold meetings.

Political groups have their own staff, the number of which has grown substantially since the first direct elections. This political group staff must be differentiated from both the Parliament's own officials and from the MEPs' personal assistants. The members are given money from the Parliament's budget to hire personal assistants. The average MEP normally has an assistant both in Brussels and/or Strasbourg and in the constituency.

The Parliament has precise rules concerning the hiring of staff. Each party group is entitled to a fixed total of two A grade (administrative) posts, with a further such post for every four MEPs within the group, and another A grade post for each language up to three languages, two posts for four and five languages, three posts for six and seven languages and four posts for eight and nine languages. The total number of A posts to which a party group is entitled then provides the key to the number of B (assistant) and C (secretarial) posts within each group, with 1.4 B and C posts funded for each A grade post. The total number of posts per party group may not exceed the number of members within that group. In 1994 the party groups were budgeted a total of 477 posts.

The input and workload of the party group staff should not be underestimated. The staff performs a whole variety of functions inside the groups. An important duty is following proceedings in the committees. The larger party groups are able to have one or even two persons following the work done in each committee, whereas an official in a smaller party group may be forced to follow the work of three or four committees. These officials assist the group's MEPs in that committee, help to ensure a unified group line in the committee, and follow the general developments in that committee. Officials are involved in preparing the debates within the group meetings, and draft studies and reports for the group. The staff also helps in drawing up group whips both in the committee and in the plenary. It is difficult to estimate the actual influence and power of these officials. Nevertheless, by assisting the individual MEPs and the party groups the officials without a doubt greatly increase the functional capacity of the groups.[4]

The internal structure of the EP political groups varies from one group to another, with the larger groups having because of reasons of size more need to develop institutionalised hierarchical organisation in order to co-ordinate their activities. Figure 3.1. shows the basic internal structure of an EP party group. The structure can be divided into two closely related and partially overlapping (in terms of membership) levels: the group leadership and the ordinary members ('backbenchers'). The former category includes the Chairman and the Vice-Chairmen and the group Bureau. The latter consists of the group meetings and the national delegations. Their roles and the significance is analysed below. The significance of committee-based division of labour is in turn explained in the next section.

Figure 3.1. The internal structure of an EP party group

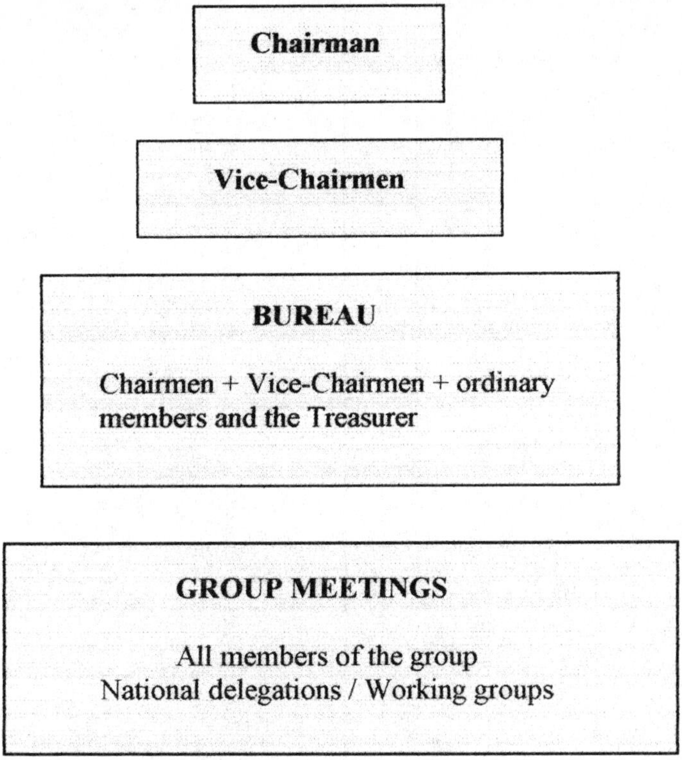

```
┌─────────────────────────┐
│        Chairman         │
│                         │
└─────────────────────────┘

┌─────────────────────────────┐
│       Vice-Chairmen         │
│                             │
└─────────────────────────────┘

┌──────────────────────────────────────┐
│               BUREAU                  │
│                                      │
│  Chairmen + Vice-Chairmen + ordinary │
│  members and the Treasurer           │
│                                      │
└──────────────────────────────────────┘

┌────────────────────────────────────────┐
│           GROUP MEETINGS               │
│                                        │
│        All members of the group        │
│   National delegations / Working groups │
│                                        │
└────────────────────────────────────────┘
```

Table 3.1. shows that each party group has developed its own internal hierarchical structure, with much variation between the groups. Notable is the difference between the Socialists and the EPP. Whereas only 17.7 % of the Socialists' MEPs were members of the group Bureau, the EPP Bureau operates on a much wider membership, including 38 % of the group's MEPs. The smaller groups have less members, and the demarcation line between the Bureau and the rest of the group is bound to be less rigid and of lesser importance than in larger party groups where the sheer size of the groups necessitates more organised and institutionalised mechanisms of co-ordination.

Table 3.1. The leadership and Bureaux of the EP party groups, 1993

Party Groups	MEPs	Chairmen and Vice-Chairmen	Total Bureau Members	Bureau MEPs (%)
PES	198	1+12	35	17.7
PPE	163	1+6	62	38.0
ELDR	44	1+10	12	27.3
Greens	28	2+2	5	17.9
EDA	20	1+5	9	45.0
Rainbow	16	2+0	6	37.5
ER	14	1+3	9	64.3
LU	13	1+2	3	23.1
NA	22			
Total EP	518	50	141	27.2

Party groups: see the list of abbreviations.

Total Bureau Members: As Bureau members were counted the Chairmen, the Vice-Chairmen, the ordinary members of the Bureau and the Treasurer. The ELDR Group, the Greens, and the Left Unity did not report having any ordinary Bureau members. The European Right also had a Deputy-Treasurer and he is included in the ER Bureau. In two groups (LU and Rainbow) the same individual acted as both a Treasurer and as a member of the Bureau (Rainbow) or as a Vice-Chairman (LU).

Bureau MEPs: The percentage figure shows the share of the group's MEPs belonging to the group Bureau.

Source: European Parliament: *List of Members* (21.6.1993).

Just over 27 % of the 518 MEPs in 1993 were members of the party group Bureaux, with 9.7 % of MEPs being either Chairmen or Vice-Chairmen of their political groups. The role of the group Chairman is important since this person represents the group in the powerful Conference of Presidents, the body largely responsible for organising the work of the legislature (see section 3.4.).

The most important intra-group body is the Bureau which is composed of the group's Chairman (often referred to as the group President), its Vice-Chairmen, ordinary members of the Bureau and the group's Treasurer. The Bureaux are largely responsible for handling issues relating to the groups' internal organisation and administration, but they also take decisions on matters appearing on the agenda of the Parliament. The size of the Bureau in relation to the whole group tends to vary from one party group to another (Table 3.1.).

Places in the Bureaux are distributed between the group's national party delegations on the basis of the respective sizes of the delegations (d'Hondt system). In practice the leaders of these national party contingents are automatically members of the Bureau. In case of larger national party delegations, the leader of the delegation is the Chairman or one of the Vice-Chairmen of the party group, with the party delegation also having additional seats in the Bureau (see Westlake, 1994a: 140).

National party delegations

National party delegations, in particular the larger ones, often have their own hierarchical structures. The importance of these national party delegations is considerable inside the party groups. The influence of a national party delegation depends mainly on its size, with the largest delegations in a very strong position. National party delegations elect their own leaders, and these persons represent their parties in intra-group negotiations, and often take decisions in the Bureaux on behalf of their delegations. Negotiations at the group level are often preceded by similar discussions within the national party delegations. When a party group is unable to act cohesively, the blame usually lies with a national party delegation that has decided not to follow the recommended group position. Reasons behind these 'opt-outs' are often domestic, with the delegations choosing to go their own way because of national concerns.

While the importance of national party delegations must not be underestimated, it must by no means be taken for granted that these party delegations are unitary actors themselves. Many national parties are divided over Europe, and these cleavages are also present inside the Parliament. The obvious examples are the two main British parties: both the Conservative and the Labour contingents in the EP have experienced splits when anti/pro-integration votes have been on the agenda of the plenary.

Group meetings

Research on parliamentary parties in national legislatures has shown that party group meetings - that is, a meeting in which all members of the group can participate - play an important role. These meetings provide the opportunity for exchanging opinions, presenting arguments, and letting off steam. The group meetings serve thus as fora for intra-group conflict-resolution and compromise-seeking before the topics appear on the agenda of the plenary.[5]

The EP party groups have in a similar fashion their own group meetings in which to discuss matters and to try to iron out differences of opinion. The groups convene regularly both in Brussels prior to the plenary week and also during the plenary held in Strasbourg. The meetings in Brussels constitute a 'Group week', lasting normally two to three days. During the Group week groups primarily discuss the topics appearing on the agenda of the plenary to be held the next week. During the plenary in Strasbourg political groups convene as they consider necessary.

These group discussions are important since they provide the individual members with a chance to express their points of view. This does obviously not mean that a group meeting would be a forum where all members may participate in discussion and decision-making with equal weight and influence. Decisions on group positions may in practice have been taken in advance of the group meeting, with the group leadership using the meeting to inform the backbenchers of such decisions agreed in the committees or in inter-party negotiations. Alternatively group spokesmen on particular issues use the group meeting to present their reports, with the opinion of the spokesman often constituting also the final party group position.

The size of the party group is of importance here: in group meetings of the smaller party groups the individual member has a better chance to receive his or her desired share of speaking time since the overall number of participants is lower. Due to sheer reasons of size, group meetings of the larger groups - at least if well-attended - are bound to be more formal and organised than the meetings of smaller party groups. However, in group meetings the individual members at least have the opportunity to hear the arguments and positions of their colleagues, and may then make up their minds whether to support the majority view or not.

When MEPs have in advance decided not to follow the official group position, they may use the forum offered by these group meetings to explain the reason behind their decision.[6] To quote Bay Brzinski:

"Group week contributes to group unity by working out differences and conflicts before the plenary session and by providing an alternative forum for disagreements to be aired. Some votes are delayed or measures are amended when group meetings show significant disagreement. Though group members accept that disagreements will exist, voting against the group position without first expressing concerns during group meetings is frowned upon and reportedly rarely occurs among the large groups." (Bay Brzinski, 1995: 154)

Bay Brzinski cites the example provided by a member of the EPP Group secretariat:

"On issues on which members would not feel very strongly, they will vote with the majority. If they feel strongly, they find other ways of demonstrating it. Very rarely they will vote against the group line in plenary. According to our rules it is possible [voting against the group line], *only they have to state it before in the group.* Not just behind curtains, suddenly voting against the group. That gives very negative voices in the group. They state their reasons, and why they have to do it." (Bay Brzinski, 1995: 149) (emphasis in the original)

Whips

Political groups, at least the larger ones, have their own whips. These whips are employed to perform the same role as their counterparts in national legislatures: to give voting instructions, to instil voting discipline on the members, and to mobilise members to be present in the chamber during voting periods. However, the position of the whip should not be overestimated:

"In terms of mechanics, the 'Whip' is normally nothing more than a list, prepared by the group secretariats and circulated to members' benches in the hemicycle before voting periods, setting out the recommended group position on each amendment as well as on final resolutions and reports...On most uncontroversial business the group position is determined and indicated by the group's spokesman. (That is, members sitting in the competent committee and designated as being responsible for co-ordinating the group's work on that particular subject matter.) More controversial business would normally be taken to a discussion in the group, and a group line decided, frequently by a vote." (Westlake, 1994a: 238)

Whips keep a check on both the attendance and voting records of their groups' representatives. But the job of the whip is made difficult by lack of available formal sanctions. Individuals who constantly dissent from the group line can expect not to receive nominations of their choice within the Parliament. In the run-up to the vote on Jacques Santer's nomination as the Commission President in July 1994, with the outcome of the vote by no means clear, the President of the EPP group, Wilfried Martens, in fact indicated to his group that "failure to support Santer would be met with sanctions, including possible expulsion from the group." (Hix and Lord, 1996: 66; Johansson, 1997). The use of this kind of threat is extremely rare in the Parliament.

With no governing majority to defend or challenge, with very high overall levels of absenteeism (see chapter 4), with national parties in control of selecting candidates to the party lists in the European elections, and with issues of national importance undermining group consensus, the whip's role is less authoritative than in many national parliaments.[7] And moreover, not all groups have whips. The following account by Winnie Ewing, the Scottish National Party MEP for Highlands and Islands, who here recalls her experience from the EDA Group in the 1984-89 Parliament, is very informative:

"Now the essential about our group is that we don't have a whip. Obviously, the RPR is too right wing for me, so I wouldn't be able to vote with them on many things, although, on the whole, I don't have much difficulty. On fish, agricultural, regional and many, many subjects I don't have much difficulty at all, but when there is difficulty you'll find in our group that there's a split with the French, particularly now, but we don't have a problem because we who want vote one way and they vote another way and I don't have any personal problems with that." (Ewing, 1989: 20)[8]

52

3.3. Controlled Specialisation: MEPs and the Committee System

Recent literature on parliaments - mainly of American origin - has paid much attention to the position of committees inside legislatures. How autonomous are they from parliamentary parties? Does a system of committee-based specialisation facilitate or undermine the cohesion of parties? Who controls appointments to committees?

While much of the literature (at least those works focusing on Congressional politics) has tended to view committees as relatively independent arenas of decision-making vis-à-vis the parliamentary parties, the argument here emphasises the interdependence of the EP committees and the EP party groups, with the ascendancy of the latter over the former contributing to the cohesion of the party groups. This hypothesis conforms with a study on Western European legislatures which concluded that while - or indeed because - committees were important actors in legislatures, parliamentary party groups held the upper hand, primarily by controlling appointments to committees (Damgaard, 1995).[9] This ability to control assignments (and not only committees) is significant since it provides the parties with an excellent means to threaten, punish, and reward individual members.

There are currently 626 representatives in the Parliament, each of them facing demands from various intra- and extra-parliamentary actors. Considering the amount of legislative and own-initiative resolutions prepared and voted on in the chamber, the party groups have been forced to develop ways of allocating rights and responsibilities in the Parliament without losing control over outcomes.

The argument here is that the *committee-based division of labour* performs that role by delegating rights and duties within groups while facilitating group cohesion. Naturally the larger groups are in a much better position to achieve this than the smaller groups given their larger share of seats in the committees. The MEPs sitting on the respective committees also normally act as spokesperson(s) on the issues handled in their committee. By discussions within their party groups, these members brief the rest of the group of developments in their committee, and the other MEPs have the opportunity to keep track of what is happening in that particular committee and have the chance to put forward questions and to present their arguments.

Political groups, in particular the larger ones, have adopted the practice of setting up specialised working groups to deal with specific policy questions. The EPP, for example, has currently five such working parties, with each focusing on selected issue areas. These working groups then report to the full group meeting.

The decision of the group is often based on the expert opinion of the spokesperson(s) or a working group. This practice mirrors the situation found in the majority of Western European legislatures. While there is naturally great variation between individual countries, party positions are influenced, or even determined, by the committee members or the party specialists on the issue. This increases party groups' need to have some control vis-à-vis the committees and individual members (see Damgaard, 1995).

In the Parliament the role of the committees has strengthened in parallel to a rise in the workload and competences of the EP. Committees are the arenas in which the bulk of the Parliament's legislative work is carried out, and much of the administrative oversight also takes place there. Committees consider legislative documents sent from the Commission and the Council (Rule 51); draft own-initiative reports (Rule 148; after having been authorised to do so by the Conference of Presidents); frequently organise hearings during which they question commissioners and/or civil servants working in the Commission; and invite experts to come and give their opinions on various issues. The Parliament may even decide to grant a committee the authority to adopt a report on behalf of the whole parent chamber (Rule 52). However, up till now this procedure has been used sparingly.

The division of responsibilities between the committees is found in the Annex VI of the EP Rules of Procedure. Some committees are obviously regarded by MEPs as more prestigious than others, with the Foreign Affairs Committee probably topping the list. While Parliament's formal powers in the field of foreign policy are limited, membership in the Foreign Affairs Committee provides the MEPs with the chance to debate topical foreign policy and security issues. Other prestigious committees include the Agriculture, Fisheries and Rural Development Committee, the Committee on Budgets, the Economic and Monetary Affairs and Industrial Policy Committee, and the Environment, Public Health and Consumer Protection Committee.

Table 3.2. Committees and subcommittees of the European Parliament, 1992

Name of the committee	MEPs
Foreign Affairs and Security	56
Subcommittee on Security and Disarmament	25
Subcommittee on Human Rights	20
Agriculture, Fisheries and Rural Development	45
Subcommittee on Fisheries	20
Budgets	30
Economic and Monetary Affairs and Industrial Policy	49
Energy, Research and Technology	31
External Economic Relations	25
Legal Affairs and Citizens' Rights	30
Social Affairs, Employment and the Working Environment	36
Regional Policy, Regional Planning and Relations with Regional and Local Authorities	35
Transport and Tourism	30
Environment, Public Health and Consumer Protection	50
Culture, Youth, Education and the Media	30
Development and Co-operation	40
Civil Liberties and Internal Affairs	30
Budgetary Control	25
Institutional Affairs	37
Rules of Procedure, the Verification of Credentials and Immunities	25
Women's Rights	30
Petitions	25

Sources: European Parliament: *List of Members*; *Official Journal of the European Communities.*

Particular individual committees are known for their constant scrutiny of the formulation and implementation of EU legislation. The Environment, Public Health and Consumer Protection Committee has been particularly active, engaging in a "conscious strategy of agenda setting" by producing regularly its own-initiative reports, and by actively scrutinising the implementation of EU environmental legislation (Judge, 1993: 191; Judge and Earnshaw, 1994).

Table 3.2. shows a list of the Parliament's committees and subcommittees in 1992 (the year used in the content analysis of parliamentary questions in chapter 5). The average size of a permanent committee in 1992 was 34.7 members. The most popular committees were the Committee on Foreign Affairs and Security with 56, Committee on the Environment, Public Health and Consumer Protection with 50, Committee on Economic and Monetary Affairs and Industrial Policy with 49, and Committee on Agriculture, Fisheries and Rural Development with 45 MEPs.

Apart from the standing committees and their subcommittees, the Parliament may also set up temporary committees[10] and committees of inquiry.[11] In 1992 the Parliament's committee system consisted of 19 permanent committees and four subcommittees. Already in 1953 the ECSC Common Assembly had seven committees, and since then the number of committees has gradually increased.

The committee system offers the member an opportunity to specialise, and an MEP's influence within the Parliament is often largely dependent (apart from holding a leadership position within a party group) on his or her activity and influence within the committee, thus compensating for the gradual curtailment of individual MEPs' rights.

According to Parliament's Rules committee members

"shall be elected during the first part-session following the re-election of Parliament and again two and a half years thereafter." (Rule 135)

In the 1989-94 Parliament nominations to committees took place in the first plenary held after the third European elections, and in the first part-session of the second half of the five-year term in January 1992.

The majority of MEPs are full members of one committee, with some being given an additional seat in another committee, and are substitutes in a second one. In 1992 the 518 MEPs shared between them 659 committee seats, with the average representative having 1.27 committee assignments (excluding subcommittees).[12] The role of a substitute should not be underestimated, for a substitute has almost equal rights with a full member. According to Rule 138/1 "the political groups and the Non-attached Members may appoint a number of permanent substitutes for each committee equal to the number of full members representing them on the committee...These permanent substitutes shall be entitled to attend and speak at committee meetings and, in the event of the absence of the full member, to take part in the vote."

Substitutes have indeed even become rapporteurs in the committees. Due to the limited number of places available, the party groups often cannot accommodate members' wishes, and representatives are forced to accept assignments to other committees. Moreover, members with seats in two committees often concentrate their energy on work in one of the committees while paying much less attention to the work of the second one. Members may also focus on work done in the committee in which they are substitutes, especially if they were not given full memberships in their favoured committees. However, such data on members' committee preferences and actual committee appointments is not available, and therefore it is difficult to draw any conclusions.

It is assumed here that most MEPs take an active interest in the work of their committee and develop expertise in that policy area vis-à-vis other issue areas, excluding, of course, the expertise the members brought with them to the Parliament (that is, expertise based on work outside the Parliament). According to Mattson and Strøm (1995: 271) restrictions on multiple committee memberships increase the legislature's specialisation and expertise by allowing the member to concentrate on one policy field only. This kind of specialisation is obviously further enhanced if that member retains his seat over a long period of time and remains on the same committee. While there is little empirical data available on the Parliament, it seems that members often choose to continue on the same committee after re-election (see Westlake, 1994a).

Membership in EP committees is largely a result of inter-group negotiation, with places being "decided upon by the Political Groups in such a way as to ensure that each committee reflects the overall political balance between the groups in plenary." (Jacobs, Corbett, and Shackleton, 1995: 109)[13] This is also formally recognised in the Parliament's Rules of Procedure:

"Members of committees and temporary committees of inquiry shall be elected after nominations have been submitted by the political groups and the Non-attached Members. The Conference of Presidents shall submit to

Parliament proposals designed to ensure fair representation of Member States and of political views." (Rule 137/1)

The rule of proportionality is also used in appointing committee Chairmen, Vice-Chairmen, and in allocating rapporteurships. To quote Westlake (1994a: 180): "the election of committee office-holders is almost always the result of a prior arrangement between all the mainstream political groups. First, on the basis of their d'Hondt-calculated strengths, the political groups 'choose' their committees. Second, on the basis of their numerical strengths, the national contingents within the political groups choose their preferred committees. Lastly, the national contingents choose preferred chairmen from within their ranks."

Rapporteur is the person responsible for drafting a report on an issue handled in the committee. When drafting the report, the rapporteur must be prepared to compromise his or her own preferences in order to accommodate the views of the other committee members. This need to compromise results from the fact that no party group controls the majority of the seats in the Parliament, and from the inter-related fact that conflict-resolution inside the chamber is mainly based on consensual negotiations within and between the groups. It often happens, however, that a skilful rapporteur (probably a person recognised for his expertise in the area) is able to leave his imprint on the report approved by the committee.

Rapporteurships are highly valued by the members, and often provide the main avenue for building a reputation in the Parliament. If a member succeeds in producing a report that is well received in the committee and later in the plenary, he will develop a policy reputation and his chances of gaining further rapporteurships and other intra-parliamentary nominations will be much improved. Moreover, rapporteurs are also an important counterweight to committee chairmen who are highly influential in their respective policy areas. The rapporteur system guarantees that individual members - and not the committee chairs - are the key persons in the passage of legislation.

Empirical research on the Parliament's committee system in 1990-1992 confirmed that the composition of the committees was informationally efficient: representative in terms of nationality and party affiliation, attracting opposing sides of the argument, and with rapporteurs needing to take into account the preferences of the rest of the committee. Bowler and Farrell have termed this as a "process of co-ordinated - even controlled - specialisation": "the individual members may specialise in their own favoured areas, but they do so under party-group scrutiny and control." (Bowler and Farrell, 1995: 241, 243)

Thus by the time the report reaches the plenary, it is usually representative of the views of the committee, with expertise and representativeness vis-à-vis the whole chamber facilitated by the heterogeneous composition of the committees. Once the report is presented to the plenary, party groups - at least the larger ones - often engage in another majoritarian exercise, coalition-building, in order to reach the legislative majorities needed to pass, reject, or amend pieces of legislation.

In both the committees and in the plenary the emphasis is on working out compromises acceptable to the majority. This often leaves a minority of MEPs, mainly those representing both extremes of the left-right dimension and/or the anti-federalist bloc, dissatisfied with the outcome. However, it must be noted that this minority is in most cases far smaller than in national parliaments. The oversized majorities that characterise decision-making in the EP stand in contrast to national legislatures where governments often enjoy only small majorities and where votes are far more contested, with the opposition eager to exploit any available opportunity to challenge the ruling majority.

3.4. The Conference of Presidents and Intra-Parliamentary Efficiency

This section focuses on the current (post-Maastricht) standing of the party groups. While no longitudinal analysis is presented here, the present ascendancy of the party groups is the result of gradual and piecemeal, but consistent changes introduced as EP's formal powers have been increased in the overall EU decision-making system (see Williams, 1995).

Inside the Parliament appointments to committees (Rule 137) and intra-parliamentary leadership positions (Rule 13) and the allocation of speaking time (Rule 106) are according to the Rules of Procedure based on the rule of proportionality, an arrangement consolidating the position of the larger groups.

Certain procedural rights, some of which were previously also enjoyed by individual members, are now reserved for the party groups (or a committee, or 29 MEPs). These procedural rights include for example the possibility to request a debate to be held on a topical and urgent subject of major importance (Rule 47), the right to table amendments to the Council's common position during the processing of EU legislation (Rule 72), the right to table resolutions in the context of debates on the implementation of common foreign and security policy (Rule 92) and on co-operation in the fields of justice and home affairs (Rule 94), the right to request that an amendment be put to the vote in plenary (Rule 124), and the right to submit an oral question to the Council or the Commission (Rule 40).[14]

The dominant role of party groups inside the Parliament can also be understood as a process of procedural rationalisation aiming at higher institutional efficiency.

> "Once the ball started rolling, i.e. once the EP had finally wrestled some decision-making powers from the other two institutions, it needed more and more regulations and constraints to make its performance functional. What this in fact boiled down to was a curtailing of the once abundant minority and individual rights in a streamlining of procedures and a rationalisation of parliamentary activities. Thus, the political groups of the EP have become the institutional cement pasting together the different units of the Parliament." (Williams, 1995: 395)

When considering the time limitations the Parliament is forced to cope with, it is clear that concern over efficiency and the need to agree on a smooth-running and well-organised internal structure have been crucial in curtailing the procedural rights of the individual MEPs. With a full part-session held once a month and lasting only four to five days, it is important that enough time is reserved for debating legislative matters, and that most of the other topics appearing on the agenda reflect the concerns of the majority of the legislature.

In 1993, "in an act symbolising the gradual concentration of political power within the Parliament in the political groups", the *Conference of Presidents* replaced the enlarged Bureau (Westlake, 1994c: 190). The Rules of Procedure states the composition and decisional rule used in the body:

> 1. The Conference of Presidents shall consist of the President of Parliament and the chairmen of the political groups. The chairman of a political group may arrange to be represented by a member of his group.
> 2. The non-attached Members shall delegate two of their number to attend meetings of the Conference of Presidents, without having the right to vote.
> 3. The Conference of Presidents shall endeavour to reach a consensus on matters referred to it. Where a consensus cannot be reached, the matter shall

be put to a vote subject to a weighting based on the number of Members in each political group. (Rule 23)

The duties of the Conference of Presidents are:

(a): It shall take decisions on the organisation of Parliament's work and matters relating to legislative planning.
(b) It shall be the authority responsible for matters relating to relations with the other institutions and bodies of the European Community and with the national parliaments of Member States.
(c) The Conference shall be the authority responsible for matters relating to relations with non-member countries and with non-Community institutions and organisations.
(d) It shall draw up the draft agenda of Parliament's part-sessions.
(e) The Conference of Presidents shall be the authority responsible for the composition and competence of committees and temporary committees of inquiry and of joint parliamentary committees, standing delegations and ad hoc delegations.
(f) It shall decide how seats in the Chamber are to be allocated.
(g) The Conference shall be the authority responsible for authorising the drawing up of own-initiative reports.
(h) The Conference of Presidents shall submit proposals to the Bureau concerning administrative and budgetary matters relating to the political groups. (Rule 24)

The list shows that the Conference of Presidents is the body responsible for organising the work of the Parliament. The decisional rule used in the Conference and the powers given to it point to the strengthened position of party groups in the chamber. While the individual representative still has several channels available for pursuing his or her interests (see chapter 5), power inside the Parliament is firmly in the hands of the political groups.

Having analysed the internal structure of the EP party groups, their position vis-à-vis the committees, and their dominance inside the chamber, it is essential to examine the evolution of the EP party system in order to understand the main cleavage and coalition structures inside the Parliament. Which groups are most influential in the Parliament? Has the enlargement of the EC/EU resulted in an increase in the number of party groups? How much voting power has each party group had in the directly elected Parliament? It is to these questions that we turn next.

3.5. Fragmentation and Consolidation:
Party Groups in the Parliament, 1979-1996

The three groups formed in the ECSC Common Assembly in June 1953 - Christian Democrats, Liberals, and the Socialists - remained the only groups until 1965 when an internal split in the Liberal group resulted in the founding by the French Gaullists of the European Democratic Union, a predecessor of the European Democratic Alliance (EDA). The entry of three new member states to the Community in 1973 altered the balance in the chamber, with two completely new groups being formed: European Conservatives group, established by the British Conservative Party MEPs, and a Communist Group. In the directly elected EP the number of political groups has varied between eight and eleven.

Political groups and the distribution of seats between them in the directly elected EP is shown in Tables 3.3. and 3.4. The picture that emerges has elements of both stability and change. Stability and continuity is represented by the consolidation of the two largest groups and the number of groups; change by emergence and disappearance of smaller party groups both at elections and during the legislative term.

The Socialists and the EPP emerged as the two largest groups after the first direct elections in 1979, and these mainstream party groups have maintained their positions throughout the period under analysis. Accession of Greece into the Community in 1981 brought little changes in the respective sizes of the groups. The forming of the far-right European Right in 1984 led to protests inside the chamber, and despite having gained official group status, the group was excluded from receiving its share of intra-parliamentary appointments during its ten-year existence (1984-1994) in the Parliament. The Rainbow Group, like the CDI in the 1979-84 EP, was very much a product of the Parliament's Rules of Procedure, bringing together a variety of regionalist members, a Green sub-group, and anti-marketeers. The Iberian enlargement in 1986 brought 84 new MEPs to the chamber, with the main beneficiaries being the Socialists and the Liberals.

Table 3.3. Party groups in the 1979-1987 EP

Date / Group	1979	seats (%)	1981	seats (%)	1984	seats (%)	1987	seats (%)
PES	113	27.6	123	28.3	130	30.0	165	31.9
EPP	107	26.1	117	27.0	110	25.3	115	22.2
ELDR	40	9.8	39	9.0	31	7.1	44	8.5
EDG	64	15.6	63	14.5	50	11.5	66	12.7
EDA	22	5.4	22	5.1	29	6.7	29	5.6
COM	44	10.7	48	11.1	41	9.4	48	9.3
CDI	11	2.7	11	2.5				
RB					20	4.6	20	3.9
ER					16	3.7	16	3.1
NA	9	2.2	11	2.5	7	1.6	15	2.9
Total	410		434		434		518	

Party groups: see the list of abbreviations.
Date: 1979 = following EE; 1981 = following the first European elections in Greece on 18 October 1981; 1984 = following EE; 1987 = situation 31.12.1987. First European elections in Spain were on 10 June 1987, and in Portugal on 19 July 1987. In September 12 MEPs, the minimum number required at that point to form a group, formed the Group for the Technical Co-ordination and Defence of Independent Groups and Members (TCDI), but this group was dissolved already in the following month.
Source: *Official Journal of the European Communities*, and European Parliament: *List of Members*.

Table 3.4. Party groups in the 1989-1994 EP

Date Group	1989	seats (%)	1992	seats (%)	1993	seats (%)	1994	seats (%)
PES	180	34.7	180	34.7	198	38.2	198	34.9
EPP	121	23.4	162	31.3	162	31.3	157	27.7
ELDR	49	9.5	45	8.7	46	8.9	43	7.6
EDG	34	6.6						
V	30	5.8	27	5.2	28	5.4	23	4.1
EUL	28	5.4	29	5.6			28	4.9
EDA	20	3.9	21	4.1	20	3.9	26	4.6
ER	17	3.3	14	2.7	14	2.7		
LU	14	2.7	13	2.5	13	2.5		
RB	13	2.5	15	2.9	16	3.1		
EN							19	3.4
FE							27	4.8
ERA							19	3.4
NA	12	2.3	12	2.3	21	4.1	27	4.8
Total	518		518		518		567	

Party groups: see the list of abbreviations.
Date: 1989 = following EE; 1992 = situation in May 1992 following the merger between EPP and EDG; 1993 = situation in January 1993 after the EUL had ceased to exist, and the majority of the group had joined the Socialists; 1994 = following EE.
Source: *Official Journal of the European Communities*, and European Parliament: *List of Members.*

Third European elections in 1989 led to a split in the Communist (COM) camp, with the EUL and LU groups formed in the aftermath of the elections, the EUL representing the moderate and the LU the extreme wing of European communism.[15] Following their success in the elections, the Greens were able to form a group of their own. The EPP suffered a setback in the elections, but the fusion with the EDG in May 1992 helped them regain their numerical strength. Similarly in January 1993 the Socialists increased their share of the seats when the EUL group was dissolved and the majority of the group joined the Socialists.

The 1994 elections led to further changes among the smaller groups. The Rainbow Group and the ER no longer exist in the fourth Parliament, while three new party groups were formed: the mononational Forza Europa, the anti-Maastricht Europe of the Nations (EN), and the left-wing splinter group European Radical Alliance (ERA).

Table 3.5. shows the fractionalisation of the directly elected Parliament between 1979 and 1995. The fractionalisation of a decision-making body can be measured in many ways. In the second column is the increase in EU member states since the first European elections. The third column shows the number of party groups during the same period. In the fourth column is the percentage of seats held by the two largest groups, PES and EPP. The final column reports the Rae-indices (Rae, 1967). The Rae-index is the probability that a randomly selected pair of representatives belong to different party groups. The index ranges from 0 (= one party alone forms the decision-making body) to 1 (total fragmentation: the decision-making body consists of individual representatives only). Thus the higher the index, the more fragmented the Parliament is.[16]

The number of political groups and the degree of fractionalization have remained almost constant throughout the 1979-1995 period, despite the fact that six member states have joined the EC/EU since 1979. The number of political groups has remained between eight and eleven, and the Parliament has been dominated by its two heavyweights - the Socialists and the EPP. They have at every point controlled over half of the seats in the chamber, with their share of the seats even reaching and staying above 60 % since 1992.

The Rae-indices show that while the Parliament has been a fragmented legislature since the first direct elections, the level of fragmentation is lower since the 1989 elections. However, while there has been a decline in the level of fragmentation, the change has not been significant, and the EP can still be considered to be a fragmented body.

Table 3.5. The fractionalisation of the EP, 1979-1995

EP	Member states	Party Groups	PES / EPP	Rae's index
1979	9	8	53.7 %	.806
1981	10	8	55.3 %	.801
1984	10	9	55.3 %	.812
1987	12	9	54.1 %	.810
1989	12	11	58.1 %	.800
1992	12	10	66.0 %	.762
1993	12	9	69.5 %	.738
1994	12	10	62.6 %	.783
1995	15	10	63.2 %	.775

Date: 1979 = after the European Elections (EE); 1981 = following the first EP elections in Greece on 18 October 1981; 1984 = after the second EE; 1987 = situation 31.12.1987 following first European elections in Spain and in Portugal; 1989 = after the third EE; 1992 = situation in May 1992 following the merger between EPP and the EDG; 1993 = situation in January 1993 after the EUL had ceased to exist, and the majority of the group had joined the Socialists; 1994 = after the fourth EE; 1995 = situation in January 1995 after the latest EU enlargement.
Party groups: Including the non-attached (NA) members as one group.
PES / EPP: The percentage of seats held by the two largest groups, the Socialists and the EPP.
Rae's index: The formula for computing Rae's index is $F = 1 - \sum p_i^2$, where p is the party group's share of seats.
Source: Wiberg and Raunio (1997).

Each successive EC/EU enlargement has presented both a challenge and an opportunity to the Parliament and its political groups. The national parties of the new member states have entered the Strasbourg chamber, and their successful incorporation into the pre-existing party groups shows the ability of the party groups to accommodate new party delegations. Since the EP party groups are based on the traditional party families found in most Western European societies and recognised in the political science literature[17], this incorporation of new member parties has been eased by *ideological homogeneity* between the national parties making up a transnational party group. Indeed, in several cases the new national parties entering the Parliament have been members of the respective transnational party federations long before their country joined the European Union.

The interests of the new national party delegations and the party groups coincide: EP groups are interested in gaining new members as this will increase their numerical strength and influence in the Parliament. The national parties, on the other hand, benefit from belonging to a party group, increasing thereby their chances of gaining preferred intra-parliamentary appointments, and preventing them from being marginalised in the Parliament. Sometimes the incorporation of new parties has proven difficult, with new entrants needing their time to settle in. However, such problems are hardly avoidable, considering the diversity of political ideologies and geopolitical realities represented in the Strasbourg Parliament.

The larger groups like the Socialists and the EPP accommodate national party delegations from all member states, while smaller groups are often dominated by or even formed around one national party delegation. Parliament's Rules encourage the formation of groups by providing them with procedural rights not enjoyed by individual members and by granting them considerable financial help. This has led to the birth of some ideologically notoriously heterogeneous groups, such as the Technical Group of Co-ordination and Defence of Independent MEPs (CDI) in the 1979-84 EP and the Rainbow Group in the 1984-89 and 1989-94 Parliaments, and also to the existence of groups formed around one national party such as the European Democratic Group (EDG) which was dominated by the British Conservatives. An extreme example was the Forza Europa (FE) group, which consisted exclusively of the representatives of the Forza Italia-party. Formed after the 1994 European elections, the group merged with EDA in the summer of 1995.

National party delegations and/or individual MEPs have often changed from one group to another either just after the elections or during the legislative term, thus slowing the institutionalisation of EP party groups. European elections can also be regarded as a negative factor in the consolidation of the EP party system, with smaller political groups particularly vulnerable should their member party delegations suffer heavy electoral defeats (Bardi, 1996). Not surprisingly there have been calls for raising the numerical and nationality thresholds needed to form a group.

The EP party groups are a heterogeneous collection of well-established groups and more temporary alliances. Outside observers may regard the larger groups as more 'European' and more representative than the smaller political groups that are often formed around one or two national parties and include MEPs from only a small number of member states. However, considering the diversity of party systems in the EU member countries, it is simply not possible at the moment to have the Parliament housing truly transnational party groups; that is each group having one national party from each member state. To quote Mogens N. Pedersen:

"The great variety of party systems in Western Europe - ranging from '2 ½'-party systems to highly fragmented, even atomised multi-party systems - precludes the formation of a relatively simple system of political groups in the European Parliament." (Pedersen, 1996: 23)

Voting power in the Parliament

How much voting power do the party groups have in the EP?[18] If we do not have any specific knowledge neither on the actors' policy positions nor on the relevant policy dimensions, we can get some insight on the various party groups' power vis-à-vis each other by computing these party groups' voting power indices.

Several voting power indices have been constructed. The most common ones are the Banzhaf-index and the Shapley-Shubik-index (Banzhaf, 1965; Shapley and Shubik, 1954). Voting power analysis is important since parliamentary party groups' voting power can deviate quite remarkably from their distribution of seats. More votes mean more power, as measured by the voting indices, but not necessarily in direct proportion. Although the power indices do not model the players' actual behaviour, they do measure each player's potential ability to change the result of the vote.

Voting power indices have been normalised for reasons of comparability so that they range from 0 to 1. An actor which does not have any voting power at all (index value = 0) is called a 'dummy'. The intuitive ideas behind both the Banzhaf- and Shapley-Shubik-indices are straightforward and clear.

The Banzhaf-index simply counts the number of coalitions in which an actor i is a swing voter. A swing occurs when the defection of voter i changes a coalition from winning to losing. Briefly, if C is a winning coalition under a given decision rule d with actor $i \in C$, then i swings if C - $\{i\}$ is losing, that is, if the same coalition without i would be losing. The Banzhaf-voting power of a voter is the proportion of winning coalitions that would turn into losing coalitions were the voter to leave it. This exit out of a coalition is also called a critical defection, and the voter's critical defections are divided by the total number of critical defections for all voters.

The Shapley-Shubik-index is computed by listing first all permutations of voters and then calculating the relative frequency with which a particular voter is in a pivotal position. The Shapley-Shubik-index draws our attention to the notion of players who can convert losing coalitions into winning ones. The Shapley-Shubik-index of a voter i in voting body v (also called a weighted voting game) is equal to the number of permutations of N voters in v in which i is pivotal divided by n! which is the total number of possible permutations for the game v. Player i is pivotal only if her membership turns the losing coalition into a winning coalition. All permutations are taken equally likely. Since neither the issues nor the preferences of the actors are specified, we can ascribe by the principle of insufficient reason equal probability to any issue and corresponding preference ordering, i.e. the permutation of voters.

The formula for computing Player i's Shapley-Shubik-index is the following:

$$SS = \sum_{S^* \subset N} ((s-1)!(n-s)!/n!) \, [v(S^*)-v(S^*-\{i\})]$$

where N is the set of players $(1,...,n)$ and s is the number of players in $S^* \subset N$ $v(S^*) = 0$ if the coalition is losing, and 1 if the coalition is winning.

The formula for computing the (standardised) Banzhaf-index for Player i is:

$$B = \sum_{S^* \subset N} [v(S^*)-v(S^*-\{i\})] / \sum_{i} \sum_{S^* \subset N} [v(S^*- v(S^*-\{i\})]$$

69

Table 3.6.   Voting power of EP party groups in the 1979-1987 Parliament under simple majority rule

Date Group	1979 B	1979 S-S	1981 B	1981 S-S	1984 B	1984 S-S	1987 B	1987 S-S
PES	.2931	.3095	.2931	.3095	.3075	.3310	.3613	.3778
EPP	.2586	.2810	.2586	.2810	.2138	.2440	.1765	.2063
ELDR	.1034	.0952	.1034	.0952	.0794	.0690	.0756	.0683
EDG	.1724	.1619	.1724	.1619	.1324	.1202	.1429	.1349
EDA	.0345	.0286	.0345	.0286	.0631	.0548	.0504	.0468
COM	.1034	.0952	.1034	.0952	.1079	.0988	.0840	.0754
CDI	.0172	.0143	.0172	.0143				
RB					.0468	.0405	.0420	.0349
ER					.0346	.0298	.0336	.0278
NA	.0172	.0143	.0172	.0143	.0143	.0119	.0336	.0278

Abbreviations: B = Banzhaf-index; S-S = Shapley-Shubik-index.
Date: 1979 = following EE; 1981 = following the first EP elections in Greece on 18 October 1981; 1984 = after the second EE; 1987 = situation 31.12.1987 following first European elections in Spain and in Portugal.
Source: Wiberg and Raunio (1997).

Table 3.7. Voting power of EP party groups in the 1989-1994 Parliament under simple majority rule

Date Group	1989 B	1989 S-S	1992 B	1992 S-S	1993 B	1993 S-S	1994 B	1994 S-S
PES	.4041	.4066	.2978	.3250	.3817	.3948	.3620	.3762
EPP	.1347	.1753	.2071	.2421	.1642	.1937	.1500	.1937
ELDR	.1095	.1062	.1460	.1290	.1386	.1341	.1060	.0984
EDG	.0737	.0677						
V	.0632	.0566	.0769	.0675	.0832	.0734	.0500	.0429
EUL	.0568	.0495	.0789	.0690			.0580	.0508
EDA	.0453	.0404	.0454	.0401	.0576	.0520	.0580	.0508
ER	.0358	.0316	.0394	.0341	.0362	.0294		
LU	.0284	.0245	.0355	.0306	.0320	.0258		
RB	.0253	.0217	.0394	.0341	.0448	.0413		
EN							.0500	.0429
FE							.0580	.0508
ERA							.0500	.0429
NA	.0232	.0197	.0335	.0286	.0618	.0556	.0580	.0508

Abbreviations: B = Banzhaf-index; S-S = Shapley-Shubik-index.

Date: 1989 = after the third EE; 1992 = situation in May 1992 following the merger between EPP and the EDG; 1993 = situation in January 1993 after the EUL had ceased to exist, and the majority of the group had joined the Socialists; 1994 = after the fourth EE.

Source: Wiberg and Raunio (1997).

71

Tables 3.6. and 3.7. show the distribution of normalised a priori voting power in the 1979-1994 EP under simple majority decision rule. It is assumed that all representatives (a) cast their vote, and that they (b) cast their vote identically with their party.

No party group has at any point in time between 1979-1995 alone controlled the majority. The PES is the strongest party group, but even its all time maximum has been only .4066 after the 1989 European elections. There are no dummies, i.e. all party groups have some voting power in influencing the outcomes of votes in the EP. It is, however, quite clear that the small party groups have so far had only a marginal impact on the voting results.

Comparing each party group's share of seats with its share of voting power, we find that no party group gets systematically at every instance more or less voting power than its share of seats would indicate. The PES gets a larger share of voting power in all instances except in 1992 after the fusion between EPP and EDG. Thus the largest party group is favoured under simple majority rule. Significantly, the EPP got a smaller share of voting power than of the seats in all instances except in 1979 and in 1981 in the case of its Shapley-Shubik-value. The ELDR got in most cases a larger share of voting power than of seats.

The smallest party groups were marginalised up to the third European elections in 1989, but their situation has improved since then. After 1992 the smaller party groups have in the majority of cases a larger share of a priori voting power than of seats. But, on the other hand, their voting power is nevertheless very weak. The two 'giants', PES and EPP, can together control the voting outcomes under the simple majority decision-making rule.

While the above analysis looked at voting power between the EP party groups, an equally interesting question is the distribution of (voting) power inside the political groups. Quite naturally the larger national party delegations within the groups carry more weight in intra-group decision-making, with the smaller parties having less influence on the outcomes. Analysing the voting power of national delegations (and not national party delegations) inside the Socialist and EPP groups in the 1994 and 1995 Parliaments, Torsten Peters (1996b) shows how a coalition by the British, Spanish, and German delegations would be able to decide the position of these two party groups. This conclusion is based on the usual assumptions that these national delegations (i) vote as unitary actors, (ii) vote together, and (iii) that absolute majority rule applies in intra-group decision-making.

While decision-making inside the groups is a much more complicated process, the analysis nevertheless shows how the larger national delegations inside the two largest groups are clearly strategically well-placed to influence the outcomes. To quote Attinà (1997): "dispersion may bring 'parliamentary weakness' to a national delegation but this is the more true the less the deputies of a country are concentrated in the largest Groups of the Parliament because these Groups are the most important actors in the formation of parliamentary majorities." The French and Italian delegations are in this sense in the weakest position, with the dispersion of their representatives throughout the party groups leading to a weaker role in intra-chamber decision-making.

Further results of the EP party group voting power analysis show that the two largest groups' share of voting power increases as the decision rule becomes more stringent. Thus the Socialists and the EPP are largely able to control the results of the votes in the chamber, with their position being further consolidated by the majority requirements of the various legislative procedures. Moreover, it has to be kept in mind that these two mainstream groups are in broad agreement over the future of European integration.

Building legislative majorities

In order to make the most of its existing powers, to maximise its own influence, and to fulfil its inter-institutional role in passing, amending, or rejecting legislation, the decision-making rules of the European Union require the Parliament to muster so-called *legislative majorities.*[19] The co-decision, co-operation, assent, and budget procedures normally require the chamber to achieve absolute majorities. Therefore in the 1989-1994 EP of 518 MEPs the need to reach the threshold figure of 260 became a pressing concern.

Since the ability of the Parliament to build those majorities depends to a great extent on co-operation between the two largest party groups, the Socialists and the EPP, the leaders of these two groups soon recognised the necessity of consensual decision-making and extensive negotiations in search of mutually acceptable compromises. The following is the way in which Rudi Arndt, the chairman of the Socialist group from 1984 to 1989, described collaboration between the two large groups:

"Then there was the second legislative period of the directly elected Parliament. It started with the Brussels meeting of the major groupings. It subsequently became known in many quarters as 'the meeting of the giants' at which it was agreed that there was no point in a mutual flexing of ideological muscles: the only sensible strategy was to achieve appropriate majorities. At that meeting in Brussels - I remember it well - both the Christian Democrats and the Socialists said: 'that's the right approach, let's try it'. The agreement in Brussels was that the Socialist Group would be responsible for discussing details with the left wing in Parliament and the Christian Democrats had the tasks of doing the same with the right wing, to ensure that a majority could be created. We agreed that the working parties would keep in touch with each other on a permanent basis and that whenever there was an issue on which a joint approach was not possible in the working parties, there would be a co-ordinating meeting in Strasbourg...Our problem was not so much to get the majority, but to involve enough MEPs in the vote to show that we could reach the figure of 260. We had problems in our own groups of course: there were plenty of people who objected to their policies being 'watered down'. I know for a fact that if the chairman of the Christian Democratic Group wanted to introduce something he would say to his group: 'if we don't do this, we won't get Arndt's support'. And I'd agreed with him beforehand that I would say to my group: 'if we don't do this then we won't get the support of Klepsch'. That, more or less, is how things operated." (Arndt, 1992: 66-67)[20]

This approach, even though understandable from procedural point of view, has not been without its negative consequences. Smaller and less influential groups have often felt neglected and pushed aside, accusing the largest groups of 'oligopoly' or 'duopoly'.[21] Arndt (1992: 67) also admitted this fact, agreeing that "it has meant steamrolling the smaller factions in the group and, of course, the smaller groups who often got very annoyed, because they regarded Parliament as a forum for making known their views, whereas we regarded it as a forum for achieving majorities."

The requirement to achieve legislative majorities has led to what Weiler (1991: 429) has called "neutralisation of ideology", with the result that certain MEPs have become ideologically marginalised within the chamber, a factor contributing to high levels of absenteeism from the hemicycle when votes are taken. However, these majority requirements have a positive impact on party group cohesion. Since the Parliament is forced to rally the required number of MEPs behind its resolution, members have an incentive to show up and insert their cards into the voting machines. Without such contribution from the party groups, the reputation and policy input of the Parliament would be undermined if it turned out to be the case that the Strasbourg Parliament could not mobilise its members either to be present in the chamber or to form required majorities on a consistent basis.[22]

The party system in the European Parliament is characterised by a core of permanent political groups that are accompanied by smaller less stable groups. The more established mainstream party groups - the Socialists (PES) and the Christian Democrats and Conservatives (EPP) - have over the years strengthened and subsequently consolidated their position in the legislature. Every EP resolution is supported by at least one of these two giants. Smaller groups have on the other hand come and gone, with much depending on the electoral success of individual national parties. This fragmentation of opposition has led and is bound to lead in the future to centripetal moves in the chamber, with some of the smaller groups aligning with the larger groups in order to increase their power.[23]

Political groups rule in Strasbourg. This chapter has analysed the evolution, internal structure, and standing of transnational political groups in the European Parliament. Party groups enjoy considerable material benefits in the chamber; they have developed their internal organisation in a way which enables them to delegate authority to individual members without surrendering control over outcomes; and they have increased their power at the expense of individual MEPs' rights. But are EP political groups capable of unitary action? Does conflict-resolution inside party groups lead to cohesive action in the plenary when votes are taken?

Notes

[1] The arguments presented in this chapter benefited from discussions in the workshop on Parliamentary Party Groups at the ECPR Oslo Joint Sessions of Workshops, March-April 1996 (Raunio, 1996c). I am grateful to the workshop participants for their insightful comments.

[2] Already "in the constitutive meeting of the Common Assembly, the first important vote, over the election of the President, showed an alignment along party lines. The German Socialists voted together with all the other Socialists for the Belgian Socialist candidate, Mr Spaak, rather than for the German Christian Democrat candidate, von Brentano." (Henig and Pinder, 1969: 478) For information on the emergence and role of party groups in the ECSC Common Assembly, see Henig and Pinder (1969), and Van Oudenhove (1965).

[3] Note that these numerical criteria have changed over the years as the total number of seats has increased.

[4] The information on party group staff and financial resources has been taken from Jacobs, Corbett, and Shackleton (1995: 86-88).

[5] See for example Andeweg (1996), Hagevi (1996), Ilonszki (1996), Kopecký (1996), Müller and Steininger (1996), and Thiebault and Dolez (1996). Note, however, that the respective roles of group meetings, party group leadership, and spokesmen are at least to a certain extent overlapping and complementary, and that this may have an effect on the reliability and comparability of these various surveys. For example, spokesmen and/or the leadership may present their reports to the group meeting where the final decision on the issue is taken. In such cases the position of the spokesman or the group leadership probably often carries the day, but the final decision is nevertheless taken at the group meeting. Much depends on the exact wording used in the questions, and on the choice of answer categories presented to the respondents.

[6] According to Luciano Bardi (1994, 1996) these meetings have the stated purpose of reducing internal conflict, thus 'concealing' the lack of agreement: "These [roll call] analyses appear to reveal a very high degree of intra-group cohesiveness, but such conclusions should be treated very cautiously. In fact, intra-group quasi-unanimity is usually guaranteed by long preparatory committee and party group sessions which have the stated purpose of smoothing out most disagreements. Indeed, the symbolic rather than politically concrete significance of most EP decisions lowers the level of internal dissent and facilitates quasi-unanimous decisions." (Bardi, 1996: 104) I don't find these arguments convincing. First of all, if agreement is reached during the meetings, surely then the meetings are working. Secondly, considering Parliament's increased influence, it is wrong to explain such quasi-unanimity by referring to EP's lack of powers, especially in the post-Maastricht period.

[7] The account by the former chief whip of the British Tory contingent in the EPP group, Mr Simmonds, emphasises the difference between Strasbourg and Westminster: "Of course, the whip does not have the same power and patronage as at Westminster, because there is no European government to defend or bring down. From time to time all national sections of the EPP decline the group whip, when their individual party or national interest is in conflict with it. Long may that practice continue." (Johansson, 1997)

[8] Mrs Ewing changed to the Rainbow Group after the 1989 elections and is currently in the European Radical Alliance (ERA) group.

[9] "In sum, if the parliamentary party leadership is not in charge of committee assignments then it seems, generally, at least to heavily influence appointments to committees. Member preferences are taken into account everywhere, but the party is also concerned with the seniority, loyalty and expertise of its MPs as well as with the need to satisfy systemic demands on the party group as a whole. In addition, geographical and intra-party group considerations play a role in a number of countries, including Germany, Austria, Belgium and Norway." (Damgaard, 1995: 315)

[10] The setting up of temporary committees is regulated in Rule 135/2 of the Rules of Procedure: "Parliament may at any time set up temporary committees, whose powers, composition and term of office shall be defined at the same time as the decision to set them up is taken; their term of office may not exceed twelve months, except where Parliament extends that term on its expiry." These temporary committees are set up to look into matters of major topical concern. Six temporary committees have so far been established (see Jacobs, Corbett, and Shackleton, 1995: 140).

[11] Committees of inquiry have been established to enable the Parliament to study in depth a particular problem or issue. So far nine such committees have been set up (see Jacobs, Corbett, and Shackleton, 1995: 276-278). Committees of inquiry were given Treaty status in article 138c of the Maastricht Treaty: "In the course of its duties, the European Parliament may, at the request of a quarter of its members, set up a temporary Committee of Inquiry to investigate, without prejudice to the powers conferred by this Treaty on other institutions or bodies, alleged contraventions or maladministration in the implementation of Community law, except where the alleged facts are being examined before a court and while the case is still subject to legal proceedings."

[12] This average number of committee assignments per MEP has remained pretty constant in the directly elected Parliament. During the period 1983-1992 the figure has been between 1.17 and 1.29 committee places per representative (Bowler and Farrell, 1995: 224-225). According to Martin Westlake (1994a: 162) the number of committee places per member between 1979 and 1992 has varied between 1.12 and 1.31.

[13] This reflects the consensual practice used in Western European legislatures: "Although committee assignment contains an element of potential conflict, it appears to be dealt with by consensus in most parliaments and for most of the time. Membership composition is, in principle, proportional all over Western Europe, with seat allocations based on the relative size of the party groups in the plenary." (Mattson and Strøm, 1995: 276)

[14] For detailed information on such procedural rights, see the EP Rules of Procedure.

[15] Note that the EUL group in the current EP is very different from the one that merged with the Socialists in 1993. With the Italian MEPs representing the PDS now in the Socialist camp, the group can in fact be regarded more as a successor of the Left Unity Group.

[16] An alternative method for measuring the fragmentation of a legislature is using the so-called 'effective' parties index, which analyses the relative size of parties in a parliament (Laakso and Taagepera, 1979). Luciano Bardi (1996: 108-110) computed this index for the 1979, 1984, 1989, and 1994 Parliaments, and found that the index declines since 1984, thus showing the increase in the relative weight of the larger party groups.

[17] While there is some variation in categorisation, these party families are now recognised in the standard literature on parties and party systems. See for example Gallagher, Laver, and Mair (1992), Seiler (1980), and Von Beyme (1985).

[18] This section is based on the voting power analysis in Wiberg and Raunio (1997). While the analysis is here limited to the simple majority decision-making rule, the analysis in the original source covers also the party groups' voting power under 3/5, 2/3, and 3/4-majority rules.

[19] For a list of the required parliamentary majorities, see Westlake (1994c: 261-263).

[20] Arndt called this institutionalised co-operation 'the European Alliance'.

[21] Such accusations were aired, for example, in connection with the deal between EPP and the Socialists over the choice of EP President in July 1994. According to this deal, reflecting a similar deal made in the 1989-94 Parliament, the Socialists were to hold EP Presidency for the first half of the five-year term (Klaus Hänsch), with the EPP in turn providing the President for the latter part of the 1994-99 legislative term. Not surprisingly, the smaller groups were anxious to voice their concern over such informal behind-the-scenes deals.

[22] The necessity of co-operation between the Socialists and the EPP has been emphasised by Attinà (1997): "... without such a collaboration the Parliament risks not to accomplish its assignment in the government of the Union: in fact, without such a collaboration, the Parliament may cause the co-operation and co-decision procedures not to work in the right way. In fact, without such a deal, each proposal put before the Parliament by the executive (the Commission and the Council) will be approved by the occasional majority of the day and not by a stable parliamentary majority because such a majority has not been formed. If such a stable majority implies that some national parties have to co-operate in the Union Parliament while they conflict in the national government and parliament arenas, such a condition - created by the specific institutional imperatives of the distinct government levels of the European Union, is, however, the condition that allows all federal systems to work."

[23] As argued by Johansson (1997): "... it seems that when making the key choice between preserving autonomy by staying in a smaller Group, or perhaps being independent, or seeking transnational alliances and risk being subdued in a larger but more powerful Group national contingents increasingly opt for the latter choice."

4 Aggregating Interests Within and Between Party Groups in the European Parliament: MEP Voting Behaviour, 1989-1994

4.1. Introduction: Research on Legislative Voting Behaviour[1]

The cohesion of parliamentary parties is often taken for granted in the literature on the national legislatures of the EU member states. While there are occasional splits within party groups, roll-call studies have shown that parliamentary parties can usually be treated as unitary actors. But how cohesive are the party groups in the European Parliament? This chapter analyses the voting behaviour of the transnational political groups in the European Parliament. The temporal scope of the research covers the third directly elected Parliament of 1989-1994. The sample consists of 159 roll-call votes.

Voting behaviour analysis is obviously only one among the many methods with which to measure party cohesion in various representative institutions. With the help of voting records students of legislatures can not only measure the cohesion of collective entities such as parliamentary parties, but we can also increase our knowledge on issues such as the distances between parties, and the importance of variables - such as the socio-economic profile of the member's constituency - that affect representatives' voting behaviour. Voting in committees and the extent to which specific policy areas determine coalition behaviour have likewise been the focus of attention. So far legislative voting behaviour analyses have mainly concentrated on the U.S. Congress, with the method receiving significantly less attention here in Europe (see Collie, 1984).

According to Jacobs, Corbett, and Shackleton:

"whatever the reason for a recorded roll-call vote, it provides a very valuable but currently under-utilised source for assessing the political positions taken by a Political Group and by individual members." (Jacobs, Corbett, and Shackleton, 1995: 160)

So far five scholars have entered the laborious task of studying party group behaviour by going through EP's voting records. The pioneering work of Zellentin (1967) covers the 1958-66 period. Menno Wolters (1982) has traced what he calls 'European interspaces', and his research is based on 40 votes in the 1979-81 Parliament. In subsequent work with Marcel Quanjel (Quanjel and Wolters, 1992, 1993), the 'interspace' approach is applied to sets of roll-call votes from the 1983, 1985 and 1990 Parliaments. Leon Hurwitz (1983, 1987) has measured the cohesion of party groups, national delegations, and largest national party delegations, and the voting similarity of the groups in the 1979-80 EP, but his sample is too small, only 19 votes, to enable us to draw any reliable conclusions.

The most important work is that by Fulvio Attinà (1990, 1992a). Attinà has analysed the cohesiveness of the groups, and the way different decision-making rules and policy areas affect party group unity in both the first (1979-84) and the second (1984-89) terms of the directly elected Parliament. Attinà's sample in his analysis of the 1984-89 EP included 110 votes, with votes categorised according to policy areas (international, institutional, political-economic, social-cultural, sectional-solidaristic) and their formal basis (legislative/budgetary acts, own-initiative resolutions). His research increases substantially our understanding of the party groups in the 1979-89 Parliament.

Finally, Joanne Bay Brzinski (1995) has measured party group cohesion in the 1989-94 EP by a roll-call analysis, supplemented by interviews with EP staff, and by examining members' absenteeism from the plenary when votes were taken. A serious limitation in her voting behaviour analysis is the very small number of votes included in the final sample, on average only 14 votes per party group. As Bay Brzinski (1995: 139) admits: "Because the number of votes used to determine the index of agreement is small, the findings are somewhat tentative." The availability of these earlier works makes possible the longitudinal comparisons included in this chapter. In particular, the similarities and differences between Attinà's work and the new data presented here are highlighted.

Is voting behaviour analysis a reliable and meaningful way to measure party cohesion and the dimensionality of cleavages and alignments in legislatures? Roll-call analysis needs to be supplemented by other methods before anything close to a comprehensive picture of the nature of political groups will emerge. However, it can be argued that roll-call analysis is a particularly worthwhile exercise in the context of the EP. Considering the fact that before legislative and own-initiative resolutions are put to vote, extensive negotiations have often taken place within and between the groups, lack of unitary voting behaviour by groups can be interpreted as definite evidence of failure to reach intra-group consensus on the matter. Voting is the time when a member must make her or his stand known to others. Occasionally party groups may decide to allow a free vote, for example in subjects considered to be 'matters of conscience'.[2] Much depends on the importance of the issue and on whether the group in question has succeeded in finding consensus in its own meeting prior to the vote.

4.2. Broad Coalitions Vulnerable to Internal Dissent? Factors Undermining Party Cohesion

When analysing the level of europeanisation achieved by the transnational party groups in the EP and their respective europarties, political scientists have without exceptions agreed that we still have some way to go before we have anything really resembling true European-wide parties. Writing after the first European elections, Michael Palmer (1981: 71) described the political groups "as broad coalitions and alliances of parliamentarians with similar, but not necessarily totally shared philosophies and objectives." In a more recent account on the nature of the EPP, recognised as the most 'European' of the transnational parties, David Hanley (1994: 194-195) applied the term "an organisation which unites national parties of similar style into a loose framework for political co-operation within European institutions for the pursuit of broad goals." Regardless of the actual wording, both academics and politicians have stressed co-operation and co-ordination between the component units - national parties - as the primary tools for understanding the nature of party cohesion and discipline within the Parliament's party groups.

A number of inter-related institutional factors, most of them specific to the inter-institutional environment in which the EP and its party groups operate, affect the cohesiveness of Parliament's party groups. The various intra-group co-ordination mechanisms established to foster co-operation and cohesion were introduced and explained in the previous chapter.

Drawing mainly on existing literature on the Parliament, this section discusses in turn the mainly negative factors which have been argued to undermine the cohesion of the EP parties.

1) *Lack of meaningful government and opposition roles within the chamber*

The European Union lacks the kind of legislative-executive relationship characterising power sharing and policy-making in the individual EU member states. Even though the Parliament's power of control vis-à-vis the Commission was increased in the Maastricht Treaty, with the nomination of the President-designate and the whole Commission subject to a vote of confidence in the Parliament, the Commission is nevertheless still composed of individuals nominated by their respective member state governments.[3] Thus with no government to defend or bring down, party groups face inevitable difficulties in enforcing voting discipline.

In national legislatures the parties forming the cabinet rely on the support of their MPs. This aspect necessitates unitary voting behaviour by the parliamentary groups of the governing parties. The parties in opposition have a similar incentive to achieve unitary voting behaviour since their ability to challenge the government is dependent on their level of cohesion.[4]

2) *The distance of MEPs from the voters*

Public's general unawareness of the role and work of the Parliament has caused concern among the MEPs. Individual representatives in Strasbourg need not normally take their voters' opinions into account when voting on a specific issue, unless, of course, the issue put to vote attracts considerable media attention in the MEP's home country and is perceived important by the electorate. The *Eurobarometer*-survey (EB 31) carried out at the time of the 1989 European elections showed that a majority of the EU citizens would like to see the representatives co-operating along national lines (59%) instead of according to party group affiliation (29 %), a finding also reflecting voters' unfamiliarity with the internal organisation of the Parliament.

The insulation of MEPs' work from the public increases their freedom of manoeuvre. The impact of this variable is dependent on the attention the issue attracts and its sensitivity in the national arena. The media plays an important role here: were the national media to monitor the voting behaviour of the MEPs (at least on certain specific issues of national significance), re-election seeking MEPs might well come to reconsider their voting decisions. If the EU and the Parliament are given further competences, such monitoring could well increase.

3) *National party delegations undermining consensus within political groups*

Transnational political groups are formations uniting various national parties, and these national party delegations, especially larger ones such as the main British and German parties, carry much weight within the groups. The national party delegations are arguably in a better position than the political groups to instil voting discipline on their representatives as MEPs need their national parties' approval for nomination as candidates in the next European or national elections. Arguing that the transnational party system in the EP is unstable and unrepresentative, Rudy Andeweg (1995: 65) in a recent article emphasised the supremacy of national party delegations over current party groups by writing that "it may be better to speak of a 79 (national) party system than of a nine (transnational) party system in the European Parliament."

National party contingents have their own hierarchical structures, and intra-group decision-making is often based on compromise-building between national party delegations. According to Jacobs, Corbett, and Shackleton

> "on important issues, groups will try to negotiate compromises among their national delegations before taking a decision. When groups fail to vote cohesively, it is usually because one or more national delegations have decided to opt out of a group position." (Jacobs, Corbett, and Shackleton, 1995: 90)

While these national party delegations often cannot accept the party group line because of their different views on the issue decided upon, the reason for voting against the group position is on occasions much more straightforward: over half, 54.2 %, of the interviewed MEPs from the former West Germany identified "national egoism", and not "political-ideological" or "group-interests" as the main factor accounting for intra-group dissent (Hrbek and Schweitzer, 1989: 6).

Several writers have argued that as EP's legislative role continues to be strengthened, national parties will start paying more attention to the behaviour of their representatives in the Parliament. According to John

Fitzmaurice, writing in 1975, parties would come to re-evaluate the EP as an institution:

> "parties are about power and the exercise of power: they react to a new power centre by attempting to structure it...Members of the EP would be called to account by their national parties for their votes and actions in the EP...Party discipline would be imposed, but it might well not be the discipline of the present European party groups but of national parties."
> (Fitzmaurice, 1975: 210)

4) *Voting by nationalities and other cross-group coalitions*

Research on the concept of representation in the EP has shown that MEPs regard themselves as representing multiple interests (see section 5.1.). While members' primary allegiance is to their political groups, on occasions national party delegations join forces in a vote with significant national implications. A good example was in July 1984 when the Parliament rejected the Fontainebleau agreement which gave the United Kingdom a budget refund. All British representatives, regardless of their party group affiliation, voted against the rejection (Vallance and Davies, 1986: 29). Standard accounts on the EP are replete with individual examples of how national interests unite members across group lines, with group cohesion falling when such issues of national importance are on the agenda.

Committees play a significant part in the Parliament's internal organisation, and individual members may develop high levels of specialisation within EP's committee structure (see section 3.3. and chapter 5). Even though votes in the committees are often uncontested, cross-party alignments occur already at the committee level (Arp, 1992: 55-57; Wolters, 1988: 11-12). This can lead to splits in group cohesion in cases where the preferences of committee members are very different from those of the median members of the party groups. However, as argued in section 3.3., in most cases the opposite is expected to happen. The appointment process to committees ("specialisation under the scrutiny of party groups") was hypothesised to foster party group cohesion by organising intra-group division of labour in ways that facilitate co-operation inside the groups.

Representatives from the 15 member states also come together in the various intergroups, approximately 50 of which were in existence after the 1989 and 1994 European elections. These intergroups bring together members from different groups who share a common interest in a specific political objective or policy area.[5] Bardi (1992: 935) has argued that the proliferation of these intergroups acts as a further obstacle to the development of cohesive transnational parties since within intergroups MEPs may form issue-specific alignments on a cross-group basis: "Although they may be very important in forging cross-group alliances, intergroups, by providing MEPs with alternative instruments for the advancement of their political goals, can sometimes cause internal divisions in the party groups." Certain topics, such as the Common Agricultural Policy (CAP) and the further deepening of integration, also attract varying levels of support within the political groups, their controversial nature leading to dissent within the party groups when votes are taken.[6]

5) *The acceptability and cost of voting against the group line*

When casting his or her vote, the individual MEP must consider the potential cost of voting against the group line. Above it was argued that since their renomination as candidates in the future elections (whether local, national, or European) is dependent on their national party, the MEPs have a career motive for respecting the wishes of their national parties. On the other hand, individuals develop a certain reputation within the organisation in which they work. According to Christopher Lord (1994: 12) "national delegations, or even individual MEPs, might be able to lower the costs of making individual deals by assiduously cultivating a reputation for keeping to commitments." If the MEP's activities in the chamber, including voting behaviour, suffer from inconsistencies, the representative may not be able to cultivate support among his colleagues. Such MEPs can expect not to be given important posts within the Parliament or in their groups, nor may they receive committee assignments or rapporteurships of their own choice.

When asked to rate the "acceptability of forms of behaviour" in 1990, 53 % of the interviewed MEPs (response rate 37.6 %) considered voting against the group line as "acceptable or most acceptable". 38 % saw voting against the group line as "unacceptable or most unacceptable". Comparing the answers of the various party groups, members of the Socialist group and the EDA were most opposed to the idea of voting against the group (see Bowler and Farrell, 1993b).[7]

6) *The transnationality and fractionalisation of the political groups*

According to this often formulated view the cohesion of a party group depends on the number of national party delegations included in the group. The logic is the same as in the Council of Ministers: the more views that need to be accommodated, the more problematic it becomes to find common ground. The Socialist group is a fine example. Prior to the enlargement of the Community in 1973 the Socialists were clearly the most cohesive group, but the inclusion of the anti-integrationist Danish and British MEPs led to a drop in group cohesion (Pridham and Pridham, 1981: 54). Many of the groups, notably the Liberals, span a rather wide ideological spectrum, and some groups even include more than one party delegation from the same member state.

7) *The different cleavages found at the European level*

According to this line of reasoning the transnational party groups do not reflect the dominant cleavages characterising politics at the European level (see for example Andeweg, 1995; Bogdanor, 1986; Sweeney, 1984). The EP party groups and the transnational European parties are based on traditional national cleavages, and are therefore arguably largely irrelevant in the context of EU decision-making where many, or even most, issues are on the pro/anti-integration dimension. Therefore party groups - and national party delegations within them - are bound to experience internal problems when issues concerning the future of European integration are on the agenda.

8) *The weakness of transnational parties*

The behaviour of a legislative party at the national level is usually subjected to scrutiny by the extra-parliamentary organs of that party where the activity of the MPs is discussed and analysed. While the effectiveness and toughness of such scrutiny varies between parties, the MPs are nevertheless accountable to the extra-parliamentary organisation. No equivalent is found at the European level, where the role of the transnational parties has remained limited. While the three main party families, the Socialists (PES), the Liberals (ELDR), and the Christian Democrats/Conservatives (EPP) have all established their own transnational parties, these parties are weak in terms of resources, are financially dependent on their party groups in the European Parliament, and main policy decisions are taken by the respective member parties. Remaining organisationally weak, with limited resources, with no mass membership of their own (there is practically no direct membership), and with no control over the selection of candidates, the europarties have hardly any power and/or means available to them to exert control over 'their' MEPs.

The literature on the EP party system has on the whole been so far sceptical about the ability of the transnational party groups to achieve high levels of cohesion. Without backing their arguments with any data, the various contributors have mainly chosen to emphasise various factors which they have argued will in time, or in 'real life' situations, undermine party group cohesion. While the present author agrees that the EP party groups are definitely more vulnerable to internal dissent than party groups in the EU member state legislatures, the main cause of which is the strong role of national party delegations within political groups, we need empirical data to support or falsify the arguments that have been put forward.

4.3. Voting in the European Parliament

According to the 9th edition of the Parliament's Rules of Procedure, adopted in June 1994, "The right to vote is a personal right. Members shall cast their votes individually and in person." (Rule 117) "Normally Parliament shall vote by show of hands. If the President decides that the result is doubtful, a fresh vote shall be taken using the electronic voting system and, if the latter is not working, by sitting and standing." (Rule 118) Voting by secret ballot is primarily used in the case of appointments to Parliament's top hierarchical positions.

Votes are taken by roll-call

"if so requested in writing by at least twenty-nine Members or a political group before voting has begun...In calculating whether a motion has been adopted or rejected account shall be taken only of votes cast for and against...Voting shall be recorded in the minutes of proceedings of the sitting by political group in the alphabetical order of Members' names." (Rule 119)

Roll-call voting used to be done by word of mouth, but since the installation of electronic voting machines (in May 1980) representatives have been able to cast their 'Yes', 'No', or 'I abstain' votes by using their voting cards. If a member feels that her or his position on the matter needs to be clarified, he or she "may give an oral explanation on the final vote for not longer than one minute or give a written explanation of no more than 200 words, which shall be included in the verbatim report of proceedings." (Rule 122)

Roll-call votes are mainly requested by the political groups for the following reasons: it enables groups to make their positions known to the wider audience; it can be used by groups to highlight the opposing view adopted by other groups; and it helps the groups in checking how their own MEPs voted (Jacobs, Corbett, and Shackleton, 1995: 160). The first time voting by roll-call took place in the ECSC Common Assembly, EP's predecessor, was in May 1955 when the Socialists demanded it should be used, the matter voted upon being the rate of the levy on coal and steel production in the Community (Van Oudenhove, 1965: 50).

Absenteeism

Poor and erratic attendance is a problem frequently associated with national legislatures, and the EP is definitely no exception. There are several factors contributing to this problem: MEPs' work involves much travelling, and in some cases the representatives simply do not have the will, energy, or time to arrive in Strasbourg for the plenary session; some members still hold dual mandates, with commitments in their national parliament preventing them from coming to Strasbourg; and a large proportion of the members hold other political or administrative offices, often at the national or local level, thus placing competing demands on their time.

Attendance in the chamber during the Strasbourg plenaries tends also to vary depending on the significance of the issue voted upon. When legislative measures requiring absolute majorities are on the agenda, MEPs take their seats in the hemicycle. In fact, these votes are grouped together at noon on the Wednesday afternoon of the plenary in order to increase the probability that the required number of members is present in the chamber when votes are taken. On Fridays, on the other hand, the Hall of the Palais d'Europe is usually at most half full, with most MEPs having already left for their constituencies. There has been a small minority of members who hardly ever turn up for plenary sessions.

This high level of absenteeism creates problems for the whole Parliament, making it harder to muster the required legislative majorities, and leading to a poor image in the eyes of the media and the electorate (Green, 1994). As Bay Brzinski argues:

"Absences are also interesting because groups spend time and resources to mobilise their memberships. The high level of absences indicates a failure by political groups to enforce discipline among their members." (Bay Brzinski, 1995: 139)

Bay Brzinski (1995: 151) found that of the national delegations the Dutch and British contingents had the best attendance records, with Italians on the other hand having the worst. If participation during voting periods is taken as an indicator of the level of absenteeism, then the EP's record is rather poor. The final sample here consists of 159 roll-call votes, and on average only less than half, 48.2 % of MEPs (250 out of 518), turned out to cast their votes. What must be noted is that the final sample included only those votes in which at least one-third (173 out of 518) of the members took part. A significant proportion of the overall population of roll-call votes could not be included in the sample due to the fact that this numerical threshold was not met.

It appears that this high level of absenteeism has characterised the Parliament since the first European elections, with approximately half of the representatives present in the chamber during the 1979-1994 period.[8] This fact must be worrying from the political groups' and the whole Parliament's point of view. Despite the increase in EP's legislative powers, on average around 50 % of the elected representatives do not bother to show up.

4.4. The Sample

Parliament's voting records are published in the C-Series of the *Official Journal of the European Communities*. The temporal scope of the research is the third term of the directly elected Parliament, 1989-94, excluding, however, the plenary sessions held in the final months preceding the June 1994 European elections. The final sample consists of 159 roll-call votes. The following quantitative criteria were used in selecting votes for further analysis.

a) At least a quorum, one-third of the elected MEPs, were required to have taken part in the vote. Thus only those votes with at least 173 representatives voting are included.

b) The indices of agreement and voting likeness were calculated only when at least a quarter of the members of the group voted. Thus the number of votes on which the respective indices are based varies between the party groups - in general the larger the group, the larger the sample.

c) Not only final votes, but also votes on individual paragraphs and amendments are included in the analysis. Of the 159 votes 62 are votes on paragraphs or amendments. Outside the scope of the analysis are left votes on objections (whether a particular topic is discussed or not during the topical and urgent debate), and those votes that are not directly concerned with the contents of the report or resolution (i.e., whether the legal base of the issue is correct or not, or whether to refer the matter back to the relevant committee for further elaboration or not).[9] The reason for including votes on amendments in the sample is that often votes on specific amendments are more significant and contested than the final votes (Jacobs, Corbett, and Shackleton, 1995: 160).

d) No minimum level of conflict was required in this study. Some may wonder what point there is in including near unanimous and even unanimous votes in the analysis. However, can we for certain assert that such votes producing universal coalitions are less significant than votes with high levels of inter-party conflict? As Cox and McCubbins (1991: 550) ask: "If one were trying to measure how frequently a gang acted as a gang, would one count only the instances in which it fought another gang, or would one also include the cases in which it acted against an unorganised opponent or no opponent at all?" Similarly identifying so-called 'key votes' is far from a simple task. Certain votes, such as those on the appointments of Jacques Santer and the Parliament's first ombudsman, could perhaps be justifiably regarded as important from the groups' point of view, but after that too much would depend on the criteria one uses to select these 'key' votes (Shull and Vanderleeuw, 1987). Case studies of individual 'important' votes have nevertheless shown the 'precarious' nature of EP party cohesion, with domestic party political considerations undermining the cohesion of the groups.[10]

4.5. The Challenge of Diversity: Party Group Cohesion

After the June 1989 European elections the Strasbourg chamber housed altogether ten transnational party groups (excluding the non-attached members). As a result of the elections the two largest groups, the Socialists and the EPP, strengthened their hold inside the Parliament while the smaller political groups suffered defeats (see Tables 3.3. and 3.4.). Three of the party groups had not been present in the outgoing 1984-89 EP. The split within the communist camp resulted in the founding of the EUL and LU groups, while the Greens, following their success in the elections (Curtice, 1989), formed a group of their own, leaving the Rainbow group to which they had belonged during the previous parliamentary term. Eleven MEPs chose not to join any political group and remained as non-attached (NA) members.

Table 4.1.   Party groups in the Parliament after the 1989 European elections

Party groups	seats	seats (%)
Party of European Socialists (PES)	180	34.7
European People's Party (EPP)	121	23.4
Liberal, Democratic and Reformist Group (ELDR)	49	9.5
European Democratic Group (EDG)	34	6.6
Greens (V)	29	5.6
Group of the United European Left (EUL)	28	5.4
European Democratic Alliance (EDA)	22	4.2
Technical Group of the European Right (ER)	17	3.3
Left Unity Group (LU)	14	2.7
Rainbow Group (RB)	13	2.5
Non-attached (NA)	11	2.1
Total EP	518	100

Source: *Official Journal of the European Communities*; European Parliament: *List of Members.*

The composition and size of the party groups varied quite considerably during the 1989-94 Parliament (Table 4.2.). Two groups disappeared altogether, both joining a larger group. The EDG group, consisting almost exclusively of British Conservatives, joined the EPP in the spring of 1992. The EUL was dissolved on 12 January 1993 when its Italian PDS (Partito Democratico della Sinistra) contingent decided to join the Socialist Group, with the rest of the group continuing as non-aligned members. EPP also gained new members by welcoming into its ranks French MEPs from both the Liberal and EDA groups.

Table 4.2.   Changes in the size of party groups, 1989-1994

Date Group	7/89	6/90	6/91	4/92	6/93	6/94	+/-
PES	180	180	179	180	198	197	+17
EPP	121	121	122	128	163	162	+41
ELDR	49	49	49	45	44	44	-5
EDG	34	34	34	34			-34
V	29	29	29	27	28	28	-1
EUL	28	28	28	29			-28
EDA	22	22	22	21	20	20	-2
ER	17	17	14	14	14	12	-5
LU	14	14	14	13	13	13	-1
RB	13	14	15	15	16	16	+3
NA	11	10	12	12	22	26	+15
EP	518	518	518	518	518	518	

+/- = The change in the size of the group during the five-year term: the difference in the number of seats held by the group after the 1989 elections and before the 1994 elections.
Source: European Parliament: *List of Members*; *Official Journal of the European Communities*; *EP News.*

Table 4.2. shows that the party groups were 'alive' in the 1989-94 Parliament, with the membership of each party group undergoing changes during the five-year legislative term. On top of the more significant moves, individual members changed their allegiances during the term. In particular the smaller groups suffered as a result of these changes. The Rainbow group was the sole exception among the smaller groups in enlarging its membership during the five-year term. By the end of the 1989-94 Parliament the number of non-attached members had risen to 26.

But how cohesive are the party groups? Is the degree of group heterogeneity directly related to its level of cohesion? Are the EP party groups less cohesive than their counterparts in national legislatures? It is to these questions that we turn next.

Hypothesis 1.
The cohesion of EP transnational party groups is not dependent on their level of (a) transnationality and/or (b) fractionalisation.

Transnational party groups are composed of national party delegations, each the product of their respective political systems, and the ideology of these delegations is expected to reflect their experiences in the context of national politics. As Brigitte Boyce (1993: 464) has remarked on the whole process of European integration: "aggregation of interest is a problem whose size is directly proportional to the number of interests that need to be aggregated." However, the argument here is that there is no direct relationship between the degree of intra-group heterogeneity and the level of party cohesion. Were the national party delegations to act as obstacles to party group cohesion, the legitimacy and wisdom of supranational partisan organisation would suffer as national voting blocs would make intra-parliamentary decision-making unpredictable.

The hypothesis is confirmed if (a) the level of party group transnationality (the number of member states sending representatives to the group) and/or (b) fractionalisation (the number of national party delegations in the group) produces no systematic variation in party group cohesion. The hypothesis is rejected if there is such a direct relationship between the level of party group heterogeneity and the level of group cohesion: the more heterogeneous the group, the less cohesive it is in when votes are taken; the more homogeneous the group, the more cohesive it will be.

An *index of transnationality* (IT) is used to compute the groups' degree of transnationality. It is "based on Rae's index [Rae, 1967] of fractionalisation. The formula for its calculation is

$$IT = 1 - \left(\sum_{i=1}^{n} SC^2 \right),$$

whereby SC is the respective share of MEPs from the various countries within a group and n is the number of countries involved. The greater the index value, the higher the degree of transnationality of a political group. It should be noted, however, that the highest index value (1) is a hypothetical one. Since the number of units is an integral part of the index, the given number of member states limits the degree of transnationality a group within the EP can come up to." (Niedermayer, 1984: 241) In the 1989-1994 EC/EU of twelve member states, a political group with country delegations of exactly equal size from each member state would have the index value of .917.

The *index of fractionalisation* (IF) is computed in the same way as the IT-index, with only the number of national party delegations replacing the number of member state delegations in the formula for its calculation.

An *index-of-agreement* (IA) is used to measure the cohesion of the political groups. The index is the same as in the voting behaviour analyses of Fulvio Attinà, partly in order to introduce a longitudinal element into the research. "The index is a measure of the relation that exists between the three modalities of votes - in favour, against and abstention - cast by the members of a group; more exactly, it is the percentage measure of the relation between (a) the difference between the highest numbering modality and the sum of the other two modalities in a vote by the MEPs of a group, and (b) the total number of votes cast by the group:

IA = highest modality - sum of the other two modalities X 100
                   total number of votes.

The index is equal to 1.00 when all the deputies belonging to a group vote in the same way. Between .999 and .001 agreement decreases, but more than half of the voters express the same voting modality. At 0 we have a split in half of the votes in two modalities or, with three modalities, one of these is exactly equal to the sum of the other two. When the index has a negative value, the votes break down into three modalities, and even the

94

highest number of votes in one modality is less than half of the total group vote." In order to calculate the IAs for the EP and its party groups, the sum of the IAs of individual votes was divided by the number of votes (Attinà, 1990: 564).

A methodological problem concerns those MEPs voting 'I abstain'. As mentioned above, the Parliament's Rules of Procedure states that when counting the result of the vote, only votes cast for or against are taken into account. Thus from this point of view it would make sense to consider abstentions as neutral positions. However, the present author regards abstentions (if the minority position within the group) as failure to accept the official group line. By abstaining the representatives do not actively support the position of their groups, and thus they increase the voting power of their opposition.

Table 4.3. **Political groups' transnationality and fractionalisation after the 1989 European elections and their cohesion in the 1989-1994 EP**

Party groups	IT	IF	IA
PES	.852	.858	.786
EPP	.841	.873	.882
ELDR	.851	.917	.857
EDG	.111	.111	.922
V	.790	.837	.875
EUL	.360	.360	.923
EDA	.566	.566	.645
ER	.526	.526	.889
LU	.653	.673	.938
Rainbow	.824	.840	.695

Table 4.3. shows the transnationality and fractionalisation of the groups after the 1989 European elections and their cohesion in the 1989-94 Parliament. As expected, the larger groups have a much higher degree of transnationality and fractionalisation than the smaller political groups. The only exception to the rule is the Rainbow group, its high indices being explained by the group's 'mixed bag' - character, as it consisted of various regionalist and other smaller parties, including four Danish anti-marketeers.

The very low indices of the EDG result from the fact that 32 out of the group's 34 MEPs represented the British Conservatives. Four out of ten political groups (EDG, EUL, EDA, and ER) have coalescing transnationality- and fractionalisation-indices, none of these groups including more than one national party delegation per member state. On the other hand, six of the ten national delegations to the Liberals' group have MEPs representing two or more national parties, and the Italian MEPs in the Greens group represent four different parties.[11]

The IA of the Socialists, the largest group in the Parliament, is low, with the group remaining clearly behind EPP, the other large group in the Parliament. In both the first and second directly elected Parliaments the Socialists were in fact the least cohesive party group in the chamber (Attinà, 1990). The situation has thus changed from the days of the nominated Parliament of the six founding EC member states:

> "If any group gives the appearance of a party group in a national parliament then it is the Socialists...outright opposition to the point of voting against the party line in a roll-call vote is rare in the Socialist group. ...the Christian Democrats and the Liberals, appear a great deal less cohesive than the Socialists." (Fitzmaurice, 1975: 164-166)

The IA of the Rainbow Group comes as no surprise. The group's ideologically very diverse composition was not conducive to successful co-ordination of points of view, and the group was - as in the 1984-89 EP - very much the result of Parliament's Rules of Procedure. Since in the 1989-1994 Parliament 23 members from one member state, 18 from two member states, and only 12 from three or more member states were needed to form a group, the MEPs or national party delegations in question decided to join a group in order to increase their influence in the chamber and to gain material benefits.

The low cohesion of the EDA is also an expected result. While the group had existed in the Parliament since 1965, it functioned primarily as a loose alliance, bringing together national parties that traditionally had strong links to the agricultural sector. It is interesting to note that Socialists and the EDA both achieve low levels of party cohesion, despite their members adopting the toughest line on the unacceptability of voting against the recommended group position.

The high IAs of the EDG, ER, EUL, and LU are largely the result of these groups' rather homogeneous character. The European Democratic Group was dominated by the British Conservatives, the influence of Jean-

Marie Le Pen's National Front only increased within the ER after the departure of three German Die Republikaner-MEPs from the group, and the two communist groups, EUL and the Left Unity Group, were dominated by Italian (PDS) and French (PCF - Parti Communiste Francais) communists respectively. The unitary voting behaviour achieved by the two communist groups confirms the logic of going separate ways after having been in the same group in the previous Parliaments, when the ideological differences between the Italian and French contingents were revealed in the low level of cohesion of the Communist group (Attinà, 1990).

The EPP and the Liberals are two groups with a high degree of transnationality and fractionalisation that also achieve relatively cohesive voting behaviour. These two party families have been at the heart of the European integration process from its very beginning, and both party groups like to stress in their programmes and electoral manifestos their federalist character and their commitment to achieving a closer economic and political union. Moreover, it is understandable why these two centre-right ideological movements have found it easier than the Socialists to mobilise their member parties and electorates into supporting the integration process. The European Union is still first and foremost an economic union largely based on the logic of unregulated competition and the free movement of capital and workforce - traditional socialist priorities of social rights and restraining market forces have remained in the background.

EPP has been clearly ahead of its rival, the Socialists in all three directly elected Parliaments. This ability to maintain cohesion over the whole time period is an impressive achievement when considering the changes in the group's composition over the years. The Liberals have improved their cohesion substantially over the years. In the nominated Parliament the Liberals were the least cohesive party group, with the group having "much greater difficulties than any other group in reaching a common standpoint on issues before the parliament." (Fitzmaurice, 1975: 167) Having been the second most cohesive party group in the 1979-84 EP, the Liberals' internal heterogeneity surfaced again in the 1984-89 Parliament, when the group found it difficult to achieve consensus when votes were taken (Attinà, 1990).

The relatively high level of cohesion achieved by the Greens comes perhaps as a surprise. The Greens sat as their own group for the first time, having formed a subgroup Green Alternative European Link (GRAEL) of the Rainbow group in the 1984-89 Parliament. The GRAEL subgroup had been torn by internal conflicts caused by ideological differences, with MEPs not being able to agree on tactics or policies to be pursued in the chamber (Bomberg, 1993; Buck, 1989). While the entry of new Green representatives in the 1989 elections and the resulting growth in numerical strength had given the Greens self-confidence, this had on the other hand further increased the heterogeneity in the group. According to Bowler and Farrell (1992b: 134) "there is an absence of an adequate *group* dimension. The individual MEPs tend to bring their individual national identities with them to the EP; they seem unwilling or unable to adequately pool their strategies and resources as a group." However, the data clearly indicates that at least when votes were taken the Greens did indeed in the majority of cases act as a group. Moreover, the Greens' attendance record shows that absenteeism was not so much a problem for them as it was for the other small and medium-size groups.

The results confirm hypothesis 1: there is no direct relationship between party group heterogeneity and party group cohesion. However, the kind of analysis undertaken here does not allow us to investigate in more detail the role of national party delegations. For example, certain national parties or country delegations may vote against the group line more frequently than others. Reaching a decision or a compromise may well be more difficult in a heterogeneous group where there are more interests to be accommodated. While no such data is presented in this work, the analysis nevertheless proves that one cannot gauge the level of party group cohesion through the level of party group heterogeneity.

4.6. Party Cohesion in Comparative Perspective

But how do EP party groups fare in comparison with parliamentary parties in national legislatures? Writing just after the 1984 European elections, Oskar Niedermayer argued that

> "despite the fact that most of the groups have long experience in intra-group attitude formation, conflict resolution and decision-making, the groups of the European Parliament cannot be compared with their counterparts in national parliaments in terms of cohesion or common action." (Niedermayer, 1984: 236)

Similarly in a more recent discussion on EP parties, Mogens N. Pedersen (1996: 16) wrote that "the cohesion of such groups is not comparable to the cohesion of most national parliamentary groups. Group-consciousness is not high, and the same goes for the stability of the group's structures."

Are such evaluations completely fair? Do outside observers underestimate the cohesion of EP party groups? In order to add a comparative element into the research, the indices of agreement found in Table 4.3. are compared with cohesion indices of parties in national legislatures.

Hypothesis 2.
The EP party groups are less cohesive than parliamentary parties in national legislatures.

The hypothesis is valid if voting behaviour analyses show that the EP political groups are less cohesive than their counterparts in national legislatures. The hypothesis is rejected if the cohesion of EP party groups is equal to or higher than the unity of parliamentary parties in national parliaments. Unfortunately there is not much recent data available.[12] Comparison is made between the cohesion of parliamentary groups in the U.S. Congress, the Swiss National Council, the Norwegian Stortinget, and the West German Bundestag.

Considering the selective nature of the sample, the data does not allow us to draw any conclusions on the cohesion of EP parties vis-à-vis the whole population of parliamentary groups. However, the four selected case studies were chosen not only because of availability of recent data, but also because these parliaments operate in different political systems. The U.S. Congress has been described as a highly 'individualistic' legislature, with the parties in a much weaker role than in Western Europe. When taking into account the American system of separation of powers and the more independent role of the average Congressman, the Congress provides perhaps a better benchmark for comparison than the various European legislatures operating in the context of unitary nation-states. Switzerland is another variant of federalism, again with political parties having decentralised structures. While Germany is also a federal state, German political parties have been recognised for their organisational discipline. Norway provides an example of a Scandinavian legislature where the cohesion of parliamentary parties has often been taken for granted.

In the U.S. Congress from 1933 to 1988, the Democrats' and Republicans' average party cohesion was 79.3 and 80.7 respectively.[13] Both parties' unity scores remained between 70.0 and 90.0 throughout the period under analysis (Cox and McCubbins, 1991). In their study on roll-call voting in the Swiss National Council between 1920 and 1994, Lanfranchi and Lüthi (1995: 15) show that "there seems to be no overall trend towards increased party cohesion over time." In the 1991-94 National Council the least unitary party, the Christian Democrats, had an index value of 68.3, while four out of nine groups achieved cohesion indices higher than 90.0.[14] Moving from federal systems characterised by 'weak parties' to parliamentary systems with 'strong parties', we find the expected result of rise in party group cohesion. In his study on intraparty agreement in the two chambers of the Norwegian parliament, Storting and Odelsting, between 1979 and 1994 (data set consisting of a total of 11 393 roll-calls), Rasch (1995) shows that all parties had cohesion indices of over 93.0, with the majority of indices being even above 97.0.[15] In the West German Bundestag between 1949 and 1987 (715 roll-calls) all parliamentary parties displayed high levels of internal cohesion, with party unity indices being in the majority of Bundestags over 95.0. In particular the cohesion of the social democrats (SDP) has been impressive, with its index falling below 95.0 only once, during the 1966-69 legislative term (Saalfeld, 1990).

All of the studies mentioned above used the Rice index of cohesion in measuring party unity (Rice, 1928). It must be noted that the Rice index is not as stringent as the index-of-agreement (IA) developed by Fulvio Attinà and used in this study. The Rice index of cohesion is calculated simply by computing the difference between the proportion of the majority of the group and the proportion of the minority of the same group.[16] Thus the crucial difference is that the Rice index ignores those choosing to abstain, unlike Attinà's index. Had the unity of EP party groups therefore been measured by using the Rice index, their cohesion indices would have been higher.

Comparing the cohesion of parliamentary parties, it appears that *parties within the selected national parliaments - with the exception of the U.S. Congress - are still in general ahead of EP party groups in terms of cohesion, at least when measured by voting behaviour analyses. Hypothesis 2 is therefore valid.* However, it is equally obvious that statements characterising EP parties more as chance agglomerations than as real parliamentary parties deserve to be modified in the light of this roll-call data. While the transnational party groups in Strasbourg may still not be as cohesive as their more homogeneous counterparts in national parliaments, their cohesion is nevertheless rather impressive when considering their internal heterogeneity.

4.7. Voting Similarity Between the Groups: EP Party System, 1989-94

Transnational political groups have existed in the European Parliament for over four decades. The roll-call analysis in the two previous sections showed that the entry of new national party delegations into the party groups does not necessarily result in a decline in group cohesion. There was no direct relationship between party group cohesion and party group heterogeneity. This in itself proves that the choice to sit in ideological groupings instead of as national delegations has been a working one, with the cohesion of the groups consolidating their position inside the chamber and preventing the emergence of national voting blocs.

But how are the groups placed on the left-right dimension? And indeed, can the party groups even be placed on a left-right axis, or do the different cleavages found at the European level make the left-right dimension irrelevant in the Parliament?

Rice's index of voting likeness (IVL) is used to measure the degree of voting similarity between the political groups. The IVL between the groups is expressed as follows:

IVL = 100 - (A- B), where
A = percentage of party group A voting pro on resolution x,
B = percentage of party group B voting pro on resolution x,
(A - B) = absolute value of A - B.

The IVL ranges between 0 (maximum disagreement) and 100 (maximum voting similarity). Average IVLs are calculated by computing the sum of the IVLs on individual votes and then dividing the sum by the number of votes. (Hurwitz, 1983: 205)

Despite the inevitable differences in the ideological outlook of the national parties forming party groups in the Parliament, the EP party system is based on the traditional party families widely recognised in the political science literature. While political groups probably overlap ideologically in some cases, the voting cohesion of the groups indicates that most national parties have had few problems in finding a home in the Strasbourg chamber.

Various analyses of the left-right placement of EP parties - based on MEPs' and party activists' own coalition preferences (Niedermayer, 1983;

Rattinger, 1982), voting behaviour (Wolters, 1982; Quanjel and Wolters, 1992), combining roll-call data with party behaviour at the national level (Attinà, 1992b, 1993, 1994b), and expert statements (Steed and Hearl, 1985) - have produced similar enough results to enable us to locate the party groups from the left to right. Drawing on these works, Figure 4.1. displays the expected locations of the party groups on the left-right-dimension after the 1989 European elections.

**Figure 4.1. The expected location of EP party groups
on the left-right dimension, 1989-1994**

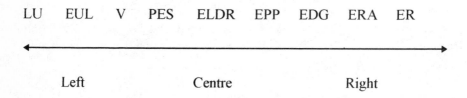

In the 1989-94 EP parties of the left were, from the extreme to the moderate centre: Left Unity Group, EUL, the Greens, and the Socialists. And the parties of the right, from the centre to far-right: Liberals, EPP, EDG, EDA, and the European Right. The Rainbow group cannot be placed on the axis due to the group's internal diversity. EDA is another somewhat problematic case because of the group's low index of cohesion indicating drifts between the leading French contingent and the rest of the group. Overlapping is particularly evident between the Liberals and the EPP, with the former's internal diversity making it virtually impossible to locate the group firmly on either side of the EPP (Attinà, 1993: 11-12; Attinà, 1994b: 296).

Hypothesis 3.
The coalition behaviour of the EP party groups is based on the left-right dimension, with the voting likeness of the party groups corresponding with their distance from each other on the left-right dimension.

The left-right division is not the only potentially existing one in the Strasbourg chamber. One can think of at least the following cleavages: northern versus southern member states, federalists versus anti-integrationists, the agricultural lobby versus those against high levels of CAP spending, and the MEPs from the central areas of the Union versus those representing geographically peripheral areas. As Hrbek (1988: 465) comments: "it would require very careful investigations - including the analysis of committee work and intra-group discussions - to give a full picture of all the different relationships and issues."

It is expected that even though - or indeed because - alternative coalitions in the EP are assumed to be of ad hoc-nature and very issue-specific (section 4.8), the left-right dimension is the dominant one in the Parliament. The hypothesis is valid if the distances (voting likeness) between EP party groups correspond with their placement on the left-right dimension as depicted in Figure 4.1. The hypothesis is rejected if it is shown that the distances between the groups do not reflect their expected places on the left-right dimension.

Hypothesis 4.
The ideologically extremist groups do not form coalitions with the other party groups in the chamber.

Writing right after the 1989 European elections, Vernon Bogdanor (1989: 213) argued that the EP party system is characterised by "an immobile centre and two incompatible extremes", with the centre parties (Socialists, EPP, Liberals) all committed to further integration, and leaving no room for effective opposition. We can identify three extremist party groups in the 1989-94 Parliament. The European Right was excluded from intra-parliamentary appointments, and the other groups refused to work with its far-right members. At the left end of the dimension, the Left Unity was regarded as hostile to the deepening of the current form of European integration, and this has also been the official position of the Greens. It is thus argued in hypothesis 4 that these three groups remain ideologically distant both from each other and from the other groups.

The hypothesis is confirmed if the voting similarity study finds these groups' voting likeness indices indicating greater distance from the other groups than in the case of the other party groups. The hypothesis is rejected if the voting likeness indices show that these groups are either grouped close to one another (or that any pair of them are), or if they show high levels of voting likeness with the other party groups or with one of the other party groups. The null hypothesis is that there is no difference between these three party groups and the other groups in their coalition behaviour.

103

Table 4.4. Party groups' voting similarity in the 1989-1994 EP

Party group	PES	EPP	ELDR	EDG	V	EUL	EDA	ER	LU	RB
PES	*	66.0	65.0	65.3	56.7	81.8	63.1	47.6	65.7	65.8
EPP	66.0	*	78.8	94.0	48.0	59.7	72.6	47.2	39.0	58.9
ELDR	65.0	78.8	*	90.3	52.6	60.1	64.0	46.1	38.9	70.3
EDG	65.3	94.0	90.3	*	43.4	55.2	72.7	43.3	32.8	55.2
V	56.7	48.0	52.6	43.4	*	66.5	49.6	53.4	75.3	72.2
EUL	81.8	59.7	60.1	55.2	66.5	*	46.1	44.9	74.3	64.4
EDA	63.1	72.6	64.0	72.7	49.6	46.1	*	58.8	37.0	57.1
ER	47.6	47.2	46.1	43.3	53.4	44.9	58.8	*	52.2	53.8
LU	65.7	39.0	38.9	32.8	75.3	74.3	37.0	52.2	*	64.5
RB	65.8	58.9	70.3	55.2	72.2	64.4	57.1	53.8	64.5	*

Table 4.4. proves conclusively the existence of a left-right cleavage in the chamber. The political groups on the left - the Socialists, EUL, LU, and the Greens - have higher voting likeness indices among them than with the groups to the right of the centre - EPP, Liberals, EDG, and EDA - and vice versa. However, the party groups forming the political centre are at the same time grouped relatively close to each other.

The Socialists are shown to be in the centre of the axis, almost equally far from six of the groups. The only group relatively close to them is the EUL, and the two indeed merged in January 1993. The Left Unity is closest to the Greens and the EUL, but remains far apart from the centre-right groups. Voting behaviour analysis also confirms the Greens' leftist position on the axis, but the group was nevertheless fairly isolated in the chamber.

On the right there is a bloc of three groups with close voting proximity, the EPP, the Liberals and the EDG. The EDG joined the EPP in May 1992, and the very high degree of voting similarity between the two groups confirms the logic of their merger after long bilateral discussions (see however Raunio, 1996b: 130-132). The EDA stands clearly to the right of the EPP and the Liberals. The European Right is very distant from the other groups, and this confirms the group's extremist ideological position at the right end of the left-right dimension. The Rainbow group behaves as expected, its voting behaviour reflecting the group's diverse membership. However, it is interesting to note that of the five party groups closest to the Rainbow group, four are positioned left of the centre on the left-right dimension.

Hypothesis 3 is confirmed - party groups' voting likeness reflects their corresponding positions on the left-right dimension.

Comparing the findings with research on the first (1979-84) and second (1984-89) directly elected Parliaments, it appears that the EP party system is fairly stable and that the left-right dimension has become even more important within the chamber (see Rattinger, 1982; Wolters, 1982; Quanjel and Wolters, 1992, 1993). Even though the number of political groups has varied between 1979 and 1994, and the compositions of the party groups have undergone significant changes over the years (see Tables 3.3. and 3.4.), the positions of the more established groups (Communists, Socialists, Liberals, EPP, EDA) on the left-right axis have remained the same.

Hypothesis 4 is also confirmed. The three party groups expected not to form coalitions with other groups in the chamber - the European Right, the Left Unity and the Greens - were all ideologically distant from the political centre. The Greens and the Left Unity were, however, also closest to each other in their voting behaviour, a finding reflecting both party groups' leftist positions on the left-right dimension and their ideological opposition to either the goals of European integration or to what the priorities of the integration process currently are.

4.8. Coalition Behaviour, Group Cohesion and Majority Requirements

A particular strand of voting behaviour research has concentrated on the question whether different policy areas produce different coalitions in parliaments. While admittedly these policy areas are probably interlocked and linked to each other in one way or another (for example, almost every vote is bound to have budgetary implications), it is thought that policy-related coalitions will be formed around such subject areas as 'agriculture', 'environment', or 'defence' (Wilcox and Clausen, 1991). Alternatively, one could assume that "policy dimensions can also break from within" so that "there is some point at which coalitions are so highly issue-specific that policy dimensions have no value." (Collie, 1984: 22-23) This section examines these arguments in the context of the EP by selecting one such policy area, 'foreign affairs', for closer analysis. Votes on the Gulf War (N = 13), on relations with Arab countries (N = 20), and on Yugoslavia (N = 37) were chosen as case studies. It is expected that coalitions in the chamber are mainly dependent on the existence of legislative majority requirements, the importance of which were explained in section 3.5.

But why focus on foreign policy votes? Since there is no prior research done on party cohesion across subject areas, it was impossible to establish for certain which issues produced most or least conflict within and between groups (see however Attinà, 1990). The choice was mainly dictated by the nature of foreign policy questions. Foreign affairs has so far constituted a problematic issue area in the context of European integration, with the EU member states finding it difficult to harmonise their viewpoints. Foreign policy questions, in particular those related to defence and security options, are also 'high profile' matters that normally command the attention of the media (and thereby of the electorate). Not surprisingly foreign policy has thus caused much debate within and between parties.

It is hypothesised that we find evidence of similar behaviour also inside the Parliament, with increased conflict both in and between the EP groups when foreign policy issues are on the agenda of the part-sessions. An obvious drawback is EP's lack of formal powers in this field. One could argue that what point is there in studying votes that result in resolutions that may go totally unnoticed outside the Parliament? The inclusion of votes on own-initiative resolutions was necessary in order to examine the relationship between legislative majority requirements and party cohesion and coalition behaviour.[17]

When defending their decisions not to grant the EP more far-reaching legislative powers, member state governments and advocates of intergovernmentalism have often questioned "MEPs ability to maintain party cohesion and to develop coherent policies." (Lodge, 1992: 49) Therefore the Parliament is often almost over-concerned with reaching consensus within and between the groups, wanting to present itself as a united institution. Foreign affairs is a particularly intriguing policy field in this respect: resolutions in this field often attract media attention, and the EP's legislative role in this policy area is limited. Thus the MEPs have been known to try to maximise opportunities in this policy field, even by adopting provocative and somewhat unconventional points of view, in order to make the Parliament's position known. As Pierre Pflimlin, the President of the Parliament from 1984 to 1987, has argued:

"...when it has been a question of adopting positions not constituting decisions, the votes that we have held in Parliament on foreign policy questions or defence questions have not been binding in any way on the Council of Ministers. There, I feel, Parliament's role is not necessarily to produce majorities, but to state positions clearly." (Pflimlin, 1992: 70)

The more weight (= more votes) EP can muster behind a resolution, the likelier it is that its opinion will be noticed by the media, the Council of Ministers, and in third countries. This is in particular the case when the Parliament adopts a different point of view from the one agreed upon at the Council of Ministers. The Parliament must try to persuade the other institutions to take its positions into account, and internal unity is a powerful tool in achieving this goal. As John Fitzmaurice (1975: 163) has argued: "disunity makes the opinions of the parliament easier to ignore."[18]

Despite its continuous calls for closer involvement in the development and formulation of European Union's common foreign and security policy, the EP's powers in the field of external relations have remained rather limited, a fact much bemoaned and criticised by the overwhelming majority of MEPs.[19] Parliament has nevertheless maintained over the years an active interest in foreign policy matters. This applies in particular to human rights questions which have always featured high on EP's agenda (Boumans and

Norbart, 1989). This 'high profile' approach in foreign policy matters has been criticised by some observers. According to this line of reasoning the EP should concentrate on the essentials, i.e. on those issue areas in which it has formal powers included in the Treaties.[20]

Foreign affairs tends to be a very politicised issue area in national legislatures, and EP party groups have behaved in corresponding fashion. In his voting behaviour analysis, Fulvio Attinà found that there is

> "an international cleavage that pits some party groups against others in the EP as it does in national parliaments. European party groups - like national political parties - choose to emphasise an affinity on international political problems, which in other areas is weak or non-existent, perhaps because the stand has more of a symbolic than a practical value." (Attinà, 1990: 572)

Interviews and surveys of MEPs and party activists have shown that while the party elites support both a stronger role for the EP and a more independent role for the EU as a whole on foreign policy issues, the exact nature of foreign and security policy co-ordination is still open to debate and is a subject with relatively high conflict potential within and particularly between the groups (Bardi, 1989; Niedermayer, 1983; Sørensen et al., 1980). In their 1994 European election manifestos the three European parties all supported the further development of a common foreign and security policy: the Socialists emphasised creating peace and security through more pan-European co-operation, while the EPP and the Liberals explicitly demanded that a genuine common security and defence policy becomes a reality.

Hypothesis 5.
Foreign policy matters do not produce lower levels of voting cohesion within EP party groups.

Foreign policy has been widely recognised as a problematic issue area in the context of European integration, with differing geopolitical contexts making it difficult for the EU member states to harmonise their viewpoints. The same happens also in the Parliament, with national considerations playing a larger than average role when foreign policy issues are on the agenda. However, it is expected that these considerations do not endanger the cohesion and credibility of EP party groups. The hypothesis is valid if the cohesion of the groups on foreign policy votes is equal to or even higher than their overall level of cohesion. The hypothesis is not proven correct if the voting cohesion of the groups falls from their overall level of cohesion when foreign policy issues are on the agenda.

Hypothesis 6.
The cohesion of party groups is not dependent on institutional imperatives (legislative majority requirements) to achieve such unitary behaviour.

The decision-making rules of the European Union require the Parliament to muster legislative (usually absolute) majorities in order to amend, approve, or reject legislation. This institutional imperative puts pressure on the political groups to achieve high levels of cohesion when votes are taken. Such cohesion is especially important when considering the high level of absenteeism that is characteristic of the Parliament. However, if the unity of party groups was found to be dependent on such institutional imperatives necessitating co-operative behaviour, then the ideological homogeneity of the groups would be undermined. The hypothesis is confirmed if the voting cohesion of the groups is not lower in the absence of majority requirements. The hypothesis is rejected if there is found a direct relationship between legislative majority requirements and party group cohesion: in the absence of majority requirements the groups are less cohesive than when the vote is accompanied by such an institutional imperative.

Hypothesis 7.
Since votes on foreign policy issues do not require the building of legislative majorities, these votes are characterised by high levels of inter-party conflict.

The Parliament's formal powers are limited in foreign affairs. Therefore a substantial proportion of the votes belonging to the three case studies chosen are either Parliament's own-initiative resolutions or urgent resolutions. An own-initiative report is a report which a committee is authorised to produce by the Conference of Presidents after the committee in question has itself requested it (Rule 148).[21] Urgent resolutions are votes following debates held on topical and urgent subjects of major importance (Rule 47). Such debates take place on Thursdays, with voting immediately at the end of the debate. Human rights questions appear almost always on the agenda. Other 'popular' subjects are natural disasters and other foreign policy crises that have taken place since the last EP plenary was held.[22]

The combination of lack of decisional rules necessitating the formation of legislative majorities and the tendency of parties to politicise foreign policy matters is expected to result in votes being highly contested, with no durable coalitions between the groups in the chamber.[23] This lack of uniformity in opinions is in turn expected to have negative implications on the Parliament's influence and bargaining position vis-à-vis the other institutions.[24] The hypothesis is confirmed if there is a direct relationship between legislative majority requirements and the level of unity in the chamber: when a vote is not accompanied with such an institutional imperative to produce winning majorities, there is more inter-party conflict between the groups in the Parliament. The null hypothesis is that there is no systematic difference between the Parliament's own resolutions and those votes in which the legislative majority requirements apply.

Table 4.5 shows the cohesion of political groups on votes on the three topics chosen as case studies. The evidence is rather inconclusive. There are no major differences when compared with the overall agreement indices of the groups. Only the EDG, with IA computed only for votes on the Gulf War, saw no decline in group cohesion. The Socialists were noticeably divided on relations with Arab countries, with the group almost evenly split in six out of the 20 votes. The EPP and the Liberals maintain their high level of cohesion, with the cohesion of the latter, however, dropping in votes on the Gulf War. The cohesion of the EUL is also much lower in votes on relations with Arab countries. The ER was internally divided when the Gulf War was on the agenda, while the Rainbow group had internal splits in votes on relations with Arab countries. Otherwise the cohesion of the groups in foreign policy questions was either more or less the same as, or higher than, their overall level of cohesion.

When controlling for the deviant cases mentioned above, *there is no general decline in the cohesion of the party groups when foreign policy issues are on the EP's agenda. Hypothesis 5 is therefore confirmed.*[25]

Comparing the differences in the cohesion of the party groups between the three issue areas, we find no general behavioural pattern. The votes on relations with Arab countries dealt mainly with financial and technical co-operation agreements between the EU and these countries, and fell therefore under the assent procedure. In these votes the unity of five groups out of nine was lower than their overall IA. The votes on the Gulf War and on Yugoslavia were on the other hand all own-initiative or urgent resolutions. In comparison with their overall IAs, the cohesion of seven out of ten groups fell in votes on Gulf War, whereas votes on the war in former Yugoslavia saw a decline in the internal unity of four out of nine EP party groups.

Table 4.5. Party groups' cohesion in votes on relations with Arab countries (1), Gulf War (2), and the situation in former Yugoslavia (3)

Group	PES	EPP	ELDR	EDG	V	EUL	EDA	ER	LU	RB
1	.516	.900	.847	*	.960	.767	.596	.912	.938	.498
2	.756	.865	.743	.959	.839	.923	.599	.565	.886	.732
3	.766	.813	.878	*	.781	*	.589	.917	.947	.818
Total IA	.786	.882	.857	.922	.875	.923	.645	.889	.938	.695

Note: IA was calculated if at least ten votes fulfilled the selection criteria.

111

Table 4.6. Party groups' voting likeness: votes on relations with Arab countries

Party group	PES	EPP	ELDR	EDG	V	EUL	EDA	ER	LU	RB
PES	*	76.4	80.9	*	51.8	78.3	77.1	52.0	58.8	69.5
EPP	76.4	*	96.2	*	43.3	67.5	69.5	50.7	52.6	57.0
ELDR	80.9	96.2	*	*	38.7	78.9	71.1	46.1	46.8	63.1
EDG	*	*	*	*	*	*	*	*	*	*
V	51.8	43.3	38.7	*	*	44.9	60.4	76.5	93.1	73.2
EUL	78.3	67.5	78.9	*	44.9	*	59.4	35.0	59.1	67.0
EDA	77.1	69.5	71.1	*	60.4	59.4	*	76.0	*	74.6
ER	52.0	50.7	46.1	*	76.5	35.0	76.0	*	63.9	59.3
LU	58.8	52.6	46.8	*	93.1	59.1	*	63.9	*	69.0
RB	69.5	57.0	63.1	*	73.2	67.0	74.6	59.3	69.0	*

IVL between political groups was calculated when at least ten votes fulfilling the selection criteria were available for comparison. Same applies to Tables 4.7. and 4.8.

112

Hypothesis 6 is proven correct: the cohesion of the party groups is not dependent on legislative majority requirements. However, as with hypothesis 7, this finding must be treated with necessary caution. Analysis was here restricted to one policy area only, and only to assent procedure, and therefore further empirical research is needed to increase our understanding of the relationship between legislative majority requirements and party group behaviour inside the European Parliament.

The category of relations with Arab countries (defined here as the countries in the Middle East, including Israel, and the southern Mediterranean countries) includes mainly votes (12 out of 20) on financial and technical co-operation agreements falling under the assent procedure. Before the Maastricht Treaty came into force an absolute majority of MEPs was required for the Parliament to give its assent to these agreements, now a majority of the votes cast will do. Thus in the case of the majority of these votes the MEPs needed to reach the threshold figure of 260 in order to approve or reject the treaty. In some cases the Parliament delayed its assent because of violations of human rights in the country in question. For example, in February and October 1992 the EP rejected financial protocols with Morocco and Syria for violation of human rights. The IA for the whole chamber on the 20 votes is .519, almost exactly the same as the total IA over 159 votes of .513.

Table 4.6. shows the effect the majority requirement has on the voting behaviour of the party groups. The political centre in the EP has voted together on most issues, with the splinter groups identified in hypothesis 4 - the European Right, the Left Unity and the Greens - staying out of the majority coalition more often than the other groups. The voting behaviour of the EPP and the Liberals is almost identical.

Both the Gulf War, following Iraq's invasion of Kuwait in 1990, and the continuing crisis in former Yugoslavia have cast serious doubts on the EU's capacity to produce collective decisions, and the question has arisen "whether collective action can be sustained over time without a further leap into federalist obligations and structures." (Hill, 1994: 123) Also the European Parliament has in numerous resolutions condemned the Union's less than satisfactory response to these crises. Hans-Gert Pöttering, the drafter of a report adopted by the Parliament on 10 June 1991, regretted the "incapacity to act jointly" on the part of the member states during the Gulf War, deploring "the fact that certain members aligned themselves with other powers, some members attempted in vain to take independent community action and some preferred not to express themselves." (Buffotot, 1994: 208-209)

Table 4.7. Party groups' voting likeness: votes on the Gulf War

Party group	PES	EPP	ELDR	EDG	V	EUL	EDA	ER	LU	RB
PES	*	47.8	41.3	45.6	66.8	81.7	59.1	66.3	66.7	77.9
EPP	47.8	*	78.1	91.4	26.8	35.0	72.5	42.8	23.0	52.5
ELDR	41.3	78.1	*	84.5	40.9	31.3	76.0	44.5	40.3	45.5
EDG	45.6	91.4	84.5	*	31.7	27.3	77.2	37.6	28.5	46.5
V	66.8	26.8	40.9	31.7	*	77.8	43.2	63.5	91.9	70.5
EUL	81.7	35.0	31.3	27.3	77.8	*	43.7	54.5	78.5	65.7
EDA	59.1	72.5	76.0	77.2	43.2	43.7	*	43.3	41.4	48.2
ER	66.3	42.8	44.5	37.6	63.5	54.5	43.3	*	54.3	87.0
LU	66.7	23.0	40.3	28.5	91.9	78.5	41.4	54.3	*	63.5
RB	77.9	52.5	45.5	46.5	70.5	65.7	48.2	87.0	63.5	*

Table 4.8. Party groups' voting likeness: votes on the situation in former Yugoslavia

Party group	PES	EPP	ELDR	EDG	V	EUL	EDA	ER	LU	RB
PES	*	47.8	31.6	*	52.0	*	60.8	27.0	64.1	48.7
EPP	47.8	*	61.8	*	67.9	*	73.9	43.7	21.3	56.7
ELDR	31.6	61.8	*	*	59.6	*	39.1	55.5	29.2	79.9
EDG	*	*	*	*	*	*	*	*	*	*
V	52.0	67.9	59.6	*	*	*	56.1	54.2	38.3	63.4
EUL	*	*	*	*	*	*	*	*	*	*
EDA	60.8	73.9	39.1	*	56.1	*	*	50.2	26.5	50.0
ER	27.0	43.7	55.5	*	54.2	*	50.2	*	46.1	39.0
LU	64.1	21.3	29.2	*	38.3	*	26.5	46.1	*	44.0
RB	48.7	56.7	79.9	*	63.4	*	50.0	39.0	44.0	*

During the crisis in former Yugoslavia the Parliament has not only simply responded to events (something that can be expected from an institution which convenes normally only once a month for the plenary session in Strasbourg), but has also sought an active role in shaping and influencing policy. For example, the EP has shown its flexibility (again something that can be expected from an institution lacking formal powers in this policy field) by arranging a joint EP session attended by the Yugoslav federal and all independent republic parliaments, and by actively discussing the issue in the Political Affairs Committee and in the plenary (Sprokkereef, 1993: 12-15). In January 1994 the Parliament adopted a joint resolution calling for the resignation of the EU mediator Lord Owen, expressing the Parliament's frustration with the lack of progress in peace negotiations.[26]

Votes on the Gulf War (N = 13) consist exclusively of Parliament's own-initiative and urgent resolutions. Table 4.7. shows the chamber divided on the left-right dimension. Groups on the left, including the Socialists, remain fairly distant from the centre-right groups, but have rather high indices of voting conformity with each other. A similar picture emerges among the centre-right groups. As in votes on relations with Arab countries, the Left Unity and the Greens, the two anti-federalist leftist groups, show a high degree of voting likeness. The 13 votes on the Gulf War were highly adversarial, with the IA for the whole EP being as low as .313.

Votes on the crisis in former Yugoslavia (N = 37) produce no coalitions in the chamber, not even on the left-right dimension as was the case with votes on the Gulf War. The IA for the whole Parliament was again low, only .307. Most of the votes took place after the EDG and EUL groups had ceased to exist, and thus they have been excluded from the analysis. In only two cases is the index of voting likeness between two groups over 70.0: between the Liberals and the Rainbow Group and between EDA and EPP. Since these votes were all Parliament's own-initiative or urgent resolutions, lacking the kind of mediation process described in section 3.5., this tendency to politicise issues by opposing one another comes as no surprise.

The findings in Tables 4.6. to 4.8. confirm hypothesis 7. Lacking formal powers, the Parliament did not speak with one voice on foreign policy matters.

In the case of votes on relations with Arab countries the requirement to reach the figure of 260 facilitated - or necessitated - the search for intra-chamber solidarity, but votes on the Gulf War and on Yugoslavia - in no way binding on the other institutions - showed lack of unity in the Parliament, with the suggested consequences on the EP's ability to make the other institutions take its opinions into account. However, one must keep in mind that the analysis in this section was limited to only one subject area and only to assent procedure, and therefore further research is needed to examine the impact of legislative majority requirements on party group cohesion and coalition behaviour.

4.9. Concluding Remarks

This chapter examined the cohesion and coalition behaviour of EP party groups by focusing on roll-call votes. Critics may argue that by analysing easily observable, recorded actions of parliamentary parties, the researcher ignores various tensions and disagreements that exist beneath the surface. However, apart from being observable, the fascinating feature of roll-call votes lies precisely in their robustness. When the vote is on the agenda of the plenary, the individual representative must make up his or her mind whether to follow the party line or not. Therefore roll-call analysis presents perhaps the most reliable indicator of party group cohesion.

The period under analysis was the third directly elected Parliament (1989-1994). We can draw the following conclusions.

1) While national parties or country delegations may vote against the group line, with some parties engaging in such activity more often than others, there was no direct relationship between party group heterogeneity and party group cohesion.

2) The cohesive party groups were the EDG, ELDR, EPP, ER, EUL, the Greens, and LU, with the EDA, Rainbow group, and the Socialists remaining clearly behind in terms of voting cohesion.

3) Parties within national parliaments - with the exception of the U.S. Congress - were still ahead of EP party groups in terms of cohesion. However, considering the selective nature of the sample, the data does not allow us to draw any definite conclusions on the cohesion of EP parties vis-à-vis the whole population of parliamentary groups.

4) Party groups' voting likeness reflected their corresponding positions on the left-right dimension. The voting similarity of the party groups forming the political centre is relatively high.

5) The three party groups expected not to form coalitions with other groups in the chamber - the European Right, the Left Unity and the Greens - were all ideologically distant from the political centre.

6) There was no major and systematic decline in the cohesion of party groups when foreign policy issues were on the agenda.

7) The cohesion of the party groups is not dependent on legislative majority requirements. However, the findings must be treated with caution since the analysis was here restricted to a rather small sample of votes and to one issue area and included only votes falling under the assent procedure.

8) Lacking formal powers, the Parliament did not speak with one voice on foreign policy matters. Votes with majority requirements saw co-operation between the mainstream political groups, otherwise votes on foreign policy issues were highly politicised in the chamber. It is argued that such lack of intra-parliamentary unity reduces EP's ability to make the other institutions take its opinions into account.

Fourth European elections held in June 1994 led to further changes in the EP's party system. Three completely new political groups emerged: Europe of the Nations (EN), an anti-Maastricht group built around representatives of the French l'Autre Europe and Danish anti-marketeers; Forza Europa (FE), a group including only MEPs from Berlusconi's Forza Italia; and European Radical Alliance (ERA), led by Bernard Tapie's Energie Radicale. The European Right and Rainbow group are not present in the current Parliament. The far-right MEPs sit now as non-attached members. The mononational FE group joined forces with the EDA group in the summer of 1995, thus making the new group - Union for Europe (UPE) - the third largest in the Parliament. The number of groups was further reduced in late 1996 when the EN lost a member and failed to meet the numerical criteria needed to constitute a group.

The larger groups continue to dominate the votes in the Parliament. With co-operation between the Socialists and the EPP necessary for building required legislative majorities, the political centre is bound to vote together on most issues falling under the assent, co-operation and co-decision procedures. On certain subject matters MEPs form coalitions on a cross-group basis. Considering the fact that EP is still an institution in search of a clear constitutional mandate, the behaviour of the party groups is still largely conditioned by the majority requirements and by the concern to present the Parliament as a united institution vis-à-vis the other EU-decision-making bodies.

The political opposition in the chamber comes mainly from members of the Left Unity, the Greens, and the far-right non-attached MEPs - that is, the predominantly anti-federalist bloc. The situation remains much the same as after 1989 - the fragmentation of opposition has only consolidated the dominance of the political centre.

Probably the most significant finding of the voting behaviour analysis was that party cohesion in the 1989-94 EP was not dependent on the transnationality and fractionalisation of the groups. Moreover, high turnover rates of members at European elections does not seem to have a negative effect on group unity. Of the 518 MEPs elected in June 1989, 251 (48.5 %) had not sat in the previous Parliament. Thus Boyce (1995: 151) is right in arguing that "very probably, new MEPs will soon be socialised into this consensual style of politics, thus largely allaying fears that inexperience may render co-operation more difficult." Either the national party delegations have little difficulty in accepting the group positions, or then the weak links between MEPs and their national parties have left representatives room for manoeuvre in the Parliament. Most probably these two factors do not cancel each other out, and it is likely that the same tendency will continue in the 1994-99 EP.

The EP parties are still less cohesive than their counterparts in selected Western European national legislatures. However, it is reasonable to claim that the cohesion of EP groups is nevertheless fairly impressive when considering their internal heterogeneity and the importance of national party delegations within them.

Notes

[1] An earlier version of this chapter was presented at the workshop on Party Discipline and the Organization of Parliaments in the ECPR Joint Sessions of Workshops in Bordeaux, 1995 (Raunio, 1995). I am grateful to the participants of that workshop for their many helpful suggestions. I would also like to thank Professor Fulvio Attinà for his insightful comments.

Parts of the text and data will be reproduced in 'Cleavages and Alignments: MEP Voting Behaviour, 1989-94', in *Transnational Party Politics in the European Union*, edited by David S. Bell and Christopher Lord, Dartmouth, Aldershot (Raunio, 1997b); and in 'The Challenge of Diversity: Party Cohesion in the European Parliament', in *Party Cohesion, Party Discipline and the Organization of Parliaments*, edited by Shaun Bowler, David M. Farrell, and Richard S. Katz, Ohio State University Press, Columbus (Raunio, 1997a).

[2] What actually constitutes a 'matter of conscience' is open to interpretation. In the Socialist group a vote with significant national importance is in fact regarded a 'matter of conscience'. "The internal rules of the Socialist Group, for example, provide for dissent from majority decisions for 'serious political reasons', often

referred to, interestingly but incorrectly, as the 'conscience clause'." (Ladrech and Brown-Pappamikail, 1995: 269)

[3] Article 158 in the Treaty on European Union. This article makes the Commission as a whole subject to a vote of approval by the Parliament. In the nomination of the Commission President the Parliament has only the right to be consulted. However, as the appointment process of Jacques Santer in 1994 showed, the various actors recognised the fact that without the support of the MEPs, the Council's nominee would in practice have to step down and an alternative nominee would have to be found. Santer himself, by no means certain of not being rejected by the EP, lobbied the Parliament and its main party groups. When the vote was held in July 1994, he won the narrow support of the MEPs, with 260 votes in favour, 238 against, and 23 abstentions. The Parliament also conducted public hearings with the Council's nominees for the Commissioners. These hearings attracted a lot of attention in the media. In the vote on the Commission in January 1995, the Parliament gave its approval with 416 votes in favour, 103 against, and 59 abstentions. The office of the Commission was also extended from four to five years in order to be linked with that of the Parliament. While the Parliament has had the right to censure the Commission as a collegiate body since the days of the ECSC Common Assembly (then the High Authority), this right has never been used. Note that because of the collegiate nature of the Commission, the Parliament cannot subject an individual Commissioner to a vote of approval or censure.

[4] In his causal analysis on party cohesion, Ozbudun (1970: 380) found that "the patterns of relationships between the executive and legislative authorities are even more closely related to the cohesion of legislative parties than are the social, cultural, and organisational factors. While cohesive legislative parties are not absolutely necessary for the proper functioning of the government under the separation of powers, the parliamentary system creates a strong incentive for maintaining party cohesion by making almost every important vote in the legislative assembly a vote of confidence in the government. In other words, effective working of a parliamentary system depends on the existence of cohesive political parties. The cohesive effects of parliamentary government are most strongly felt in two-party or moderate multiparty systems." I would like to thank Petr Kopecký for kindly sending me a copy of this regrettably little-known monograph.

[5] It is very difficult to establish the actual number of intergroups since they are not officially registered. Specific intergroups have been very influential, while others only meet very infrequently. For more information on intergroups, see Jacobs, Corbett, and Shackleton (1995: 169-178).

[6] Both federalism and CAP have caused much debate within and between the groups. MEPs from the two major British parties, for example, have at times found it difficult to accept their groups' views on federalism and have voted against the group line (see Westlake, 1994a). Similarly on agricultural issues the chamber has often been divided on a cross-group basis, one camp defending the system of high

prices and subsidies paid to the farmers, the other favouring reductions in agricultural spending. See for example Theato and Graf (1994) and Bourguignon-Wittke et al. (1985: 54).

[7] The exact question put to the respondents was: "It is generally accepted that aside from their written rules, parliaments have their unwritten rules and customs. How would you, in terms of those unwritten rules, judge the behaviour of an MEP who acted in one of the following ways?" While there was a high degree of consensus concerning what might be termed 'courtesy' norms, the survey found also considerable variation in MEPs' opinions: "And on the three questions concerning party group discipline (introducing motions without group advice, voting against the group and speaking against group leaders), opinion is much more noticeably divided, so much so that we may reasonably argue that there is no consensus of expectations, no norms, operating here." (Bowler and Farrell, 1993b)

[8] Keith Middlemas (1995: 734) writes that in the 1979-84 Parliament on average 210 MEPs (51.2 %) were present when votes were cast, and that in the 1984-89 Parliament an average of 300 members (57.9 %) were in the chamber during voting periods.

[9] However, one can argue that the request for a referral back to a committee (Rule 129) is made exactly because of the contents of the report. According to Jacobs, Corbett, and Shackleton (1995: 163) such a referral is requested "to get a controversial item off the plenary agenda, and thus to postpone or block Parliament's decision on the matter. ...This is often done by the responsible committee itself, if difficulties have emerged during a debate, or if new developments or an unsatisfactory response by the Commission require consideration of the matter within the committee."

[10] In their recent article Simon Hix and Christopher Lord (1996) examined the voting behaviour of the MEPs in the Santer vote, and found that the cohesion of the party groups was dependent on domestic party politics at the national level. Since Santer was the nominee of the Council, the MEPs sitting in party groups opposed to Santer, but representing government parties at home, had to choose between supporting Santer (and thus defying the group line), or opposing Santer (and thus defying their party back home). In the event, national considerations dominated: "In all, we found that 91.7 per cent of the voting behaviour of MEPs could be explained by means of the following hypothesis.

i) If their parent parties are in government, national delegations will vote for the nominee of the European Council, even if this means going against the majority view of their transnational party group.

ii) All MEPs from the country of the nominee will vote for him/her, such is the prize of securing the presidency of the Commission for a compatriot.

iii) With the exception of the circumstances in i) and ii), transnational party solidarity will hold and national delegations will follow the group line." (Hix and Lord, 1996: 72)

Studying the voting behaviour of EP party groups in the 'enlargement' vote (whether to accept Austria, Finland, Norway, and Sweden into the EU) held in May 1994, Johansson (1997) also shows the intrusion of domestic considerations into EP party politics: "...we can safely conclude that MEPs were subject to clear instructions from governments and mother parties to show up and vote in approval of the Accession Agreements. It is understood that MEPs faced threats of deselection from party lists contesting the European elections if they disobeyed. ...Party Group managers had been successful in orchestrating attendance and discipline but they had primarily done so at the wishes of national parties and governments, reasserting control over 'their' MEPs." Johansson analysed also the Santer vote, and his conclusion echoes that of Hix and Lord cited above: "How to explain that a majority of MEPs likely to reject Santer's appointment had changed into a, however, similarly small, majority in his favour?...The split within the PES Group reflected a clear government-opposition divide ...Reminding of May's enlargement vote it is beyond doubt that MEPs were put under heavy pressure from respective party headquarters and governments."

[11] These facts need to be treated with some caution. For example, the party affiliation of the French members within the Liberals Group is somewhat unclear - different sources, including official party documents, report different party affiliations.

[12] The forthcoming volume edited by Bowler, Farrell, and Katz (1997) focuses on party cohesion and discipline in legislatures, with contributors analysing various dimensions of party unity in parliaments. Similarly the forthcoming volume on party groups in European legislatures, edited by Heidar and Koole (1997), includes information on the cohesion of parliamentary parties. For information on the level of parliamentary party cohesion in Western democracies until the late 1960s, see Ozbudun (1970).

[13] Computed from the table in Cox and McCubbins (1991: 562). See their article for the original sources of the data.

[14] During the 1920-1994 period, excluding missing data from 1953 to 1967, there were a total of 426 roll-calls in the Swiss National Council. The 1991-94 indices were based on 163 roll-calls in the National Council. The original sources of the cohesion data is found in Lanfranchi and Lüthi (1995: 15).

[15] Comparing with data from other Scandinavian parliaments, the parliamentary parties in the Finnish Eduskunta between 1945 and 1954 had cohesion values (measured by the same Rice index) ranging from 74.5 to 95.2. See Nyholm (1961, 1972) and Nyholm and Hagfors (1968). Parties in the 1967 Swedish Riksdag had cohesion-values (again using the Rice index) between 88.0. and 95.0 (Clausen and Holmberg, 1977: 166-167). There is no reason to suspect that party cohesion has declined over the years. In the Danish Folketinget the party groups have also been cohesive in their voting behaviour (see Mikkelsen, 1994).

[16] The formula for computing the Rice index on a given vote for party X is:

$$I_X = | \%_{YES} - \%_{NO} |$$

The values range from 0 (the party is divided into two fractions of equal size) to 100 (complete party unity).

[17] Other issue areas characterised by high conflict potential include those votes that deal directly with allocation of funds within the Union, and where MEPs could thus be expected to fight hard to bring money home to their constituents. For example, votes on the distribution of structural and social funds are included in this category. Similarly votes on agriculture and fisheries policy are interesting in this respect.

[18] In her discussion on EP's role in foreign policy, Juliet Lodge (1988: 130) has also made the same point: "Clearly, the chance of a resolution either being noted by Council or influencing Council foreign policy deliberations is enhanced if significant majorities can be managed within the European Parliament."

[19] The foreign policy role of the Parliament has also received much attention from scholars despite EP's limited legislative powers in the field of foreign affairs. See Bieber (1990), Elles (1990), Lodge (1988), Neunreither (1990), Penders (1988) and Viola (1994, 1996).

[20] According to Kirchner (1984: 132) "the EP's potential to upgrade its role in decision-making is not effectively enhanced if members devote a considerable proportion of their time to EC foreign policy issues. Whilst the issue area of political affairs probably increases the image and prestige of the EP as a political and moral forum, especially outside the EC, it does not correspondingly augment its role in EC decision-making."

[21] I have included here reports following a motion for resolution tabled by an individual MEP. (Rule 45) It is up to the responsible committee to decide whether it desires to draw up a report on the basis of the motion. As in the case of own-initiative reports, the committee must first receive the approval to draft the report from the Conference of Presidents.

[22] A maximum of five topics may be discussed during the debates on topical and urgent subjects of major importance. A political group or at least 29 members may ask the President that a particular issue is placed on the agenda of the debate. Such a request must be linked with a motion for a resolution. Having consulted these requests, the topics are then selected by the Conference of Presidents. A political group or 29 members may oppose the selection of the Conference of Presidents, and request that an alternative issue of their own choice is debated. A vote without debate on the objection is then held. (Rule 47)

[23] Note however that certain policy areas often produce universalistic coalitions in the chamber even without such majority requirements. In the 1989-94 EP votes on environmental matters were often passed either unanimously or with only a few dissenting votes.

[24] On the relationship between EP's voting behaviour and its influence vis-à-vis the other European institutions, see for example the case studies in Grabitz et al. (1988).

[25] In his voting behaviour analysis on the 1984-89 EP, Attinà (1990: 572-573) found that in general the cohesion of party groups was higher than average on international issues.

[26] The Parliament was probably also annoyed with Lord Owen's refusal to address the EP on the issue. See Viola (1994: 25-28).

5 Informing and Controlling the Executive at the European Level: Questions in the European Parliament

5.1. Introduction: Representing Multiple Interests[1]

Should the representative focus on defending the interests of her or his locality, some particular interest sector, or the whole nation? Should his views reflect the mood prevailing in the constituency ('delegate') or should the member instead acquire a more independent role ('trustee')? How do members combine loyalty to their parliamentary party with the task of promoting other interests? These are the central questions that come up in the various theoretical works and empirical studies on the concept of representation.[2]

Apart from seeking to achieve his own goals, the average representative needs to cater for a variety of interests: he receives letters from individual constituents, is the subject of lobbying by interest groups and companies, must in most cases toe the official line of the party he represents, and must respect the written rules and informal norms of his workplace. Hanna Pitkin's conclusion provides a fitting summary:

> "In the first place, the political representative has a constituency and constituents...In the second place, he is a professional politician in a framework of political institutions, a member of a political party who wants to get re-elected, and a member of legislature along with other representatives. He must be sensitive to his political party (both local and national) and to various public and private groups and interests. As a member of the legislature, he occupies an office to which certain obligations and expectations are attached. He must comply with its traditions and work within the framework of the rules and mores of the legislative body. He must get along with his colleagues, especially certain important ones among them.

To act effectively he must keep in mind not only the formal and informal rules of his legislative body but also its place in the whole structure of government. In the third place, he will also have views and opinions, at least on some issues. He will feel that some measures are intrinsically unsound, immoral, or undesirable. At the same time, his opinions may, in turn, be shaped by those around him and his sources of information." (Pitkin, 1967: 219-220)

The representatives in Strasbourg face the same kind of choices and demands as their colleagues in national legislatures. The significant difference lies in the transnational composition of the Parliament. Article 137 of the Treaty establishing the European Community states that the EP

"shall consist of representatives of the peoples of the States brought together in the Community."

The Treaties thus spell out the fact that, despite being elected on national or regional lists, the "MEP's role is not confined to representing the interest of the nation which elected him." (Bieber, 1991: 400) This was also the primary reason why the first nominated delegates to the ECSC Common Assembly in 1953 decided to sit in ideological groupings instead of as national delegations. Since national interests were argued to be already safeguarded in the meetings of the Council, it was regarded important that the parliamentary assembly would offer a 'European' perspective to policy-making.

In one of the first studies on the directly elected EP, Geoffrey Pridham and Pippa Pridham wrote that

"a crucial determining factor in the development of transnational party co-operation in the EP will be the priorities which individual MEPs set themselves for their work in the Parliament, and where they see their loyalties lying." (Pridham and Pridham, 1981: 95)

MEPs may in principle see themselves as representing one of the following: the party group in the EP, national party, the constituency and/or member state, the whole European Union, or specific sectional interests. However, the most likely answer is that MEPs regard themselves as representing multiple interests. This has indeed been shown by the large-scale surveys of the directly elected Parliament that have included questions on representation.

The 1983 EUI study found that members saw contributing to policy-making at the European level and the advancement of European integration as their two main commitments, followed by looking after constituency interests, overseeing European executive bodies, and promoting national interests. When asked about whom they perceived being responsible to, the electorate came first, with EP party group coming far behind the respondent's national party (see Bardi, 1989).

The most recent data on this issue was collected as part of the 1994 European Elections Study. When asked to rate the importance of various role orientations, the candidates identified 'contribute to European policy-making' as their most important function, followed by 'represent regional interests'. 'Advance national interests' and 'help people with particular problems' came next, with the least important role being 'represent group interests'. When asked whether their primary loyalty in the case of conflict was to their national party or to their EP party group, the respondents opted for the middle ground, with the Italian delegation leaning most towards their party groups, and the Danish delegation showing most loyalty to their national parties. Finally the respondents were asked whether co-operation in the Parliament should be based on nationality or political views. With the exception of the Irish delegation, the candidates supported the idea of partisan-based co-operation. Candidates from the small EU member states were, however, on average more prone to protecting their national interests than candidates from the larger countries. However, considering the survey's very low response rate, it is questionable whether the results can be considered as representative of the chamber.[3]

Table 5.1.   Whom do the MEPs see themselves as representing?

National party	4.61
Party group	4.32
Country	4.27
Region	4.07
All the citizens of the EC	3.91
District	3.76
Interest group	1.68

Source: Bowler and Farrell (1992a: 22).

Table 5.1. shows the results of research undertaken by Shaun Bowler and David Farrell in 1990. The response rate was 37.6% (195 out of 518 MEPs). The question they presented to the respondents was "how applicable to you are the following statements about the way in which MEPs see themselves?" MEPs had seven options which they were able to mark as less or more applicable on a scale ranging from 0 (not applicable) to 6 (highly applicable). The findings in Table 5.1. are particularly interesting since the respondents of the survey were members of the 1989-94 EP.

Table 5.1. indicates that members understand their role as representing multiple interests, with six out of seven response categories clustered fairly close to each other. Only the 'interest-group'-focus received little support among the respondents, remaining clearly behind the other categories. However, a more detailed analysis of the replies shows that there are interesting differences between member state delegations, with MEPs from the smaller and geographically more peripheral countries having a stronger sense of territorial - national - representation, and with the UK contingent, elected from single-member constituencies, devoting more attention to individual voters. Bowler and Farrell concluded that

"what is somewhat surprising is that there seems little consensus among MEPs over their representative role...these results do not say that the individual MEP is necessarily confused over what his or her role might be...we argue that these results reveal a marked lack of clarity which is relevant for the EP as an institution and, more especially, an institution under construction." (Bowler and Farrell, 1992a: 23-26)

Parliamentary questions (PQs), one of the freest forms of activity in modern legislatures, gives the individual representative an excellent chance of promoting and defending those issues which he or she regards important. Thus

"the use of parliamentary questions may be considered an especially interesting indicator of how the elected understand their role as representatives." (Wiberg, 1991a: 68)

However, it must be pointed out at the very beginning that the device of parliamentary questions is only one of the many possibilities members have in pursuing their goals. Therefore the aim of this chapter is not to give a comprehensive account of the concept of representation in the Strasbourg assembly, but to study the various aspects of the institution of parliamentary questions in the EP and the usage of it by the MEPs, and thereby increase our understanding of specialisation and representation in the Parliament.

5.2. Research on Parliamentary Questions

Parliamentary questions have attracted surprisingly little attention from scholars interested in legislatures. While often mentioned in studies on various parliaments, works focusing solely on this device have been few and far between. The early articles and monographs were mainly descriptive (Ameller, 1964; Chester and Bowring, 1962; Johnson, 1961), concentrating on describing the various actors and elements involved, and explaining the formal rules of submitting questions and receiving answers to them. The qualitative analysis by David Judge (1974) on the questions of British MPs is an excellent example of the way concepts such as specialisation and representation can be studied by examining the content of MPs' questions. Recent years have seen the welcome additions of volumes edited by Mark Franklin and Philip Norton (1993a) and Matti Wiberg (1994a), with the former work focusing on the British House of Commons, and the latter consisting of chapters on the use of this device in Nordic legislatures. Finally, the recent comparative analysis of Western European parliaments included a chapter on parliamentary questions (Wiberg, 1995).

Within the context of EP the situation is similar to that prevailing in works on national parliaments. While briefly mentioned in standard texts on EP, only a few studies exist focusing on MEPs' questioning activity. Discussed as a control device by Zellentin (1967), Cohen's (1979) study on the development of question-time, highlighting the role of British MEPs, was the first proper study on parliamentary questions in Strasbourg. Question-time has also been analysed in similar fashion by Westlake (1990). Kirchner's (1984) work on the background and activity of MEPs included quantitative and content analyses of parliamentary questions from the 1979-82 EP, while rather similar information from the same time period is found in Grabitz et al. (1988). Two recent studies on specialisation and parliamentary norms by Bowler and Farrell (1993b; 1995) included an analysis on the use of oral questions by MEPs.

5.3. Parliamentary Questions in National Parliaments

First it is worth looking at the institution of parliamentary questions in the context of national parliaments, not least because many of the hypotheses put forth in this chapter originate from studies on this device in national legislatures. Parliamentary questions are multi-functional, and MPs ask questions for several reasons. Among the most important are:

a) tabling questions is something the MPs are supposed to be doing - it is a part of their job and a normal activity within the chamber;
b) asking for information;
c) getting the executive to make a formal statement and pressing it for action;
d) defending or promoting constituency or sectoral interests; and
e) informing the policy-makers of problems they might be unfamiliar with (see Franklin and Norton, 1993b; Wiberg, 1991a; Wiberg and Koura, 1994).

Parliamentary questions thus perform a variety of functions, and their attractiveness is enhanced by the fact that by submitting questions MPs may raise practically any issue they want. The more specific the issue raised or the information required, the more effective the questions usually are. Wider issues may also be tackled, although this may lead to the answer being rather non-informative and general in nature (Johnson, 1961: 143).

It should be recalled that tabling questions is just one of the channels available for individual MPs to pursue their goals. Committee work, writing letters to ministers, and using other informal and formal contacts are probably often more important avenues of communication for the average MP. Furthermore, the fact that the questions and answers to them are in most cases only published in the official records of the national parliaments, read by just a handful of interested outside observers, together with the delays involved in receiving an answer, often lead MPs to concentrate on more direct, public, and effective ways of trying to influence the course of events.

Considering that before entering the Parliament a majority of the MEPs have either sat in their national legislatures or in various regional assemblies, their work habits, at least at the beginning of their tenure in the Strasbourg Parliament, may reflect their experiences in national politics. Moreover, a number of members still hold dual mandates. Therefore it is useful to look briefly at the institution of parliamentary questions in the EU member state parliaments.

Putting questions to the executive is a well-established feature of government-parliament relations in the EU member states. However, while parliamentary questions are present in every EU national legislature, there is significant variation between the various national parliaments regarding both the types of questions used and the procedural details concerning the submission and answering of questions. It has to be remembered that parliamentary questions are constantly under evolution, with both new forms of questioning replacing older ones, and more detailed changes introduced to the legislatures' rules of procedure. Written questions are used in the national parliaments of Austria, Belgium, Denmark, Finland, France, Germany, Greece, Ireland, Italy, Luxembourg, the Netherlands, Portugal, Spain, and the UK. Currently the Swedish Riksdag is the only EU member state legislature without written questions (Wiberg, 1995).

5.4. The Sample

The data consists of all the questions for written answer MEPs tabled in 1992 to which an answer had been given by the time of conducting the research (December 1994). This was the most recent year for which the questions together with their answers were available. During that year the members asked a total of 3,526 questions: 3,051 were addressed to the Commission, 338 to the Council of Ministers, and 137 questions to the EPC. However, the total number of questions is somewhat higher (N = 4,077), due to the fact that a number of questions were signed by two or more MEPs, and in these cases also the co-signers have been credited. It would have been illogical to include in the analysis only the first signer of the question, since in this way we would have ignored the probability of MEPs co-operating already at the stage of drafting the question. For example, the Italian MEPs representing the same electoral district often joined forces in submitting a question to the Commission.

In order to acquire a better understanding of the institution of parliamentary questions, and to get some inside information on the usage of it by the members, a number of interviews with MEPs, their assistants, and EP staff were carried out by the author in Brussels and in Strasbourg in February 1996. A total of 15 members, representing eight nationalities and five party groups, and/or their assistants were interviewed. A full list of the representatives who took the time to answer the questions is found in the bibliography. All interviewed MEPs were present in the Parliament in 1992, and on average they had served in the Parliament for 10.3 years. Included in the sample were members making active use of written questions, as well as those submitting few if any parliamentary questions.

One feature confusing the picture is the different tactics adopted by MEPs in using the device of parliamentary questions. Some representatives include many points in their questions, while others prefer to use separate questions when tackling the same issues. Often the same MEP or different MEPs also ask the same question twice or even more times, thus either wanting to underline the urgency or importance of the matter, or demanding to know why no action has so far been taken to remedy the situation in question.

The French MEP Jean-Pierre Raffin, representing the Greens, commented in his question on funding a road project in the Pyrenees:

"perhaps, like the walls of Jericho, the impenetrable defences which the Commission has erected will come tumbling down if the questions are asked again."[4]

Table 5.2. shows the number of seats per political group and national delegation in the EP at the beginning of 1992. Almost half of the 518 MEPs, 46%, were elected to the Parliament for the first time in the 1989 European elections.[5] In May 1992 one significant change took place in the internal organisation of the chamber: the 34 MEPs forming the European Democratic Group joined the EPP. In the analysis of results the 32 British Conservatives and two Danes making up the group are included in the EPP group. Apart from this merger, 1992 appears to have been a rather 'normal' year in the work of the Parliament. Reflecting developments in Europe, the year's debates in the chamber were dominated by the completion of the internal market (in particular its social dimension), the Treaty on European Union, and Community's response to the crisis in former Yugoslavia.[6]

1992 was also in the middle of an electoral cycle, thus in practice ruling out the possibility of elections having any effect on the level of MEPs' questioning activity. Parliamentary questions in the EP are free from the kind of electioneering that takes place in some national legislatures, with the total number of questions rising prior to the elections (Wiberg, 1991b, 1994b), and because of the lack of meaningful opposition and government roles within the chamber, representatives questions' are not as partisan-motivated as often is the case in national parliaments.

Table 5.2. Political groups and national delegations in the EP at the beginning of 1992

Member States / Party Groups	B	DK	F	G	GR	IR	I	L	NL	P	S	UK	EP
PES	8	4	22	31	9	1	14	2	8	8	27	46	180
EPP	7	4	11	32	10	4	27	3	10	3	18	33	162
ELDR	4	3	9	5		2	3	1	4	9	5		45
EUL		1			1	1	22				4		29
V	3		8	6			7		2		1		27
EDA			12		1	6					2		21
RB	1	4	1	1		1	3			1	2	1	15
ER	1		10	3									14
LU			7		3					3			13
NA			1	3			5		1		1	1	12
Total	24	16	81	81	24	15	81	6	25	24	60	81	518

Member states: B = Belgium, DK = Denmark, F = France, G = Germany, GR = Greece, IR = Ireland, I = Italy, L = Luxembourg, NL = Netherlands, P = Portugal, S = Spain, and UK = United Kingdom.
Sources: *Official Journal of the European Communities* and European Parliament: *List of Members*.

133

5.5. The Development and Function of Questions in the European Parliament

MEPs have the right to put questions to the Commission and to the Council of Ministers. Until the Maastricht Treaty came into force in November 1993, members were also able to submit questions to the Foreign Ministers meeting in European Political Co-operation (EPC). However, this channel is not available anymore since the EPC no longer exists, having been replaced or subsumed in the current EU structure within the 'second pillar', the common foreign and security policy (CFSP). The Commission and the Council have answered questions since the founding of the Community, while Foreign Ministers meeting in EPC agreed to a similar arrangement in 1975. It must be noticed that the Commission is obliged by the Treaty to answer Parliament's questions. Article 140 of the Treaty reads:

> "The Commission shall reply orally or in writing to questions put to it by the European Parliament or by its Members."

The Council agreed in 1973 to answer questions put to it by the Parliament, and this practice was consolidated in the 1983 Stuttgart Solemn Declaration on European Union. However, only the Commission is bound by the Treaty to answer parliamentary questions.

Prior to the 1993 change of Parliament's rules there existed four different types of questions that could be tabled: written questions, oral questions without debate, oral questions with debate, and questions at question-time. Since then the two types of oral questions have been reduced to one. Due mainly to restrictions on available plenary time, oral questions (Rule 40) may nowadays only be tabled by a political group, a committee or at least 29 members. In practice the decision of whether to place an oral question on the EP's agenda is made by the Conference of Presidents. The number of oral questions has remained low since the introduction of direct elections. From 1979 until 1987 the Parliament submitted between 45 and 103 oral questions per year after which there was an upsurge in the number of questions tabled. The peak came in 1990 with 411 questions. In 1995 the Parliament tabled 297 oral questions.

Question-time (Rule 41) was introduced into the EP in 1973, but has never come close to matching the liveliness of debate which characterises this institution in the British House of Commons. According to Westlake (1994c: 176) question-time was bound to remain a pale imitation of its role-model "in a culturally diverse Parliament where debates had to be interpreted through earphones, where there was no government and opposition and, above all, where there was no prime minister." Furthermore, "requests for statistical information, or on matters requiring extensive prior research are out of order for question-time", and must therefore be submitted instead as written questions (Cohen, 1979: 45). Question-time suffers also from the fact that Commissioners take turns to be in Strasbourg to answer the questions. The Commissioner present in the chamber will thus be answering all the questions on behalf of the Commission, quite irrespective of whether the questions fall under his or her competence. This can undermine the practice of asking supplementary questions since the Commissioners cannot be experts in all issue areas. Despite these shortcomings, question-time is a permanent feature in the organisation of parliamentary work in Strasbourg. Since the introduction of direct elections the total number of questions has varied between 768 (in 1983) and 1,355 (in 1990), and the variation in questions asked per representative has ranged from a high of 2.6 per MEP (in 1990) to a low of 1.4 per MEP (in 1994).[7]

By far the most popular of the procedures is the written question. This comes as no surprise, given the advantages which the written question enjoys over the other types of questions: MEPs can raise any issue they want, and tabling a written question does not require the physical presence of the questioner in the chamber at a given hour. Rule 42 of the latest edition of the EP's Rules of Procedure lays down the rules concerning the questions for written answer:

1. Questions for written answer may be put by any Member to the Council or the Commission.
2. Questions shall be submitted in writing to the President who shall forward them to the institution concerned.
3. Questions and answers shall be published in the Official Journal.
4. If a question cannot be answered within the time limit set it shall, at the request of the author, be placed on the agenda of the next meeting of the committee responsible. Rule 41 [Question Time] shall apply mutatis mutandis.
5. Questions which require an immediate answer but no detailed research (priority questions) shall be answered within three weeks. Each Member may table one priority question each month.
6. Other questions (non-priority questions) shall be answered within six weeks.

7. Members shall indicate which type of question they are submitting. The final decision shall be taken by the President.

As in the case of national legislatures, the overall number of questions has risen steadily over the years (see Table 5.3). However, this increase is largely explained by the parallel increase in the number of MEPs. Already the members of the Common Assembly had the right to question the European Coal and Steel Community's High Authority, a right which they used 57 times during the six years of the Assembly's existence (Cohen, 1979: 41-42). Until the early 1970s the Socialists, led by the persistent questioning activity of Mr Vredeling, submitted the lion's share of the questions (Zellentin, 1967; Fitzmaurice, 1975), and in the year of the first direct elections to the EP, 1979, a total of 1,977 questions for written answer were submitted. Since the first direct elections, the average number of written questions asked per representative has usually varied between 5 and 7, dropping below five per MEP on only two occasions, in 1981 and again in 1989 when the MEPs tabled only 3.8 written questions per member. The peak was in 1993 when the 518 MEPs asked 4,111 written questions, 7.9 per representative.

Approximately 90 per cent of the questions are addressed to the Commission, which is the 'executive' branch of the Union's decision-making apparatus. One author has argued that an increase in the share of questions addressed to the Council (and the EPC) would be a sign of EP's strengthened influence since these two institutions are involved in actual policy-making, but the rationale behind this argument is very doubtful (Ollerenshaw, 1993: 37). It is logical that MEPs address most of their questions to the Commission: there is more to be gained and more information to be received as the Commission is the EU institution with the right to initiate legislation and is also responsible for overseeing the implementation of that legislation. The Commission, through its internal organisation based on division of labour between the DGs, each with its own field of competence and civil servants, and involvement in the day-to-day administration of EU affairs, is better placed to provide the kind of information MEPs want to elicit by submitting their questions.

Table 5.3. **The increase in written questions in the EP since the first direct elections (1980-1995)**

Year	C	CM	EPC	Total	per MEP
1980	1995	271	57	2323	5.7
1981	1744	210	37	1991	4.6
1982	2022	256	66	2344	5.4
1983	1946	242	49	2237	5.2
1984	1976	262	73	2311	5.3
1985	2949	258	125	3332	7.7
1986	2671	195	157	3023	5.8
1987	2591	201	150	2942	5.7
1988	2512	159	171	2842	5.5
1989	1711	144	114	1969	3.8
1990	2732	217	126	3075	5.9
1991	2905	257	119	3281	6.3
1992	3051	338	137	3526	6.8
1993	3588	354	169	4111	7.9
1994	2505	401		2906	5.1
1995	3217	444		3661	5.8

Note: Questions for written answer.
Abbreviations: C = Commission; CM = Council; EPC = European Political Co-operation.
Source: *General Report on the Activities of the European Community* (1980-1995).

When tabling a question the member must first decide whether submitting a parliamentary question is the best available strategy for pursuing a matter. If the individual member chooses the strategy of parliamentary questions, he must then make the further choice between the various types of questions (note that oral questions can only be tabled by a political group, a committee or by 29 MEPs).

Having decided to submit a question for written answer, the MEP must then choose between either presenting the question alone, or together with colleagues from her own party group or from other party groups. Sometimes members receive similar requests from their colleagues and they must decide whether to join in. The majority of written questions are submitted by a member without seeking the co-operation of fellow representatives. First of all, there is no procedural obligation - as in the case of oral questions - to seek other MEPs' signatures. Secondly, members often want to make it clear who is behind the question. As one member said: "it is my point."

Often several MEPs may deliberately submit a series of almost identical questions on the same topic, thus wanting to send a message to the Commission that the subject matter is an important one and causing concern in the Parliament. Much depends on the issue: if several members share similar interests, then co-operation may be a feasible option. As one MEP explained: "if there are specific problems related to my home region, then I seek the co-operation of other members representing our region. Otherwise I submit questions alone." Another member saw that 'European' interests are best served by co-operation: "if the question involves broad European interests, then co-operation is sought." Co-operation between members may stem from many fora. The members may represent the same constituency, or constituencies with similar concerns. Collaboration may also be the result of work in the Parliament's committees, party groups, and intergroups.

MEPs can forward the question as a "priority written question" (Rule 42/5), a practice introduced unilaterally by the Parliament in 1994. Priority questions were introduced by the Parliament as a way of speeding up the Commission's replies. In this case the question should according to the rules be answered within three weeks. Each member is entitled to one such priority question per calendar month, a maximum of 12 priority questions per MEP per year. In 1995 the MEPs submitted between them a total of 400 priority questions, 0.64 per member. Two Greek MEPs, Alavanos (EUL) and Kaklamanis (EDA), made maximum use of this right, tabling all the available 12 questions. 19 MEPs asked between four and nine, 28 members submitted three, 46 asked two, and 94 MEPs asked one priority question. The remaining 440 members out of 626 did not participate in this activity in 1995.[8] Normal questions (non-priority) should according to the rules be answered within six weeks.

The questions must be typewritten, and the maximum length of a written question is 25 lines. The member either writes the question himself, or instructs his assistant to write the question. Several MEPs told that they give a topic to the assistant who then drafts the question, after which the member reads it in order to check the final wording before adding his or her signature. Members also receive questions, or requests to submit a question on a particular topic, from various interests groups or from constituents.

Members often also initiate such contacts themselves, for example by inviting visitors from various extra-parliamentary organisations and then using the information for drafting a question. However, this does not obviously automatically lead to the member tabling that question. As one MEP explained: "I never agree to ask questions drafted by other people unless they deal with a problem which I'm very concerned about. Even then I will take the liberty of rewriting them."

Figure 5.1. depicts the various phases of submitting a question for written answer in the European Parliament.

**Figure 5.1. Submitting a question for written answer
          in the European Parliament**

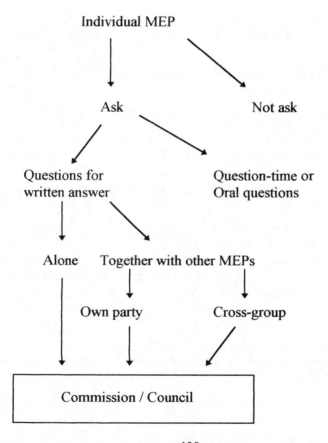

The question is then according to the Rules of Procedure submitted to the President who has the final say on the type of question used. However, in practice the questions go directly to the Commission without the intervention of the EP President. All questions go via the EP office in Luxembourg. Members either mail the question directly to Luxembourg, or send it to Luxembourg via the office for parliamentary questions located currently in the second floor of the Parliament's Leopold-building in Brussels.

There is no control by the party groups either, with the written question being one of the last formal channels available for the individual parliamentarian. As one member argued: "party groups should not interfere since the questions deal with the concerns of our constituencies." However, one MEP argued that there should be some kind of control: "there are so many written questions that MEPs don't know what others have asked. There should be some kind of summary of written questions in order to avoid identical questions."

Within the Commission the questions "are attributed to the competent Commissioners and Directorates General by the specialised unit in the Secretariat General. Replies are drafted by the services and forwarded up through the competent cabinet to the college for approval (by written procedure), before transmission back to Parliament by the Secretariat General." (Westlake, 1994b: 44) While the Commission as a whole is involved in the procedure, the answers are given by the responsible commissioner. The Commission sends the answer by mail to the member responsible for the question, and often the answer is accompanied with replies to other MEPs' questions on the same topic.

Within the Council the answers are given by the President-in-Office. The draft replies are prepared in the Secretariat of the Council and then circulated to the Permanent Representatives of the Member States as well as to the Commission for possible comments and/or objections. When there are no such comments, the reply is approved without further discussion. Otherwise the COREPER discusses the question. As an organ that represents the EU member states, the Council is more cautious than the Commission in its replies, and often tends to be less forthcoming in its replies.

The Commission has indicated to the Parliament that the deadlines for receiving an answer imposed unilaterally by the EP are not realistic, and that the Commission is not bound by them. Delays in receiving a reply from the Commission have caused frustration among the MEPs. Several interviewed members identified this as the biggest disadvantage of written questions: "it takes too long to receive an answer. Normally I want to know the answer quickly, and then the written questions offer no help." Because of these delays, by the time the reply is given, "the political message is lost." In similar vein another member argued that often "the issue is dead when the answer comes." The British Labour MEP Anita Pollack complained in her question to the Commission about the "immensely long time it takes the Commission to produce a written reply:"[9]

> "In a survey of Member States the longest period of time taken by any Parliament to provide answers to written questions is expected to be no longer than two months, although most are between one week and 20 days. In view of the immensely long time it takes the Commission to produce a written reply which is often even longer than one year, does the Commission feel it should review the excessively bureaucratic and lengthy procedure for written replies to Members' Questions and try to aim for an outside maximum of two months?"

In his reply to Mrs Pollack's question, the Commissioner Mr Pinheiro stated that:

> "the Commission always tries to answer Members' written questions as quickly as possible. However, the very large - and ever increasing - number of questions put to the Commission, coupled with the need to consult various departments on answers by reason of the principle of collective responsibility, can in some cases result in delays, which the Commission deplores. Moreover, the need for translation, which is specific to questions to Community institutions, means that more time is required than would be the case in a monolingual national procedure."

Despite the official time limit of six weeks, receiving an answer normally takes much longer. While it usually takes anything between six weeks and six months, it may occasionally take even more than one year before a question is answered. As mentioned above, translating the questions to all languages takes time. Furthermore, often the Commission needs to engage in a lot of research in order to produce a satisfactory reply, and in these cases it is obviously also in the MEPs' interests that the answer is carefully drafted and based on reliable information. The time it takes to receive an answer is often dependent on the Directorate General in the Commission to whom the question is addressed.

When asked about the quality of replies, MEPs' opinions varied. Several members complained that the Commission's record in answering the questions was inconsistent. Often the Commission fails to do its homework properly, leading to vague and imprecise answers. According to one MEP there is "not very much effort put into replying." Sometimes the Commission may shy away from answering the question, depending on the subject matter. Issues involving direct Commission responsibility are often politically sensitive issues, and the Commission may not want to share the information with the Parliament. Several MEPs also complained that the answers are often written using too "bureaucratic", "diplomatic", or "technical" language.

Other MEPs had more positive opinions. In comparison with oral questions, one member said that the answers are better because "they are given by civil servants who know the case." According to one long-serving MEP "the Commission's record in answering the questions has improved over the years." One member did not hesitate in praising the quality of replies: "We have an absolutely magnificent Commission: honest, open, and frank." The quality of the answers is often related to the quality of the question itself. As one member explained: "written questions must be drafted so that the Commission must give an answer. If they are not carefully drafted, the answer might be less than satisfactory."

The benefit of the written question is that it is a multi-functional instrument, with two of its main functions being control of the executive and sending and acquiring information. The members can use the questions to "force the Commission under control" because "they are obliged to answer." Many of the questions directly probed the Commission about its intentions or actions ("What has the Commission done?" / "What is the Commission going to do?"). This procedural obligation to answer is significant because it forces the Commission to produce a reply, and members thereby receive an official statement from the Commission which they can afterwards use for their own purposes. They can forward the answer to the interest group or constituent concerned, or can use it for further political action in the Parliament.

MEPs can use the written questions to inform the Commission of a particular problem it might be unfamiliar with, thus making the problem known in Brussels. By submitting written questions members send signals to the Commission, expressing thus their concern over a particular grievance or developments in certain country or sector. Human rights questions are good examples of such cases where members use questions to draw attention to the maltreatment of individuals or certain ethnic groups.

142

Moreover, considering the gradual curtailing of individual MEPs' rights, parliamentary questions represent one of the last rights of the backbencher and one of the last means available to the MEP to have her or his case presented in public.

Even though MEPs ask questions on all sorts of issues, certain subjects may be better addressed by relying on another channel. As mentioned above, written questions are of little use when the representatives need the information immediately without delay. Written questions are particularly useful when members want detailed and specific information, often involving technical facts. Budgetary questions fall into this category, as the answers are often lengthy, with much statistical data. Therefore several members regularly submit questions on issues such as the allocation and spending of structural funds.

Members may also highlight delays in implementing EU legislation. As one MEP explained: "when there are delays in implementing EU legislation, I can take up this point and the Commission is obliged to answer." The Commission, in its 1989 annual report to the Parliament on the implementation of EC law and its monitoring efforts, acknowledged the part played by the MEPs "in helping in the monitoring of EC law by parliamentary questions and petitions." (Arp, 1992: 17) Several members highlighted the importance of bringing up national and/or constituency concerns in their written questions. By submitting a question on such issues members are able to draw attention to these issues.

The representatives also have other avenues available for serving their constituents and pursuing their own goals. The most effective channel is direct contact with the Commission. The members can write letters, send faxes and e-mail, or simply phone or visit the Commission, asking for all kinds of information. Using these informal channels, the representatives may receive the answer in the space of just a few days or even instantly, depending on the nature of the information required. Several members had also over the years developed personal contacts inside the Commission. However, the obvious drawback of these informal channels is that the Commission is under no obligation to answer, and neither is the answer an official Commission statement as are the answers to written questions.

Representatives may concentrate on their work in the committees of the EP which have increased in significance as the Parliament's legislative position has been strengthened. Commissioners or Commission representatives are invited to the committees where the MEPs may put questions to them. The benefit of these hearings in the committees is that the members have at least the opportunity to engage in a face-to-face dialogue with the representatives of the Commission. Within committees, party groups, and the whole Parliament members may also approach their colleagues in order to rally support for their cause. Such strategy is especially useful when members have clear and specific objectives in mind and are able to present their case at the very beginning of the decision-making process.

While the tabling of parliamentary questions constitutes a well-established activity inside the Parliament, it seldom attracts the attention of the media. Several members use press releases and/or send information to local media in their constituencies. According to one member press releases are crucial since "otherwise no one would notice" their work. National papers may occasionally pick up a point that has come up in a written question. Some respondents also mentioned that media in other EU member states had paid attention to their questions. However, national or European-level media normally notices only 'grand' or 'sensational' issues, and it is in any case doubtful whether the media has become aware of the issue as a result of the written question. According to one member the likelihood of the media noticing a written question varies "depending on the general interest the issue attracts."

5.6. Questioning Activity of Party Groups and National Delegations

In this and the next two sections a number of research hypotheses are tested in order to increase our knowledge of the use of parliamentary questions in the EP. Some of the hypotheses originate from studies on parliamentary questions in national legislatures, while others emphasise the specific features of the EP. The following dimensions of parliamentary questions will be analysed:

(i) the number of questions tabled by individual members, party groups, and national delegations;
(ii) the issues MEPs raise in their questions, focusing on specialisation by individual representatives, party groups, and national delegations; and
(iii) the territorial dimension of the questions, and the differences between national delegations.

Hypothesis 8.
The smaller and least influential party groups ask more questions per MEP
than the larger and more influential political groups.

According to Ingvar Mattson (1994: 313) "a reasonable hypothesis on questioning activity is that those members who lack other, more important arenas of influence tend to be the most active on the arena of parliamentary questioning."[10] Such expectation is natural in the context of national legislatures where the demarcation line between the government and the opposition is in most cases clearly drawn, and where opposition parties often use all available means, including parliamentary questions, to attack, criticise, and control the executive. The obvious difference with regard to the European Parliament is that there is no government to defend or bring down, and therefore questions are bound to be less strategically 'planned' and partisan-oriented. However, we can expect similar behavioural patterns also in the Strasbourg chamber.

While the EP party system has been shown to be based on the left-right dimension, the pattern of EP inter-party conflict-resolution often sees co-operation between the mainstream political groups representing the political centre, especially so when the Parliament faces the need to achieve legislative majorities. In the EP committee assignments and intra-parliamentary leadership positions are primarily allocated according to the respective sizes of the political groups and the national delegations within them. Even though Fulvio Attinà (1992b: 81) has argued that "there are no anti-system groups that act as 'irresponsible' parties and consider themselves permanently excluded from decisive majorities", the combination of applying the rule of proportionality in intra-parliamentary nominations, diminutive voting power (see section 3.5.), and ideological extremism means in practice that especially members of the European Right, Left Unity, and the 12 independent representatives should make frequent use of parliamentary questions.

Table 5.4. shows the relationship between the percentage of seats held by each political group and the number of questions asked per group in 1992. The hypothesis is valid if the smaller and least influential political groups ask more questions per representative than the larger more powerful groups. The hypothesis is rejected if the smaller and least influential party groups submit less questions per MEP than the larger groups. The null hypothesis is that the size of party groups is directly related to the number of questions submitted: the questioning activity of party groups reflects their share of seats in the chamber.

Table 5.4. Political groups and their share of written questions in the 1992 Parliament

Party Group	seats	seats (%)	PQs	PQs (%)	PQs/MEP	STD
PES	180	34.7	1853	45.5	10.3	38.2
EPP	162	31.3	983	24.1	6.1	14.2
ELDR	45	8.7	198	4.9	4.4	8.4
EUL	29	5.6	155	3.8	5.3	11.0
V	27	5.2	396	9.7	14.7	14.9
EDA	21	4.1	95	2.3	4.5	4.3
RB	15	2.9	180	4.4	12.0	21.2
ER	14	2.7	16	0.4	1.1	1.8
LU	13	2.5	119	2.9	9.2	14.1
NA	12	2.3	82	2.0	6.8	12.9
EP	518	100.0	4077	100.0	7.9	

The results in Table 5.4. show that the 'distance-from-power' - hypothesis is not valid in the European Parliament.[11]

The fourteen MEPs of the group most out of line with rest of the chamber, the far-right European Right, asked between them only a meagre 16 questions. The average figure of over 9 questions per MEP in the Left Unity group is mainly explained by the fact that 82 of the group's 119 questions were asked by two men, Alexandros Alavanos (46) and Sergio Ribeiro (36). The Greek MEP Mihail Papayannakis tabled 61 of the 155 questions submitted by the EUL. Nor were the Rainbow Group's 180 questions, exactly 12 per MEP, evenly spread, with the Belgian Jaak Vandemeulebroucke alone accounting for almost half (89) of the questions. The Greens MEPs tabled on average most questions, and nor were the questions in the group concentrated on one or two chronic questioners.

As for the larger party groups, the two centre-right groups, EPP and Liberals, behaved as expected, asking less questions than their share of the seats, while the Socialists on the other hand tabled almost half of the questions. Their high level of standard deviation, as well as their high total number of questions, is partly the result of one MEP, the Greek Sotiris Kostopoulos, who alone asked 499 questions, thus being by far the most active questioner in the whole Parliament.[12]

Hypothesis 9.
There are no differences between national delegations in their frequency of questioning activity: there is a direct relationship between the share of seats held by a national delegation and its share of questions.

While representatives often have previous experience from member state national and/or regional legislatures, and while their behaviour may reflect the parliamentary and/or political culture of their home countries, it is expected that national delegations ask approximately the same number of questions per MEP. The reasons are argued to be two-fold:

(a) members are accustomed to their work in the Strasbourg parliament (1992 was in the middle of an electoral cycle), and their behaviour is conditioned more by their work environment than by previous political experience; and

(b) submitting a question for written answer is a relatively cost-free exercise in which all MEPs can participate without almost any restrictions.

Table 5.5. The distribution of seats between member states and their share of written questions, 1992

Member States	seats	seats (%)	PQs	PQs (%)	PQs / MEP	STD
Belgium	24	4.6	385	9.4	16.0	22.4
Denmark	16	3.1	32	0.8	2.0	5.5
France	81	15.6	323	7.9	4.0	7.6
Germany	81	15.6	306	7.5	3.8	4.6
Greece	24	4.6	717	17.6	29.9	99.0
Ireland	15	2.9	92	2.3	6.1	8.9
Italy	81	15.6	401	9.8	5.0	8.9
Luxembourg	6	1.2	11	0.3	1.8	2.5
Netherlands	25	4.8	246	6.0	9.8	7.8
Portugal	24	4.6	101	2.5	4.2	7.2
Spain	60	11.6	635	15.6	10.6	19.6
UK	81	15.6	828	20.3	10.2	16.4
EP	518	99.8	4077	100	7.9	

The hypothesis is confirmed if the national delegations' share of written questions corresponds with their share of seats. The hypothesis is rejected if the share of written questions tabled by national delegations is not related to their share of seats.

Table 5.5. shows the relationship between the distribution of seats between the 12 member states and their share of written questions.

As in the case of transnational party groups, the standard deviation (STD) figures shown in the last column make it difficult, if not impossible, to draw any clear conclusions. There are huge differences in the use of parliamentary questions between individual representatives (see section 5.9), and this is clearly reflected in the results in Table 5.5. Of the four large member states holding 81 seats, only the UK delegation submitted a higher share of questions than its share of seats. UK representatives asked in 1992 between them just over a fifth of all the written questions, 10.2 per member. Their total number of questions (828) was also the highest of the national delegations. France, Germany, and Italy come far behind, all submitting five questions or less per MEP. Spanish members also made frequent use of written questions, asking over ten questions (10.6) per representative.

Belgium and Greece stand out among the smaller member countries. Greek MEPs submitted four times more questions than their share of seats would indicate, asking nearly 30 questions per member. While the abovementioned 'Kostopoulos-effect' is again present, the Greek delegation included several active questioners. However, it has to be remembered that Kostopoulos alone asked 499 out of 717 written questions submitted by Greek representatives. The Belgian delegation asked 16 questions per MEP, their share of questions being twice their share of the seats. However, the high STD-value again reveals the presence of a small minority responsible for the majority of questions. Also the Dutch asked a higher share of questions than their share of the seats. The Luxembourg delegation and Danes submitted least questions, and the Danish input was heavily dominated by the PES representative Freddy Blak.

While the evidence is inconclusive due to the high STD-values, hypothesis 9 must be rejected: the questioning activity of national delegations does not reflect their size in the chamber.

5.7. Political Profiles and Specialisation

Content analysis of MEPs' parliamentary questions can increase our understanding of the concepts of representation and specialisation by providing answers to such questions as: What kinds of issues come up in the questions? Is there any variation between national delegations or party groups in the kind of issues brought up? Do representatives concentrate in their questions on issues with a European dimension or do they use them primarily to advance national concerns? This section looks at the political profiles of the party groups, national delegations, and individual representatives by focusing on the issues MEPs ask about in their questions.

The categorisation of questions according to their issue areas is shown in Table 5.6.

Subject categories reflect the committee structure of the parliament, with some categories including the spheres of competence of two or more committees.[13] In the 1992 Parliament there were 19 permanent committees and four subcommittees (see Table 3.2.). Some of the categories are unavoidably partly overlapping, and in many cases categorisation was rendered more difficult by the fact that many questions included elements from two or more categories. Despite these inevitable shortcomings, the margin of error is considered to be too diminutive to have any effect on the reliability of the results.

Two of the Parliament's 19 permanent committees are not included in the categorisation scheme: the Committee on Rules of Procedure, Verification of Credentials and Immunities, and the Committee on Petitions. The former deals with matters relating to Parliament's internal organisation, and the latter with petitions sent to the Parliament.

While most of the categories are rather straightforward, some committees proved more problematic. The inclusion of the Committee on Energy, Research and Technology in the EM category may appear rather illogical. However, it was very difficult to separate questions on industrial policy and energy and technology. Therefore questions on energy policy were included in the economic, monetary and industrial policy (EM) category. Another problematic case was questions on institutional matters. The division of labour (as described in EP's Rules of Procedure) between the Committee on Institutional Affairs and the Committee on Foreign Affairs and Security made it difficult to determine to which category a particular question belonged to.

Table 5.6. Categorisation of written questions

Category	Subject matters	EP Committees
FA	Foreign affairs; human rights in third countries; development of foreign and security policy	Foreign Affairs and Security; Subcommittee on Human Rights; Subcommittee on Security and Disarmament
AF	Agriculture; fisheries: rural development	Agriculture, Fisheries and Rural Development; Subcommittee on Fisheries
EM	Economic and monetary policy; budgetary matters; industrial policy	Budgets; Economic and Monetary Affairs and Industrial Policy; Energy, Research and Technology; Budgetary Control; Subcommittee on Monetary Affairs
S	Social policy; labour relations; human rights in the European Union	Legal Affairs and Citizens' Rights; Social Affairs, Employment and the Working Environment; Civil Liberties and Internal Affairs; Women's Rights
ED	External economic relations; development policy	External Economic Relations; Development and Co-operation
R	Regional policy	Regional Policy, Regional Planning and Relations with Regional and Local Authorities
EN	Environment; public health; consumer protection	Environment, Public Health and Consumer Protection
TT	Transport; tourism	Transport and Tourism
CE	Cultural Policy; education; media; youth	Culture, Youth, Education and the Media
IA	Institutional questions	Institutional Affairs
other		

151

Hypothesis 10.
MEPs' questioning activity shows no signs of specialisation by the EP party groups.

Content analysis of parliamentary questions can throw light on the political profile of both individual representatives and parliamentary party groups. Here the unit of analysis is first the party group: what kinds of subjects are covered by the EP party groups? Are there any differences between the political groups? With seats in the committees based on the respective sizes of the groups and the national delegations within them, it is expected that party groups develop an interest over a wide range of subjects instead of concentrating on one or two policy fields.

The hypothesis is confirmed if the content analysis shows no signs of specialisation by the EP political groups. Specialisation is defined here as a party group or a national delegation submitting a third or more of its written questions on one issue category or half or more of its questions on two issue areas. The hypothesis is incorrect if a party group concentrates in its questioning activity on one or two subject categories.

Hypothesis 11.
There is no specialisation by national delegations in their use of parliamentary questions.

Similarly the national delegations are expected to display an interest in a variety of subjects instead of focusing on one or two subject categories. The EU member states are obviously different both in terms of socio-economic profiles and geopolitical locations. Therefore one could expect, for example, a more agricultural member state to have a special interest in agricultural and regional policies, with MEPs elected from that country submitting a large share of questions on these matters. However, it is argued here that there is no such specialisation by national delegations in their written questions. First of all, through their work in the Parliament, and especially in the committees, members develop an interest also in other topics as well as those directly stemming from the needs of their electoral districts. And secondly, members forming a national delegation have their own interests to promote, belong to different parties, and have different role conceptions. Moreover, while there are differences between the member states, their similarities should not be underestimated.

Table 5.7. Questions by subject category: political groups (%)

Subject Group	FA	AF	EM	S	ED	R	EN	TT	CE	IA	other
PES	13.8	8.6	9.1	20.8	6.9	5.8	23.9	2.4	7.4	1.3	0.1
EPP	5.4	12.9	16.7	18.8	9.5	6.6	15.2	4.7	5.8	3.9	0.6
ELDR	2.5	6.6	12.1	17.2	18.2	4.5	14.6	9.1	5.1	9.6	0.5
EUL	7.7	11.0	6.5	18.1	1.3	13.5	27.1	4.5	8.4	1.3	0.6
V	11.1	3.8	2.8	17.9	7.6	2.8	42.9	4.0	4.3	2.5	0.3
EDA	4.2	17.9	9.5	11.6	9.5	17.9	18.9	3.2	5.3	2.1	0.6
RB	6.1	6.7	5.6	35.0	5.0	14.4	17.2	3.3	5.6	0.6	0.6
ER	12.5			12.5	31.3	18.8	12.5		6.3		6.3
LU	5.9	11.8	7.6	22.7	9.2	13.4	18.5	4.2	5.9	0.8	
NA	12.2	4.9	7.3	26.8	3.7	4.9	31.7	3.7	4.9		
EP	9.9	9.3	10.1	20.3	8.0	6.9	22.8	3.6	6.4	2.4	0.3

Note: Subject categories as explained in Table 5.6.

153

The hypothesis is valid if the content analysis of written questions shows no signs of specialisation by the member state delegations. As in the previous hypothesis, specialisation is defined as a national delegation submitting a third or more of its written questions on one issue category or half or more of its questions on two issue areas. The hypothesis is invalid if a national delegation concentrates in its questioning activity on one or two subject categories.

Tables 5.7. and 5.8. show the questioning activity of party groups and member state delegations broken down by subject category.

In the case of transnational political groups, the overall picture is that none of the groups with the exception of the Greens concentrate in their questioning on any particular subject category. The Greens predictably display a keen interest in environmental issues, questions on environment, public health, and consumer protection accounting for 42.9% of their total of 396 questions. The Rainbow group also displayed signs of specialisation, with members of the group tabling just over one-third (35.0%) of their questions on social issues. However, this figure results primarily from the questioning activity of Mr Vandemeulebroucke and his interest in social affairs, and therefore this focus on social issues does not constitute specialisation in that category by the whole group. The EDA group, mainly a coalition of French Gaullists and Ireland's Fianna Fáil with strong links to the farming sector, not surprisingly produced the largest share of questions on agriculture. Similarly the EPP and the Liberals were most interested in questions on economic, monetary and industrial policy. Significantly in the larger groups the questions are fairly even spread between the issue categories.

Hypothesis 10 is confirmed: only in the case of the Greens did the party groups show definite signs of specialisation - focusing in their questioning on one or two subject categories.

The results in Table 5.8. show member state delegations displaying a similar lack of specialisation. Countries from the periphery of the Union ask slightly more questions on agriculture, but otherwise it is very difficult to see any evidence of specialisation by member state delegations. Differences in percentage figures often result from one or two MEPs within a member state delegation asking a large number of questions on the same subject category.

Table 5.8. Questions by subject category: national delegations (%)

Subject Member state	FA	AF	EM	S	ED	R	EN	TT	CE	IA	other
B	10.1	3.6	5.2	35.3	11.7	7.8	16.6	1.3	6.5	1.6	0.3
DK	6.3	6.3	21.9	50.0			9.4		3.1		3.1
F	5.6	8.0	9.9	13.0	12.1	6.2	25.7	4.3	9.6	5.0	0.6
G	8.2	5.6	12.1	20.6	10.5	4.6	25.5	5.6	5.6	2.0	
GR	9.3	14.4	7.0	14.1	3.6	9.5	31.0	2.9	7.5	0.7	
IR	4.3	13.0	4.3	17.4	10.9	15.2	17.4	2.2	9.8	5.4	
I	13.5	11.7	7.5	18.5	5.5	4.7	26.2	5.5	4.7	2.2	
L	9.1		18.2	27.3				9.1	27.3	9.1	
NL	8.9	9.3	15.4	15.4	13.0		23.6	8.9	3.3	2.0	
P	7.9	6.9	7.9	43.6	5.0	5.9	8.9	2.0	10.9	1.0	
S	9.6	7.9	16.2	16.9	12.8	9.0	14.3	3.1	7.9	1.6	0.8
UK	12.4	9.3	9.8	22.8	4.0	6.3	24.4	2.7	4.0	4.0	0.4
EP	9.9	9.3	10.1	20.3	8.0	6.9	22.8	3.6	6.4	2.4	0.3

Note: Subject categories as explained in Table 5.6.

155

The Portuguese delegation focused in its questioning activity on social issues, with 43.6% of the delegation's PQs in that category. However, this finding reflects the small number of questions tabled by the Portuguese contingent, and the input among them of a couple of MEPs making active use of this form of parliamentary activity. The Danish MEP Freddy Blak asked 23 out of Denmark's 32 questions, and therefore his emphasis on economic and social issues is also reflected in Denmark's figures. Considering such 'distortion' caused by the questioning activity of only one or two individuals within national delegations, it would be wrong to speak of specialisation at the level of a whole delegation.

Hypothesis 11 is proven correct by the findings of the research: there is no specialisation by member state delegations in their use of parliamentary questions.

Hypothesis 12.
Members' questioning activity reflects their specialisation in the framework of the Parliament's committee system.

Research on parliamentary questions in national parliaments has shown that MPs tend to ask questions concerning those issue areas in which they specialise within the framework of the legislature's organisation (Judge, 1974; Damgaard, 1994; Mattson, 1994; Rasch, 1994; Wiberg, 1994b).[14] It is expected that this applies also in the European Parliament where the committees play an important role. In their study of the committee system and the level of specialisation in the EP, Bowler and Farrell (1995) have shown that the questioning activity of the members of Agriculture, Environment, and Regional Policy committees reflected their specialisation in their respective committees. It is expected that this applies also to the other committees: MEPs' questioning activity reflects their specialisation in the framework of the Parliament's committee structure. Two sets of data are presented:

(a) first at the level of the whole chamber by computing for every issue category the percentage of questions tabled by 'own' representatives, i.e. those sitting in the respective committees; and

(b) at the level of individual MEPs by computing per member the percentage of questions submitted on subjects falling under the competence of her or his committee.

The hypothesis is valid if (a) members sitting in the respective committees are twice as likely to ask questions on 'their' ('own') subject category than non-committee members, and/or (b) if on average 50% or more of individual members' written questions deal with matters handled in their respective committees. The hypothesis is rejected if it is shown that there is no such specialisation based on committee work, with members either submitting questions on a wide range of issues or in the case of MEPs asking a small number of questions, their questioning activity not reflecting their specialisation in the framework of the EP committee system.

In order to test the hypothesis, two sets of results are presented below in Tables 5.9. and 5.10. Table 5.9. presents first the findings at the level of the whole chamber by computing the percentage of written questions asked by 'own' representatives: i.e., those sitting in respective committees. The second column shows the total number of questions belonging to the subject category. In the third column is the sum of committee seats held by individual representatives sitting in the respective committees (as explained in Table 5.6.). The actual number of committee places is in most cases higher than the reported number of seats. This is due to the fact that many representatives are members of more than one committee belonging to the same subject category. For example, several MEPs sitting in the Committee on Foreign Affairs and Security are also either in the Subcommittee on Human Rights or in the Subcommittee on Disarmament. Similarly in the economic and monetary subject category (EM) and in the social affairs category (S) several representatives were appointed to more than one committee. The fourth column ('own') shows the percentage of committee seats in that subject category. The figure has been computed by dividing the number of committee places falling under that subject category by the total number of committee seats in the Parliament. The fifth column shows the percentage share of total questions asked by representatives sitting on the respective committees. The figures in the fifth column have been derived by the simple method of first computing the sum of written questions asked by members sitting on the respective committees, and then dividing that sum by the total number of questions on that subject category. And the final column shows the percentage of questions per subject category asked by other members than the ones holding seats in the respective committees. Therefore the sum of percentage shares of the fifth and sixth column is a hundred. When interpreting the results in Table 5.9., condition (a) is met when the percentage share in column five (questions asked by members sitting in the respective committees) is double the percentage share in column four (the percentage of committee seats in that subject category).

Table 5.9.   The share of written questions asked by members who sit on the respective committees

Subject category	PQs	seats	seats (%)	own (%)	other (%)
FA	404	67	12.9	17.6	82.4
AF	378	55	10.6	23.3	76.7
EM	412	117	22.6	35.4	64.6
S	829	115	22.2	30.4	69.6
ED	325	65	12.5	19.7	80.3
R	280	35	6.8	17.1	82.9
EN	931	50	9.7	23.8	76.2
TT	148	30	5.8	19.6	80.4
CE	261	30	5.8	11.5	88.5
IA	97	37	7.1	9.3	90.7
other	12				

The findings in Table 5.9. indicate that members sitting in respective committees are considerably more likely to ask questions on their 'own' issue areas. However, only in five out of ten of the subject categories were the members sitting in respective committees twice as likely to submit questions on that issue area. The tendency to table questions on 'own' areas was found to apply in the case of Agriculture, Fisheries, and Rural Development Committee, Regional Policy, Regional Planning, and Relations with Regional and Local Authorities Committee, Environment, Public Health and Consumer Protection Committee, Transport and Tourism Committee, and Culture, Youth, Education and the Media Committee. In no subject category were the members sitting in respective committee(s) less likely to ask questions on subjects within that issue area. Moreover, while the EM-category, for example, did not meet the criterion, the members still were almost twice as likely to ask questions on economic, financial, budgetary, and industrial policy matters. This is in the opinion of the author a rather large share, considering that such general issues are bound to attract interest among the whole population of MEPs.

Table 5.10. looks at the question of specialisation at the level of an individual representative by presenting the average percentage figures per subject category that MEPs asked questions concerning their 'own' issue areas. The second column ('own') shows the average percentage of written questions members submitted on the subject category falling under the sphere of competence of their committees. The third column shows the average percentage of questions representatives tabled on other topics than those handled by their committees. Again the sum of percentage figures in the second and third columns is hundred. The average percentage figures reported in the second column were computed by first counting for each individual MEP sitting in the respective committees the percentage of questions the member asked on her or his 'own' subject category. Then the sum of these individual percentage figures were computed and divided by the number of questioners. Those not asking questions were omitted from the analysis.

The findings in the second column of Table 5.10. show that while representatives submit questions to pursue matters handled within their respective committees, the level of specialisation is not as high as expected. Comparing the subject categories we find that in no category do MEPs come even close to tabling 50% of their questions on the subjects falling under the competence of their respective committees. The 'fit' between questions and committees was most marked in the case of the Agriculture, Fisheries, and Rural Development Committee, Environment, Public Health, and Consumer Protection Committee, and Culture, Youth, Education and the Media Committee.

Table 5.10. Specialisation by individual MEPs:
the percentage of questions on own subject category

Subject Category	Own (%)	Other (%)
FA	20.6	79.4
AF	31.4	68.6
EM	19.1	80.9
S	29.9	70.1
ED	13.4	86.6
R	21.3	78.7
EN	32.7	67.3
TT	18.7	81.3
CE	31.6	68.4
IA	4.1	95.9

A number of factors need to be taken into account in the interpretation of results. Members' questioning activity is to a certain extent dependent on the kinds of requests they receive from their constituents and various interest groups. Therefore MEPs do not necessarily ask questions on issues handled in their committees: questioning behaviour reflects more the general pattern of demands placed upon them and the overall balance of issues coming up in their daily work. For example, all members are bound to be concerned with economic and social issues, as such matters are sure to be on the agenda in every corner of the Union.

Secondly, considering the fact that there is only a limited number of committee places available, with members often having to settle for committee assignments of their second or third choice, it is natural that MEPs do not ask questions on those issues in which they are not interested. Considering the powerful position of the substitute members, with almost equal rights with full members, it is also possible that some members specialise in the work of the committee in which they are substitutes, probably because they did not receive full membership in committees of their choice (see section 3.3.). However, gathering such information would be an enormous undertaking, requiring extensive interviews with the members themselves. Needless to add, such data on committee preferences and actual committee assignments is not available. Moreover, one could argue that if parliamentarians already sit on a particular committee, why would they submit questions on issues falling under the competence of that committee? Since they can influence events, and acquire information, through their work in the committee, they don't necessarily have to resort to parliamentary questions to elicit information on these issues.

Content analysis of parliamentary questions has shown the tendency by the MEPs to submit questions on subjects handled in their respective committees. However, this specialisation was not as marked as was expected. Hypothesis 12 must therefore be rejected.

When analysing the questioning activity of those members who tabled five questions or more, it is evident that while some concentrated on only one or two subject categories, the overall record shows that MEPs behave more like 'generalists' than 'specialists', tabling questions on a wider range of issues (Searing, 1987, 1991, 1995). The exceptions to this rule were primarily the most active questioners in the chamber who tended to focus on one or two subject categories. Whereas specialists seek influence in a small number of issues, generalists on the other hand prefer not to focus on one issue area at the expense of other topics, but instead choose to get engaged in a variety of matters appearing on the legislature's agenda.

MEPs' choice of priorities appears to have changed somewhat since the first term of the directly elected Parliament.[15] From 1976 to 1983 questions on agriculture and on economic and monetary matters were the most common ones, with environment lagging far behind its current status. In 1992 the two by far most popular categories were social affairs and environment (including public health and consumer protection), making up 20.3% and 22.8% of the questions respectively. Questions on foreign affairs, agriculture and fisheries, and economic and monetary union came next, with each policy area attracting around 10% of the questions.

5.8. Combining National and European Perspectives? Territorial Dimension

The parliamentary questions were further analysed according to their territorial dimension. By 'territorial dimension' is meant the geographical area specifically mentioned in the question. Table 5.11. lists the territorial categories in which the representatives' questions were divided.

The territorial categories are rather straightforward but require explanation. Included in the member state (MS)-category are questions that had a national or a subnational (local, regional) dimension. The EU-category consists of questions that had a European dimension. For example, a question concerning the formulation of specific EU measures to combat unemployment throughout the Union. Some of the questions were difficult to categorise since they often dealt with relations between two territorial categories. For example, many MEPs were interested in the relationship between their own member state and the EU. In such cases the question was interpreted as having a national (MS) dimension. Similarly several MEPs were concerned with the development of contacts between EU and a third country. In such cases the question was understood as focusing primarily on the third country referred to in the member's question. The reason for including Arab countries on the southern coast of Mediterranean in the Near East-category instead of the Africa-category was that many questions treated the 'Arab world' as one single entity. The geopolitical situation of Mediterranean Arab countries makes them very different from the rest of Africa.

Table 5.11. Categorisation of written questions: territorial dimension

Category	Geographical areas included
MS	The member state from which the MEP was elected to the Parliament
AM	Another member state of the European Union
EU	The European Union
AF	Africa, excluding the Arab countries on the Mediterranean coast
Asia	Asia
NA	North America (USA, Canada)
SA	South America (Central and Latin America)
AP	Australia, New Zealand, and the Pacific Islands
EE	Central and Eastern Europe, including the successor states of the Soviet Union
NE	Arab countries in the Near East and on the southern coast of the Mediterranean, and Israel
other	

Hypothesis 13.
The questioning activity shows that the category with a European (EU) dimension has the highest share of questions.

Representatives may choose to focus in their work on defending regional or national interests, while others may understand their role more as builders of European integration. Naturally these territorial categories do not cancel each other out. Surveys of MEPs (see section 5.1.) have shown that members see themselves as representing multiple interests, with contributing to European policy-making seen as the priority, followed by defending the interests of their respective constituencies and/or member states.

It is hypothesised that MEPs' questioning activity shows in similar fashion that members understand their role as one of representing multiple territorial interests. Since the Parliament is an EU institution, with the bulk of its work concerning the scrutiny and passage of EU legislation, questions with a European (EU) dimension should make up the biggest single category of questions, followed by questions dealing with national or subnational concerns. The hypothesis is valid if the categorisation of the written questions according to their territorial dimension shows that the EU-category has the highest share of written questions. The hypothesis is incorrect if members instead submit the highest share of questions on national or subnational issues (or indeed on any other territorial category).

Hypothesis 14.
MEPs from the Benelux countries, France and Germany are expected to submit a higher than the average share of questions with a European dimension, while representatives from the geographically peripheral regions of the Union are expected to see themselves more as champions of regional or national interests.

The member states forming the European Union are naturally different from each other, each with its own history, national economic structure, and geopolitical situation. These differences are bound to affect the kind of politics the representatives of these nations pursue in the Parliament and in the Council of Ministers. An often mentioned line of division is that between more central and richer member countries and the more geographically peripheral countries of the Union. The countries on the periphery are expected to focus more on defending their national concerns, while MEPs from the six founding members of the European Community should on the other hand see themselves as representing wider European interests given their longer participation in European integration. To quote Bowler and Farrell:

> "Members from the Original Six states (Benelux, France, Germany and Italy) should perhaps be more pro-European in their attitudes. This set of attitudes may well be associated with the fact that it is these states that comprise in whole or in part the fast growing hub of Community operations. These states represent the crossroads of European trade and also provide a home to European institutions themselves. Italy does present the possibility of being something of an exception." (Bowler and Farrell, 1992a: 29)[16]

Here also Italy is treated as an exception, the country is a major recipient of the Union's regional aid and its southern parts are heavily reliant on agriculture. Thus while it is expected that MEPs from the Original Six excluding Italy concern themselves mainly with European-wide issues, representatives from the peripheral regions of the Union (Portugal, Spain, Italy, Greece, and Ireland) are expected to see themselves mainly as champions of national or regional interests.[17] The hypothesis does not imply that representatives from these geographically more peripheral member states would be less 'European' than their colleagues from the central countries. Such expected tendency to focus on local and national concerns is indeed natural given these member states' socio-economic profiles.

The hypothesis is confirmed if the MEPs from the more central states ask a higher than the average share of questions with a European dimension, and the representatives from the more peripheral member countries submit a higher than the average share of questions on national and/or subnational issues. The null hypothesis is that there are no differences, or no such systematic centre-periphery division, between national delegations in the territorial dimension of their written questions.

Hypothesis 15.
MEPs make frequent use of parliamentary questions to defend and promote constituency issues.

Studies on parliamentary questions in the British House of Commons have shown that MPs make active use of PQs to promote the interests of their constituents.[18] Parliamentary questions offer the individual representative an excellent opportunity to raise any issue she or he wants, and thus it is expected that members use the device of questioning to pursue the interests of their constituents. The hypothesis is rejected if the content analysis of written questions shows no such use by the representatives, with constituency concerns being promoted by alternative strategies.

An obvious problem is the fact that MEPs do not necessarily mention their electoral district or member state when submitting a question on behalf of their constituents. For this reason this point relies heavily on information from the interviews. The MEP may phrase his or her question so as not to make it evident that he is acting on behalf of a particular voter or an interest group, perhaps because he or she wants to emphasise the European dimension of the issue in order to make it more relevant in the context of policy-making at European level. For example, Irish MEPs seldom referred to their country or electoral district when asking questions on agriculture, even though they may well have acted on behalf of a constituent back in Ireland. I have followed here the logic of David Judge (1974: 181), who, in his analysis on parliamentary questions in the British House of Commons, argued that "it may be taken that if the MP specifically mentions his constituency then his primary concern is with the geographical region. For example, if the Member for North East Derbyshire asks a PQ on

164

unemployment in his constituency it is assumed that this member is primarily concerned with North East Derbyshire. If his interest lies in the problem of unemployment generally, the question tabled will not have the specific geographical restriction."

Table 5.12. shows the 4,077 questions broken down by national delegations according to their territorial dimension.

41% of MEPs' questions had a European-wide dimension. The figure reflects the Parliament's involvement in decision-making at the European level and its role as the agent of integration, and it clearly indicates that a large percentage of the MEPs regard themselves as representing European-wide interests. This tendency to give priority to EU-wide issues corresponds with the results of the surveys reported at the beginning of this chapter.[19]

Since the Single Market was due to be completed by 1 January 1993, many of the questions dealt with the consequences of the internal market. For example, the Socialist Mr Lode Van Outrive expressed his concern for the social effects of the EMU and the need to meet the convergence criteria:

"Application of the stringent monetary criteria for membership of EMU may have a serious impact on social protection, employment and income in the Member States. It is, of course, the weakest groups in society which are likely to be hardest hit by these measures. What measures does the Commission envisage to tackle these problems? Does it have a means of establishing the impact on the population of the application of the "Maastricht" standards?"[20]

Among other topics that appeared regularly were CAP, Common Fisheries Policy, the mutual recognition of educational qualifications, and the future of student exchange programmes.

33.7% of the questions had a national or sub-national dimension. Questions included for example inquiries about the availability of financial assistance from the EU for various projects, and requests for information on the use and allocation of regional and social funds. MEPs may also use parliamentary questions to criticise the policies of their home government, in particular if the member's national party is in opposition at national level (Hrbek, 1976: 375; Kuper, 1991: 634). For example, the Spanish MEP Valverde López (EPP) submitted a series of questions to the Commission on the failure of the Spanish authorities to implement the provisions of the internal market.[21] Similarly several representatives used questions to give information on environmental damage in their member states.

Table 5.12. Questions by territorial dimension: national delegations (%)

Category Member State	MS	AM	EU	AF	Asia	NA	SA	AP	EE	NE	other
B	14.0	7.5	57.4	3.9	1.8	1.6	3.1		4.9	1.8	3.9
DK	28.1	34.4	31.3							6.3	
F	22.6	7.4	51.1	0.9	2.2	2.5			5.6	5.0	2.8
G	17.6	13.7	47.7	2.6	0.3	2.6	0.7		9.8	2.9	2.0
GR	67.4	1.5	17.6	1.1	0.6	0.6	0.1		6.7	3.8	0.7
IR	28.3	7.6	48.9	2.2	4.3	1.1			3.3	1.1	3.3
I	48.1	5.5	27.9	1.2	1.0		0.3		9.5	4.0	2.5
L		9.1	81.8					.		9.1	
NL	19.1	13.4	41.1	2.8	3.3	6.1	2.8		4.1	2.8	4.5
P	58.4	11.9	17.8		5.9		1.0		1.0		4.0
S	34.5	3.8	38.7	1.7	2.5	1.9	5.2	0.2	3.0	5.8	2.7
UK	19.1	6.6	57.1	1.3	1.4	1.0	0.4		1.4	8.5	3.1
EP	33.7	6.6	41.0	1.7	1.7	1.5	1.5	0.0	4.9	4.7	2.6

Note: Territorial categories as explained in Table 5.11.

Members of the Original Six excluding Italy all behave as expected: MEPs from Belgium (57.4%), Germany (47.7%), France (51.1%), the Netherlands (41.1%), and Luxembourg (81.8%) asked a higher than the average percentage of questions on 'European' issues. The other part of the hypothesis, that MEPs from the outlying regions of the Union concentrate in their questioning activity on national issues, is also validated by the findings. Questions tabled by MEPs from Portugal (58.4%), Spain (34.5%), Italy (48.1%), Ireland (28.3%), and particularly Greece[22] (67.4%) had all, with the exception of Ireland, a higher than the average share of PQs with a national and/or a subnational dimension. However, the centre-periphery-difference between member state delegations is not as marked as expected.

Of the two countries not included in hypothesis 14, Denmark's figures again reflect the small number of questions tabled by the Danish delegation and the input of Mr Blak who tabled several questions on events in other EU member states. The figures for the UK delegation are very interesting considering the electoral system used in Britain. With single-member constituencies, it could be expected that UK representatives submit a higher than average share of questions with a constituency (subnational)-dimension. However, 57.1% of their questions had a EU-dimension, with only 19.1% of the questions having a national or subnational focus. While it is probable that many of the questions in the EU-category are in fact 'hidden' MS-entries, the results nevertheless show that the UK MEPs' expected tendency to focus on constituency issues is far less pronounced than anticipated.

Hypothesis 14 is valid: representatives from the geographically peripheral regions of the Union concentrate more on defending the interests of their constituencies and/or member states, while MEPs from the central areas of the Union see themselves more as champions of questions with a European dimension.[23]

The constituency-dimension of questions could be expected to be dependent on the kind of electoral system used in the member states. However, whether the electoral system has any effect on the level of constituency-orientation of parliamentary questions is difficult to measure. As explained above, the main problem is that representatives do not necessarily mention their electoral district in the question even though they may be acting on behalf of a constituent. Moreover, "though many MEPs are elected on national lists...the majority are elected in distinct territorial subdivisions of their states and from the formal view if MEPs from the UK represent sub-national constituencies, a majority of the EP does so also." (Steed, 1985: 268) For example, several of the Spanish MEPs, elected on national lists, focused in their questions on the problems of their home region. While the system of single-member constituencies leaves its mark on British MEPs' behaviour, the differences between the UK delegation and other national contingents should not be overestimated.[24]

A more important variable than the type of electoral system is the specific economic and cultural situation in the constituency the member represents. The region or electoral district may have special cultural problems relating to the protection of minority rights. In such cases the representatives of these areas often submitted questions on language. A significant number of MEPs represent constituencies that face severe economic problems and are therefore beneficiaries of the EU's structural fund schemes. These members are likely to spend much resources in defending the interests of their constituencies, and tabling questions on the needs of their regions is part of their strategy. As one MEP representing a mainly rural district pointed out in relation to his work: "I am one of those mean politicians who concentrate solely on one's own constituency."

It is evident that parliamentarians in Strasbourg do make active use of questions in order to raise matters important to their constituents. Often the MEPs' questions deal with issues that are of minor importance at the European level, but which are significant to the local inhabitants. Take, for example, the following question on noise pollution from road surfaces by the British Conservative MEP Mr Madron Seligman:

"The Commission has introduced much valuable legislation designed to protect citizens of the Community from various forms of noise pollution. Constituents of mine have drawn attention to the excessive noise generated by traffic travelling on the brushed concrete surface of the Chichester-Havant section of the A 27 trunk road which causes distress to hundreds of local residents. Financial compensation has been paid to some of those living nearest the road in question. It is known that the noise generated by a Tarmacadam surface would be far less. Is the Commission aware of the scope of this problem? Has it arisen in other Member States? Is it prepared to adopt an initiative to eliminate further suffering by local residents near the A 27 from this avoidable cause?"[25]

Hypothesis 15 is confirmed: while also using other more direct and probably more effective tactics, MEPs do make frequent use of parliamentary questions to defend the interests of their constituents.

Less than 20% of the questions concerned relations with or events in third countries. Not surprisingly the Near East (4.7%) and Central and

Eastern Europe (4.9%) were referred to in as many questions as Africa and Asia, North and South America, and Australia and the Pacific put together.

The phrase "representatives of the peoples" can also be interpreted to mean that a MEP is at the same time representing the citizens of the other member states as well as the country from which he or she was elected. Thus they have the opportunity to legitimately question or demand knowledge on events occurring within the borders of these states. A German MEP, for example, may seek to redress grievances on behalf of a fellow-national mistreated by authorities in Finland. Or a British representative can question the wisdom of heavy agricultural spending in the Mediterranean countries. During negotiations on the Maastricht Treaty, the Socialists and the EPP condemned the British government's decision to opt out of the social charter, with the Liberals even going as far as to demand that British MEPs should not be allowed to take part in votes on social issues (Mengelberg, 1994). As Hedetoft points out:

> "EC institutions...allow politicians from each of the member states to monitor and influence decision-making and legislative processes in the other eleven [now fourteen] countries on a formally recognised and permanent basis...If one member-state gains influence in the rest of Europe, then the other eleven [fourteen] in turn gain more influence over the domestic affairs of this member-state." (Hedetoft, 1994: 26-27)

While this legitimate right of "interference" is the "natural course of things" in the EU, the issue remains sensitive, especially to the average citizens who "tend to resist changes to the political we-image, even if the political unit is no longer capable of fulfilling the survival functions of the individual or the group." (Zetterholm, 1994: 79) The EP is not unique among the EU institutions in offering this possibility, but what makes this forum different is the openness of the Parliament. Behind the closed doors of the Council of Ministers delegates may challenge the policies of their colleagues and try to force them to toe the line (particularly now with increased use of qualified majority voting), but little of this is ever transmitted to the public, with the odd exception of a disgruntled, often defeated, minister revealing to the electorate his or her true stand.

6.6% of MEPs' questions dealt with events in member states other than the one from which the MEP asking the question was elected to the Parliament. These questions were rather diverse in nature: among them were requests for information, demands to protect the environment, the failure by the state in question to respect the Treaties, and the treatment of the questioner's fellow nationals in the state in question. Take the following question to the Commission by the German MEP Manfred Vohrer, representing the Liberals:

"Is the Commission aware of the substance of the new Italian Hunting Law No. 157 of 11 February 1992, published in the *Official Gazette* of 25 February 1992, and will it initiate proceedings before the European Court of Justice for infringement of Council Directive 79/409/EEC?[26]

Vohrer's question is a fine example of a member expressing his concern on conflict between national - this time Italian - and EU legislation. Another illustrative example is the question to the Commission by the Danish Socialist Freddy Blak:

"In Greece, conscientious objectors are persistently treated like criminals and imprisoned in military gaols for long terms. Despite repeated calls by the European Parliament, among others, the Greek Government continues to refuse to comply with general human rights requirements. This should no longer be tolerated in a State which belongs to the European Community. What action does the Commission propose to take to put an end to this unacceptable practice and ensure that Greece's rules on military service come into line with those in the other Member States of the Community?"[27]

Categorising the written questions on the basis of their territorial dimension alas confirms hypothesis 13: the EU-category had the highest share of questions. While there are differences between national delegations and also naturally between individual members, the overall situation shows the members combining European policy-making with promoting national and local concerns.

5.9. Is Questioning a Minority Activity?

Hypothesis 16.
Small minority of MEPs ask the majority of questions.

While tabling parliamentary questions is 'something the MPs are supposed to be doing' as 'part of their job' and 'normal activity in the chamber', a small minority of MPs are known to specialise in this form of parliamentary activity in national parliaments. Studies on question-time and oral questions in the EP have shown that representatives in Strasbourg are no exception to this rule. Question-time procedure has since its inception been actively used by British MEPs, accustomed to this form of control device in their own Westminster parliament, with the Greek contingent also asking a disproportionately high share of questions (Westlake, 1990). Written questions don't have such cultural influences, and all MEPs can participate. In the case of oral questions "there is not a typical MEP who asks a given number of questions. There are many who do not, or who do so rarely (nearly two-thirds of MEPs for example asked one question or less in this period). At the other extreme are chronic questioners. The top five questioners accounted for 17% of the total number of questions asked during this period." (Bowler and Farrell, 1993b: 16)[28] As mentioned above, oral questions can nowadays only be tabled by a political group, a committee, or by 29 members.

Table 5.13. shows the varying use of written questions by the 518 MEPs. The hypothesis is valid if a minority of members ask the majority of questions. The hypothesis is invalid if there is no such dominance by an active minority, with a majority of MEPs also responsible for the majority of questions. The null hypothesis is that there is little variation between individual members in their use of written questions.

Table 5.13. The number of written questions asked by MEPs in 1992

questions	MEPs	MEPs (%)
0	115	22.2
1	67	12.9
2-5	171	33.0
6-10	77	14.9
11-20	48	9.3
21-50	29	5.6
51-100	9	1.7
100+	2	0.4

It appears that an analysis of written questions produces much the same result as research on oral questions. Including those questions with more than one signatory (N = 4,077), the MEPs asked in 1992 on average 7.9 written questions per parliamentarian. Over one-fifth (22.2%) of the MEPs did not ask any questions at all, while over two-thirds (68.1%) of the representatives asked five questions or less. 17% of members submitted eleven or more written questions.[29] Each national delegation and party group included both active questioners as well as members who chose not to submit any questions at all. Thus the remark by John Fitzmaurice (1978: 214) from the days of the nominated Parliament is still valid: the written question "is the device of a small number of backbenchers, many of whom have specialised in this form of parliamentary activity over a long period."

In 1992 7.7% of MEPs tabled over 20 questions, and the top six questioners are found in Table 5.14.

Table 5.14. The six most active questioners in 1992: written questions

MEP	Party group	Member State	PQs
Kostopoulos	PES	Greece	499
Valverde López	EPP	Spain	117
Robles Piquer	EPP	Spain	90
Vandemeulebroucke	RB	Belgium	89
O'Hagan	EPP	UK	84
Smith Llewellyn	PES	UK	81

The most active questioner, Mr Sotiris Kostopoulos, accounted alone for 12.2% of the written questions submitted in 1992. Most of the members making frequent use of parliamentary questions specialised in their questions on one or two subject categories. Mr Jaak Vandemeulebroucke, for example, asked mainly questions on the Union's social policy, while Mr Llewellyn Smith, as well as Mr Alex Smith who asked 70 questions, concentrated on nuclear safety. Lord O'Hagan's inclusion among the top six questioners is particularly interesting, for already in the 1970s he was an active figure during question-time (Cohen, 1979: 51).

Hypothesis 16 is valid: a small minority of members ask the majority of written questions in the EP.

While members are free to make as much use of written questions as they wish, it should also be kept in mind that drafting a reply may sometimes involve a lot of work. The staff in the Commission are thus required to spend considerable amounts of time in producing a satisfactory reply. From this point of view it may well be that submitting too many questions also has its drawbacks. As one MEP pointed out about the questioning activity of Mr Kostopoulos: "In the last Parliament we had a member who asked really a lot of questions. I think this was not very good as it consumed so much of the resources and time of the Commission." Another member said that "asking too many written questions" leads to a "degeneration" of the instrument of written questions.

Writing on the eve of the first direct elections to the Parliament, Cohen (1979: 57-58) commented on "the high degree of co-operation between European parliamentarians on question-time topics of common interest. This co-operation can exist within the European party groups or it can be both cross-group and cross-national. The question-time also serves to reflect the considerable degree of personal co-operation that can be achieved by Members seeking a common goal." Such co-operation between representatives may be crucial in giving much needed added weight to what might otherwise remain a marginal issue.

In 1992 148 written questions were signed by two or more MEPs. Co-operation took place mainly between members of the same political group, but 41 questions were the result of cross-group co-operation, including several cases of cross-national co-operation as well. For example, in their question to the Commission, the Socialist MEP Léon Schwartzenberg and 54 others from four different political groups wanted information on "the damage to artistic creativity and the European broadcasting and film industry caused by different interpretations of the Berne Convention by its signatories."[30] In another question, addressed to the Council, Josep Pons Grau and 9 other MEPs from three party groups enquired about the "establishment of Co-operation Councils with the Maghreb and Mashreq countries."[31] Transnational co-operation, both within and between the political groups of EP, also features regularly in the context of parliamentary questioning in the Parliament. MEPs are exposed to new sources of information, and "participation in the parliamentary work at Strasbourg makes the Members better informed about European questions, in terms of sheer quantity as well as diversity of information." (Kerr, 1973: 65)

5.10. Concluding Remarks

Parliamentary questions are an interesting indicator of the way the MEPs in Strasbourg understand their role as the "representatives of the peoples" of the European Union. The device of parliamentary questions is one of the freest forms of parliamentary activity: all MEPs can participate, their questions may concern anything, ranging from the plight of an individual constituent to general issues such as removal of trade barriers and the protection of rain forests, and drafting and submitting a question is not a very time-consuming exercise, even less so given that MEPs have secretarial staff to assist them. While it is probably true that members sometimes gain relatively little by asking questions, the cost of making use of them is equally small.

In the context of national legislatures the total number of parliamentary questions asked has increased rapidly. A similar trend has occurred in the EP, reflecting the parallel increase in the number of seats in the chamber. In fact, the number of questions asked per MEP has not risen during the past decade despite the substantial increase in the powers of the EU and the Parliament. The delays in receiving replies frustrate members who choose to exploit alternative channels when pursuing their interests.

In this chapter a content analysis of parliamentary questions (questions for written answer) was undertaken in order to increase our understanding of the political profiles of the EP party groups and national delegations, and in order to examine the concepts of specialisation and representation in the Parliament. The analysis produced the following results.

1) Party groups' questioning activity is not related to their size and influence within the chamber. The 'distance-from-power'-hypothesis is not valid in the European Parliament. Probably the lack of a government-opposition dimension, together with the input of certain individual MEPs, explains the fact that the 'distance-from-power'-hypothesis does not hold.

2) The questioning activity of national delegations does not reflect their size in the chamber. There was quite significant variation between the member state delegations, with Greek, British, Spanish, and Belgian MEPs making active use of written questions. However, much of the difference between country delegations was the result of a small number of 'chronic' questioners.

3) There was hardly any specialisation by party groups. Only in the case of the Greens did the party groups show definite signs of specialisation - focusing in their questioning on one or two subject categories.

4) Member state delegations displayed similar lack of specialisation.

5) MEPs are considerably more likely to submit questions on subjects handled in their respective committees than on other issue areas.

6) Representatives from the geographically peripheral regions of the Union concentrate more on defending the interests of their constituencies and member states, while MEPs from the central areas of the Union see themselves more as champions of questions with a European dimension. However, this centre-periphery division was not as marked as expected.

7) Parliamentarians in Strasbourg make active use of questions in order to raise matters important to their constituents. Often the MEPs' questions deal with issues that are of minor importance at the European level, but which are significant to the local inhabitants.

8) A relatively small minority of members ask the majority of questions, with members often co-operating on a cross-group and cross-national basis to pursue common goals.

9) While there are differences between national delegations and also naturally between individual members, the overall situation shows the members combining European policy-making with promoting national and local concerns.

MEPs table questions for much the same reasons as in the case of national legislatures. The questions serve mainly as a two-way information channel, MEPs both receive information and can use questions to inform the other institutions of problems they might be unfamiliar with. In their answers the relevant Commissioners often replied that "the Commission was unaware of the problem referred to by the Honourable Member."

It is very difficult to evaluate the actual impact the questions have on policy-making in the Commission and the Council. Indeed, the two institutions often fail to answer questions addressed to them, stating simply that the subject matter does not fall within their competence. However, the mere fact that the Commission is obliged by the Treaty to produce answers to MEPs' questions is significant. The Commission (and the Council) are forced to look into matters and to familiarise themselves with the concerns of the MEPs and the people they represent.

An important difference between the EU political system and national politics is that the relationship between the Commission and the Parliament is far less antagonistic and conflictual than executive-legislature relations in member-states. Therefore the Commission is much more forthcoming and co-operative in its replies than the governments are in the context of national politics. The method of parliamentary questions is important to the EP because it enables the assembly to "convey signals, moods, and impressions and to make others take its interpretations into account." (Mattson, 1994: 348) Parliamentary questions have a well-established and important part to play in inter-institutional relations, especially between the Commission and the Parliament.

Notes

[1] Several colleagues have contributed to the development of arguments found in this chapter. I am indebted to David Farrell for his constructive criticism on an earlier version of this text. Results of the analysis were presented at the Colloquy on Parliamentarism in International Relations: Significance and Function of Transnational Parliamentary Assemblies in the Peaceful Management of International Conflict, Göttingen, May 1995. I am grateful to the participants, in particular to Fulvio Attinà and Carl Einar Stålvant, for their insightful comments and criticism. Subsequent draft was presented at the meeting of the Nordic Political Science Association (NOPSA), Helsinki, August, 1996, where the contribution of Peter Esaiasson was of great help.

Parts of this chapter have appeared in 'Parliamentary Questions in the European Parliament: Representation, Information, and Control', *The Journal of Legislative Studies* 2:4, pp. 356-382; and 'Parliamentary Questions and the Concept of Representation in the European Parliament', in *National Interest and Integrative Politics in Transnational Assemblies*, edited by Ernst Kuper and Uwe Jun, Frank Cass, London (forthcoming). The criticism and suggestions of both the editor, Philip Norton, and the two anonymous reviewers of *The Journal of Legislative Studies* offered valuable assistance when writing the final version of this chapter.

[2] The standard texts on the theory of representation are Birch (1971) and Pitkin (1967). For an excellent recent empirical analysis, see Esaiasson and Holmberg (1996).

[3] The response rate was unfortunately only 19.3%. Among the respondents were 157 who eventually won a seat in the elections, that is, 27.7% of the members. Moreover, Greek and Portuguese candidates were omitted from the survey. For an early presentation of the results, see Katz (1996).

[4] *Official Journal of the European Communities* C 258, 22 September 1993, Written Question No. 3349/92, p. 12. A number of other MEPs have also addressed a series of questions to the Commission on the delays in receiving replies.

[5] Information on MEPs and the political groups has been taken from the following sources: European Parliament: *List of Members, Official Journal of the European Communities,* Wood ed. (1989), and Jacobs, Corbett and Shackleton (1992, 1995).

[6] The subjects of EP debates as reported in *Official Journal: Annex: Debates of the European Parliament, Bulletin of the European Communities,* and the *General Report on the Activities of the European Communities* (1992).

[7] Information taken from the annually published *General Report on the Activities of the European Community* (1980-1995).

[8] Commission's internal statistics.

[9] *Official Journal of the European Communities* C 145, 25 May 1993, Written Question No. 3394/92, p.36.

[10] This was one of the hypotheses tested in the individual chapters in the volume on parliamentary questions in the Nordic countries (Wiberg, 1994a). This 'distance-from-power'-hypothesis was found to be valid in the Danish Folketinget (Damgaard, 1994), in the Swedish Riksdag (Mattson, 1994), and in the Norwegian Stortinget (Rasch, 1994), while in Finland no such behavioural differences were discernible (Wiberg, 1994b).

[11] During the first three years of the directly elected EP, from July 1979 to July 1982, EDA - then the group of European Progressive Democrats - had the highest average of questions asked per MEP, 14.46 written questions per representative. No other political group reached an average of over ten questions per MEP. See Kirchner (1984: 96-99).

[12] I have included Kostopoulos in the Socialist Group, even though he served as a non-attached member for the second half of 1992. Mr Kostopoulos was forced to leave the Socialist Group with effect from 8 June 1992 after having been suspended from his national party PASOK for one year (*Official Journal of the European Communities* C 176, 13 July 1992, p. 2). Mr Kostopoulos rejoined the Socialists in June 1993 (*Official Journal of the European Communities* C 194, 19 July 1993, p. 198).

[13] Information on EP's committees was taken from the following sources: European Parliament: *List of Members;* EP Rules of Procedure; Jacobs, Corbett, and Shackleton (1992, 1995).

[14] Studying the institution in the Norwegian Stortinget, Rasch (1994: 262) found that "all committees direct more questions to their own minister than we should expect in the case of statistical independence." Mattson (1994: 325) observed similar specialisation in the Swedish Riksdag: "The high figures indicate that there is a tendency for questions and interpellations to accumulate in the same field in which the MPs' committee specialises. The conclusion, then, is that the specialisation is reflected in parliamentary questioning." In the Danish Folketinget, "the scarce evidence available further indicates that the questioning activity of MPs tends to follow a general pattern of specialisation in legislative work, which is tied to the jurisdictions of parliamentary committees." (Damgaard, 1994: 71) In the 1987-1990

Finnish Eduskunta, however, "only 14 per cent of the oral questions and 15 per cent of the written questions come from representatives who are members of the respective committee. This is not much. It is thus rather the exception than the rule that ministers have to answer questions that are put to them by representatives who are members of the respective committee." (Wiberg, 1994b: 154) Having analysed PQs in the British House of Commons, David Judge (1974: 186) found such specialisation surprising: "This paper has shown that the vast proportion of backbenchers do specialise in asking Parliamentary Questions, and that only a small percentage are generalists. Given the facts that Question Time is one of the 'freest' procedures in the House: allowing the backbencher a wide range of issues on which to raise Questions, and that the stimuli to table PQs are numerous - the observation that most backbenchers do specialise is perhaps surprising. For the combination of 'freedom' with a variety of reasons for tabling Questions might have led one to expect a greater diversification of activity than appears to occur in the 1970-71 session."

[15] Comparison with the figures from 1976-1983 is complicated by the fact that of the two studies from that period one has broken down the questions by subject category on the basis of the internal organisation of the Commission, while the other has categorised the questions on the basis of the EP's committee structure. See Grabitz et al. (1988: 410-413), and Kirchner (1984: 105).

[16] Bowler and Farrell (1992a: 33-34) found that "MEPs from the smaller, peripheral states have a keener sense of territorial [national] rather than ideological representation", and that members from the central states "are much more positive in stressing they represent EC citizens than a party group."

[17] The hypothesis has the drawback of treating the centre and periphery member countries as unitary entities. As the Italian case demonstrates, there are naturally great differences also within - and not just between - states. For example, what is often referred to as the 'core-region' or 'dynamic part' of the Union cuts across several member states, including the Benelux countries, France, Germany, and Italy. While it would have been most interesting to pay more attention to these important intra-state differences, the investigation of such factors would have been methodologically very complicated and difficult. Moreover, the fact that several member states have the whole country as one electoral district obviously has an impact on members' behaviour.

[18] David Judge (1974: 185) found that "in both parties [the Conservative and the Labour Parties] constituency problems account for the largest percentage of Questions." When asked about their reasons for submitting written parliamentary questions, British MPs identified 'making ministers aware of points of concern to constituents' and 'defending or promoting constituency interests' as the third and fifth most commonest reasons respectively. 76% of the interviewed members thought that written questions were helpful in pursuing constituency casework. (Franklin and Norton, 1993b: 109, 121). While the British electoral system, with its

winner-takes-all single-member electoral districts, may be considered as producing exceptionally constituency-oriented behaviour, it is expected that similar tendency to submit questions on constituency-issues prevails also in other national legislatures. Unfortunately there is no comparative data available on this topic.

[19] See section 5.1. The interviews carried out by Ionescu (1996: 347) reveal a similar attitude: "While 'negative' and utilitarian motives probably come first in the pro-EU stance of the MEPs interviewed, it must be acknowledged that in almost every case we found a powerful and idealistic predisposition towards a European mentality."

[20] *Official Journal of the European Communities* C 195, 19 July 1993, Written Question No. 3482/92, p. 41.

[21] See for example *Official Journal of the European Communities* C 274, 22 October 1992, pp. 21-27, and *Official Journal of the European Communities* C 141, 19 May 1993, pp. 3-10.

[22] Wenturis (1996: 296-300) reports similar behaviour on the part of Greek MEPs: "An analysis of questions put by Greek MEPs between 1981 and 1989 shows that their content was almost without exception related to specifically Greek attitudes. ...The content of these questions may be summarised as follows: questions of economic policy came up in the context of criticism directed to the EC organs, for instance, in the form of critical interpellations about the failure to provide financial support or about alleged EC intervention in national economic policy-making by the Greek government. ...Parliamentary questions related to national interests concentrated on Greece's problem with Turkey, particularly with regard to Cyprus and the Aegean. As far as speeches and the voting behaviour of Greek MEPs are concerned, it can be said that between 1981 and 1989 national perspectives again dominated. This took the form of an exaggerated emphasis on national sovereignty, national identity and national culture on the part of all Greek MEPs, with hardly any distinction of party. ...national economic interests were constantly invoked: all Greek MEPs referred in their remarks to the useful function of the EC for the national interests of their country, and even underlined this function." Wenturis notes that in the 1990s "there is a significant structural contrast to the previous period, in that the degree of intensity of European consciousness among the Greek MEPs, as well as the qualitative and quantitative growth of 'Europe-centred' policies in their parliamentary activity, have grown markedly. ...the Greek MEPs since 1989 have developed a substantially 'Europe-centred' attitude which has allowed them to play more fully the role of a European parliamentarian."

[23] Further analysis shows that there was little variation between the EP party groups in the territorial dimension of their questions. What difference was found resulted mainly from the composition of the group, thus underlining the explanatory value of the MEPs' member state when analysing their behaviour in the chamber (Raunio, 1996b).

[24] The UK representatives perceive constituency-oriented activity as more important than their continental colleagues. See Bowler and Farrell (1992a, 1993a).

[25] *Official Journal of the European Communities* C 247, 24 September 1992, Written Question No. 788/92, p. 39.

[26] *Official Journal of the European Communities* C 65, 8 March 1993, Written Question No. 955/92, p. 8.

[27] *Official Journal of the European Communities* C 317, 3 December 1992, Written Question No. 268/92, p. 16.

[28] The findings of Bowler and Farrell (1993b) are based on a sample of oral questions asked during the first year (1989-1990) of the third directly elected EP.

[29] Comparison with 1995 statistics shows similar findings. In 1995 five MEPs tabled over hundred written questions: Alavanos (EUL, Greece) 183, Amadeo (NA, Italy) 155, Raffarin (EPP, France) 146, and Crampton (PES, UK) and Le Gallou (NA, France) 104 each. 66.6% of the representatives (417 out of 626) asked 10 questions or less. When comparing the list of most active questioners in 1992 and in 1995, same names come up, thus confirming the fact that representatives tend to specialise in this form of parliamentary activity over a period of time, probably throughout their tenure in the Parliament. Source: Commission's internal statistics.

[30] *Official Journal of the European Communities* C 61, 3 March 1993, Written Question No. 2175/92, p. 19.

[31] *Official Journal of the European Communities* C 112, 30 April 1992, Written Question No. 17/92, p. 52.

6 Concluding Discussion: Future Problems and Prospects of Europarties

6.1. A Summary of the Results

The European Parliament is the institution normally regarded as strengthening parliamentarism and democracy in what otherwise is considered an overtly bureaucratic and secretive EU system. The EP is indeed democratic, being directly elected by the EU citizens in elections held every five years. But being directly elected by the people is only the first part of the process. What happens once the Parliament gets down to do its work is an equally important matter. Considering the Parliament's influential role in the EU decision-making system, it is important that attention is paid to the question of how decision-making is conducted inside the Strasbourg Parliament.

This work has sought to increase our understanding of the Parliament by focusing on the relationship between the legislature's structural properties and the behaviour of transnational political groups. The European Parliament is responsible for its own internal organisation, a right formally recognised in the Treaties. The internal structure of a legislature is significant since it channels members' activities by organising division of labour among the representatives and by providing continuity and clarity to the proceedings by spelling the rules of the game. Clearly defined practices make it easier for the individual members to conduct their business. The internal organisation of the Parliament has a direct effect on agenda formation, transmission of information, and on the choice of final policy choices.

The internal organisation of the Parliament shows the ascendancy of party groups. The Conference of Presidents is the body responsible for organising the work of the Strasbourg Parliament. The decisional rule used in the Conference (votes weighted according to the respective sizes of the groups) and the powers given to the Conference point to the dominant position of party groups in the chamber. While an individual MEP may succeed in achieving her or his goals without the support of a party group, members are increasingly reliant on their party groups. Alas *intra-parliamentary power is concentrated in the hands of the party groups*.

The members of the ECSC Common Assembly decided in 1953 to sit as supranational party groups instead of as national delegations. Such an arrangement was considered necessary in order to avoid the emergence and consolidation of national blocs inside the chamber: national interests were seen as protected by the intergovernmentalist method employed in the Council. While national considerations unavoidably surface every once in a while, uniting national delegations on a cross-group basis, political groups have been the backbone of the Parliament's organisation throughout its existence. Based mainly on traditional party families found in the EU member states, *ideological homogeneity* facilitates the internal cohesion of EP party groups.

Party groups have their own hierarchical structures, with the group Bureaux, whips, internal group meetings, and national party delegations each playing an essential role. In particular the group meetings provide important fora in which to discuss matters. These group discussions are important since they offer the individual members a chance to express their points of view. When MEPs have in advance decided not to follow the official group position, they may use group meetings to explain the reason behind their decision. Naturally the degree of *intra-party institutionalised co-operation* varies from one group to another. Some party groups have not invested much resources in working out unitary positions, while larger and more established groups - Socialists and the EPP - have on the other hand clearly defined practices and intra-group procedures.

Even though group hierarchy and internal division of labour have been emphasised throughout this work, the *will to build compromises* is an essential factor in the search for intra-group solidarity. Without such willingness and readiness to adjust and compromise the cohesion and logic of transnational party groups would be endangered as national parties would start reconsidering the value of party co-operation at the European level.

These group-level discussions are often preceded by similar negotiations within the *national party delegations* that make up the EP transnational party groups. Formulating a party group position is thereby in practice often left to the heads of national party delegations who have received their mandates from their respective delegations. However, one must not draw the conclusion that an EP party group is a mere umbrella organisation bringing together various national party delegations. After all, while a national party delegation may sometimes decide en bloc to defy the group line, these national party delegations are by no means unitary actors themselves, with individual MEPs representing the same national party often unable to agree on a common position. While literature on the Parliament has so far tended to emphasise the strength of either the national party delegations or the party groups, most contributors overestimate the cohesion and ideological homogeneity of the former. Sweeping generalisations should be avoided and more attention paid to factors uniting MEPs across national party delegations.

The most important form of intra-party co-operation is *committee-based division of labour*. Considering the amount of legislative and own-initiative reports simultaneously processed inside the Parliament, party groups have been forced to develop ways of allocating rights and responsibilities in order to increase their functional and political efficiency. Facilitated by ideological homogeneity, party groups delegate rights and duties to individual members sitting on the various committees. These MEPs sitting in the respective committees act often as spokesperson(s) on the issues handled in their committee. Such committee-based specialisation constitutes the primary means of intra-group 'cue-taking'. Division of labour based on the EP committee system thus facilitates co-operation and cohesion within party groups.

Institutional features are also important in the reduction of uncertainty over outcomes and in the development of specialisation among the MEPs, the party groups, and in the whole legislature. The main problem is how the whole legislature and the party groups can benefit from members' asymmetric information? While the role of transnational party groups has been emphasised, the Parliament's informational efficiency (and legitimacy) is dependent on the *accommodation of both partisan and territorial interests*. The appointment process to committees and other intra-group/parliamentary positions is in a key role. By striving for a 'fair representation of member states and of political views', the duality principle enshrined in the official Rules of Procedure helps the Parliament in 'striking a balance' between partisan and territorial representation. Considering the powers of the party groups and the committees, a nomination process based on the twin pillars of proportionality between party groups and transnationality of the chamber's membership reduces external risks associated with Parliament's policy choices.

Roll-call analysis showed that *there was quite substantial variation in the cohesion of the EP party groups*. While some groups had achieved similar levels of cohesion as parliamentary parties within national legislatures, others remained far behind, a finding at least partly explained by the fact that not all groups even try to agree on a common group line before votes are taken.

In contradiction of the arguments presented in the literature on EP/EU politics, *the number of national parties included in a political group does not explain variation in party group cohesion.* There was no direct relationship between party group heterogeneity and party group cohesion. This clearly proves that the hypothesis 'aggregation of interest is a problem whose size is directly proportional to the number of interests that need to be aggregated' does not hold. Working out compromises between the various interests represented in a large party group may well be an arduous undertaking, with long and extensive negotiations needed before a majority position acceptable to the members of the group is found. However, the cohesion indices show that most groups are successful in building intra-group consensus.

Critical observers have also tended to argue that, reflecting the situation in the Council of Ministers, the decision arrived at is in most cases no more than a compromise at the level of the 'lowest common denominator'. Such subjective judgements must be treated with necessary caution. After all, as widely recognised, the Parliament has been the EU institution responsible for adopting positions regarded by other actors as ambitious, radical, or unconventional.

The more cohesive EP party groups were also consistent in their performance: *internal disagreement was limited to a small number of votes,* and *in the overwhelming majority of cases these party groups were able to achieve unitary or almost unitary voting behaviour.* Sceptical observers may point out that a closer investigation of the votes would reveal that internal disagreement surfaced in those votes considered as 'important' or 'key' votes. The identification of such significant votes is no easy task in the first place. Secondly, roll-call analysis of votes on foreign policy issues - a policy field recognised for its high conflict potential - produced hardly any variation from the groups' overall level of cohesion.

Comparative analysis demonstrated that *EP party groups are not as cohesive as parliamentary parties in the national legislatures of Western Europe.* This is largely explained by the heterogeneity of EP groups and by the lack of government-legislative linkage. The success of party groups in national legislatures in either staying in power or in challenging the executive is dependent on their unity. But with no government to defend or bring down, EP parties do not have similar institutional incentives to seek unity. Moreover, it must be kept in mind that national parties - and not EP groups or transnational parties - control the selection of candidates in Euroelections. EP parties thus lack an important tool of punishment and reward available to, and used by, most national party organisations. Nevertheless, the cohesion of EP groups is impressive considering their inevitable internal heterogeneity. Statements characterising EP parties more as chance agglomerations than as real parliamentary parties need to be modified in the light of this roll-call data.

Party groups are without a doubt vulnerable to internal splits, especially so when domestic party political considerations intrude into the chamber. The example of the vote on Jacques Santer is illustrative in showing what happens when mother parties back in the member states decide to exert control over their MEPs. Since members' political careers are in most cases dependent on their reputation within their national parties, disobeying voting instructions from national party headquarters is more self-destructive than defying the group whip inside the Strasbourg chamber.

An important question is whether national parties should exert control over their MEPs? Such a close supervision can be defended by arguments stressing the need to ensure the compatibility of views between the electorate and the elected representatives. However, the counter-argument is that since the MEPs were elected to the Parliament to contribute to European policy-making, national parties should instead concentrate on doing their part in the framework of domestic party politics. Moreover, if a party is in the government, it is able to influence EU-legislation at the negotiation table of the Councils of Ministers. Through their work MEPs are exposed to a diversity of information not found in, and not easily available to, politicians working within the borders of a member state, and therefore members in Strasbourg should be given freedom of manoeuvre by their mother parties. To put it simply, national parties should not give binding voting instructions to their MEPs. After all, if the elected member chooses to disregard the mood prevailing in the constituency, the voters may use the opportunity provided by the European elections to oust the member from office.

The party system in the European Parliament has elements of both continuity and fragmentation. While the number of party groups has remained around ten during the 1979-1996 period, there has been a gradual but steady trend towards increasing bipolarisation. The two largest groups, the Socialists and the EPP, control around two-thirds of the seats, and further centripetal moves are bound to take place in the future. Past experience has shown that ideological arguments are sacrificed in return for gaining more power in the chamber.

At the time of writing (January 1997) the consolidated groups appear to be the EPP, the Socialists, the Liberals, and the Greens. Recently, however, even the fate of the Liberals has been questioned, and while the group has been ever-present in the chamber its future seems uncertain. Roll-call data showed that the ELDR group was cohesive in the 1989-94 EP, but both before that, and since the latest EU enlargement in 1995, the group has been far less cohesive. Considering the variety of national party delegations that make up the group, it is difficult to establish what actually constitutes the binding force that keeps the group together. The recent decision in the summer of 1995 by the EDA and Forza Europa to form the Union for Europe group (UPE) is also difficult to understand in terms of ideological affinity. While the national parties making up the group are undoubtedly right-wing conservative parties, it is possible that these parties, as well as some parties within the ELDR group, seek in the near future membership in the EPP group.

The smaller groups have been vulnerable to the electoral fortunes of their member parties. The Communists, for example, have formed their own group in the Parliament since 1973, but their ability to get enough like-minded members elected at each European election to form a political group is always a question-mark prior to the elections. While the Greens were able to form a group of their own only after the 1989 elections, their internal coherence and sustained activity in the Parliament point to their ambition of becoming a force to be reckoned with at the European level. However, the same vulnerability to electoral misfortune applies in the case of the Greens as well.

Coalition behaviour inside the chamber is based on the left-right dimension and on legislative majority requirements. The left-right dimension is the dominant one. While MEPs form coalitions on a cross-group basis, these alignments are not durable, and thus they only serve to strengthen the value of the left-right dimension in explaining the voting similarity of the EP party groups.

The various EU legislative procedures put a pressure on the Parliament to muster absolute majorities if it wants to amend, reject, or pass a piece of legislation. In practice this has mainly happened through inter-party negotiations, with institutionalised co-operation between the EPP and the Socialists. Without majority requirements, the left-right cleavage becomes much sharper. Such lack of intra-parliamentary unity reduces EP's ability to make the other institutions take its opinions into account. However, one must keep in mind that the analysis was limited here to only one subject area (foreign policy), and therefore further research is needed to measure the impact of legislative majority requirements on party group cohesion and coalition behaviour.

Content analysis of parliamentary questions was undertaken in order to increase our understanding of the political profiles of the EP party groups and national delegations, and in order to examine the concepts of specialisation and representation inside the Parliament. While submitting questions to the Commission and the Council is part and parcel of a member's job, there was wide variation among the MEPs in their use of this instrument. Some members have specialised in this form of parliamentary activity over a long period of time, whereas other members refrain from asking questions altogether. A minority of MEPs table the majority of questions.

Analysing the variables in explaining the differences in the level of questioning activity between party groups and national delegations, the results show that the input of individual MEPs makes it difficult to establish any 'norms' prevailing within groups or national delegations. *The Greens submitted most questions per representative*, and their written questions were also fairly evenly divided among the members of the group. Of the national delegations *the most active questioners were the Greek, British, Spanish, and Belgian delegations.* However, much of the difference between country delegations is explained by the presence of a few 'chronic' questioners within these contingents.

Since places in the committees are divided between the party groups according to their respective sizes, it was expected that categorising questions into issue areas would show that there is no specialisation by the groups, and that MEPs' specialisation would reflect their committee membership. Content analysis proved these expectations correct.

In the case of transnational political groups, *none of the groups with the exception of the Greens concentrated in their questioning on any particular subject category.* The Greens predictably displayed an active interest in environmental issues. *Member state delegations displayed a similar lack of specialisation.* Differences in percentage figures often resulted from one or two MEPs within a member state delegation asking a large number of questions on the same subject category. In 1992 *the two by far most popular categories were social affairs and environment* (including public health and consumer protection), making up 20.3% and 22.8% of the questions respectively. Questions on foreign affairs, agriculture and fisheries, and economic and monetary union came next, with each policy area attracting around 10% of the questions.

The findings indicate that *members sitting in the respective committees were more likely to ask questions on their 'own' issue areas (i.e. those subject matters falling under the competence of their committee).* Categorising MEPs' written questions according to their subject categories shows therefore that the practice of ensuring a 'fair representation of member states and of political views' in the committees is significant since it channels party groups' and members' activities in ways that ensure that members bring their partisan preferences (membership in a party group) and knowledge of local conditions (territorial interests) to the committees. The representativeness of EP's decisions increases when party groups and national delegations develop an active interest in all policy areas.

Categorising the questions according to their territorial dimension showed that while there are differences between national delegations and individual members, *the overall situation sees members combining European policy-making with promoting national and local interests.* Over 40 per cent of the questions had a European dimension, with one-third of the questions having a national or a subnational dimension.

MEPs from Belgium, Germany, France, the Netherlands, and Luxembourg asked a higher than the average percentage of questions on 'European' issues. MEPs from Portugal, Spain, Italy, and particularly Greece submitted a higher than the average share of questions with a national or a subnational dimension. This centre-periphery division is mainly explained by the socio-economic profiles of the members' constituencies. While MEPs from the founding members of the EC have often questioned the 'European' vocation of their colleagues from the southern member states, the tendency by MEPs representing the more 'peripheral' regions to focus more on promoting their national or local interests is understandable considering the needs of their constituents.

Parliamentarians in Strasbourg make active use of questions to raise matters important to their constituents. Often the MEPs' questions deal with issues that are of minor importance at the European level but are significant to local inhabitants. But should members act as channels through which issues of local nature are brought to the European level? According to many observers, including several MEPs, local problems should be addressed at the local level. However, MEPs have the important duty of 'conveying moods and signals' from their constituencies, and parliamentary questions provide an excellent opportunity for such transmission of information. While MEPs' top priority must be contributing to European-level policy-making, by informing the Commission of problems arising at local level (perhaps in connection with implementation of EU-legislation), MEPs are performing an important function as representatives of the people.

This book has increased our understanding of the European Parliament - a legislature whose internal workings have remained seriously under-researched - by analysing the behaviour of the EP party groups in a very data-rich fashion. Considering the limited amount of research done on the Strasbourg Parliament, the collecting of such data, and subjecting it to meaningful theoretical investigation, is essential from the point of view of both scholarly interest and practical relevance. Party groups inside the European Parliament are important actors in the EU-decision-making process, and *the evidence presented here indicates that they can be considered cohesive actors, with internal organisation, facilitated by ideological homogeneity, providing the key for their cohesion.* However, *there are great differences between the groups*, with the above statement needing to be qualified in the case of the smaller political groups.

But what does the future hold for the European Parliament and for the party groups? Do we have the foundation of a European party system? What are the prospects for the development of such a continent-spanning party structure? Does representative democracy work in the context of European integration?

6.2. Public Opinion and Europolitics: No Shortcuts For Europarties

In recent years the magic word 'subsidiarity' has attracted a lot of attention, with the general interpretation of the concept being that decisions should be taken at the European level only if there is a genuine need for such a transfer of competences. When discussing subsidiarity in connection with party politics in the European Union, two inter-related problems deserve the attention of both politicians and academics interested in Europe's future political organisation: the involvement of the public in EU/EP politics, and the adoption of majority decision-making by the EU institutions, including the European Parliament.[1] In this concluding section, both of these issues will be analysed briefly.

Eurobarometer-surveys show the contradictory answers the respondents give to questions put to them. EU citizens are in general supportive of

European integration, but more detailed survey items reveal that voters possess very limited knowledge on EU governance. Not much appears to have changed since 1982 when Martin Slater wrote:

> "There is little public understanding of or interest in the Community. Clearly, the work of the Community is not something that has captured the imagination or interest of the public. A difficult problem for the Community is that where it has attracted public attention, the publicity is all too often negative...A high level of diffuse support for European unification seems to have little relevance for public attitudes towards more concrete aspects of European integration." (Slater, 1982: 77)

Attitudes towards, and knowledge of, the Parliament reflects to a great extent the overall public opinion on European integration. EU citizens are used to their national political systems, and adjustment to and familiarisation with the new political entity is bound to take time. To quote Geoffrey Pridham:

> "the political and institutional development of the Community requires a very long haul and cannot depend on any 'great leap forward' or even the kind of small leap that some expected of the first elections in 1979. Accordingly, European elections cannot by themselves be expected to grant the desired legitimacy, for their own future potential depends first and foremost on the EC system itself acquiring more authority and projecting itself more effectively." (Pridham, 1986: 295)

But with four direct elections already behind us, how much longer can the current situation go on? The European Parliament proclaims to be the 'voice of the people', but it hardly contributes to its legitimacy when citizen interest in and knowledge of its proceedings are at such a low level. Most probably the current situation will persist in the foreseeable future. The Parliament has a positive image in the eyes of the majority of Europeans: but for how long can it maintain this image?

How can the EP party groups and their respective transnational parties increase their visibility in the eyes of the electorates? According to one line of argument the parties and party groups should strive to develop clear programmatic identities. Were the parties to offer to the electorates competing policy packages, the voters would find it easier to 'pick' their party at the European level. Armed with such identifiable profiles, the Euro-parties would thus perform the same function as parties in national politics.[2] However, such arguments focusing on the traditional left-right cleavage underestimate the complexity of EP/EU politics. While the voting likeness of the EP party groups reflects their positions on the left-right continuum, the multi-dimensionality of cleavages, the much contested nature of the future EU polity, and the fact that there is no government elected from or accountable to the Parliament, means in practice that the nature of EP politics hardly conforms with such proposals advocating increased politicisation and conflict between two opposing homogeneous camps, the left and the right.

The future may well see more adversarial party competition at the European level (including in the European Parliament), but the present author regards the (i) mobilisation of electorates and (ii) the exchange of ideas in the context of transnational party co-operation as the two primary functions of political parties in the integration process.

Considering the weakly developed European or EU identity, it is questionable whether active support for further integrationist moves is forthcoming from the electorates. Indeed, the atmosphere of the current IGC seems to be one of caution and careful consideration. But is similar constraint exercised also inside the Parliament? While the strongly federalist arguments of the MEPs should be understood in the light of EP's continuing power-struggle vis-à-vis the Council of Ministers, it matters little to the public whether the final decision is taken by the Council or the Parliament if the electorate in question feels that its opinion has been neglected. Dehousse (1995; 119, 134) has rightly emphasised that majoritarian features of parliamentary decision-making are ill-suited for centre-periphery relations within federations such as the EU. As argued by Weiler:

> "...the European electorate (in most member states) only grudgingly accepts the notion that crucial areas of public life should be governed by a decisional process in which their national voice becomes a minority which may be overridden by a majority of representatives from other European countries...even a beefed up EP (which also operates on a majority principle) will not necessarily solve that legitimacy problem since in my analysis the legitimacy crisis does not derive principally from the accountability at the European level but from the very redefinition of the European polity." (Weiler, 1991: 420-421)

Naturally decision-making by unanimity rule has its inherent problems, and therefore less stringent decision-making rules are required simply for the sake of efficiency and for keeping the wheels turning. While analysing the effects of various majority rules in the Council of Ministers has recently become a popular theme among political scientists, less attention has been paid to similar considerations in the Parliament. The fact that the EP is directly elected - and thereby receives its mandate directly from the people - is no guarantee that citizens regard decisions taken by it as any more legitimate than decisions taken by another EU body.

The deepening of European integration has forced even the most reluctant parties to take part in the discussion on the future of the continent. While several parties are hampered by the fact that the EU-dimension has revealed or caused splits within the parties, the essential function of the parties, as intermediaries between the voters and the system of governance, is to stimulate debate on Europe. When formulating their positions, national parties are aided in this process by their links with sister parties in fellow EU member states.

The evolution of European integration and direct elections to the EP have led to more regular meetings between party leaders, to the formulation of common electoral manifestos and party programmes - no matter how vague they may be - and thus to ideological harmonisation. By offering competing visions on the nature of European polity, transnational parties are not only contributing to discussion, but these policy packages can and have been implemented in EU decision-making (Hix, 1995).

The simple fact that party representatives from various states get together on a regular basis has facilitated the exchange of ideas and deeper appreciation of each others' concerns (see Kuper, 1995). Transnational parties are open to national parties from non-EU countries and thereby they provide important fora for such parties wishing to develop and maintain contacts with like-minded sister parties. During recent years this aspect of co-operation has acquired particular significance as parties from the former communist states of Eastern Europe have joined these transnational parties.

It would be premature to conclude that transnational party co-operation has a dynamic of its own. The fate of transnational parties is tied to progress in European integration, with the most important arena for transnational party co-operation being and remaining the European Parliament.

The purpose of these concluding remarks has not been to argue against moves strengthening the supranational elements in European integration, but simply to make it clear that the way democracy is exercised inside the Strasbourg Parliament has implications for the legitimacy and functioning of the whole EU decision-making system. Since the success and future of the European Union is dependent on support from the citizens and national political elites of its constituent units (member states), this aspect deserves to be taken seriously. Much research remains to be done on life inside the Parliament: decision-making in the committees and inside the party groups, the impact of intergroups, the work and contact networks of the MEPs, and agenda formation are features of which far too little is known.

Notes

[1] More attention needs to be paid on the linkage between public opinion and EP's role in the decision-making system, and on the EP as a majoritarian institution. Public opinion on the Parliament has been investigated in articles by Niedermayer (1991) and Niedermayer and Sinnott (1995a). Based on *Eurobarometer*-surveys, the articles include longitudinal analyses of the development of public support for the Parliament, and measure citizens' knowledge of the EP. The report by Hofrichter and Klein (1993) contains similar analysis with data from the 1988-1992 period. All three articles show citizens' very limited knowledge on the Parliament. Stavridis (1992) argues in his brief article that increasing the powers of the Parliament will not cure the democratic deficit as long as the legitimacy of the Parliament and of the whole Union, based on European public opinion, is questionable. In his excellent discussion on the legitimacy of the Union, Weiler (1991) warns of the dangers involved in transferring competences to any majoritarian EU institution, including the Parliament, without first making sure that approval from the citizens is forthcoming. Similarly Dehousse (1995) has argued that the EU cannot ignore the legitimacy enjoyed by member states. Relying on majoritarian decision-making may deteriorate centre-periphery relations in the Union. According to Dehousse majoritarianism may not work in a decentralised federalist system characterised by strong national feelings.

[2] According to Robert Ladrech (1996: 295) "this is an important point, for, in the light of the heterogeneity of the groups and the absence of a government/opposition polarity, the left-right division could serve as the means by which public opinion comprehends not only the role of party groups within the EP but EU policy issues in general. ...the choice offered by a broad distinction between two competing groups (or coalitions) traditionally expressed in left-right terms, could have allowed for some semblance of a parliamentary identity, at least on the part of the major party groups." See also the works by Simon Hix mentioned in the bibliography.

Bibliography

Interviews

Interviews with MEPs, their assistants, and EP staff were carried out by the author in Brussels and in Strasbourg in February 1996. The following MEPs and/or their staff took the time to answer the questions: Mary Banotti (EPP, Ireland), Jan Willem Bertens (ELDR, Netherlands), Raphael Chanterie (EPP, Belgium), Ben Fayot (PES, Luxembourg), Carles Alfred Gasoliba i Böhm (ELDR, Spain), Fernand Herman (EPP, Belgium), Mark Killilea (EDA, Ireland), Annemarie Kuhn (PES, Germany), Manuel Medina Ortega (PES, Spain), Maria Oomen-Ruijten (EPP, Netherlands), Carlos Pimenta (ELDR, Portugal), Jannis Sakellariou (PES, Germany), Alex Smith (PES, UK), Ken Stewart (PES, UK), Jaak Vandemeulebroucke (ERA, Belgium). The author is grateful to the representatives for their co-operation.

European Parliament Documents

1988: Political Parties in the EC and European Unification, *Research and Documentation Papers, Political Series* no. 14, DG for Research, October 1988.

1989a: European Parliament and the Trans-European Policy Studies Association (TEPSA): Symposium on the European Parliament in the Community system, November 1988. Summary report and Plenary debates, *Research and Documentation Papers, National Parliaments Series* No. 5, DG for Research, March 1989.

1989b: *Forging Ahead: European Parliament 1952-1988*, Third edition, DG for Research.

1992: *The European Community in the Historical Context of its Parliament*, Proceedings of the 40th Anniversary Symposium, Strasbourg.

EP News (1989-1996).

List of Members (1989-1996).

Rules of Procedure 8th provisional edition, October 1993; 9th edition, June 1994.

Commission Documents

Bulletin of the European Communities (1989-1996).

Eurobarometer: Public Opinion in the European Union, Directorate-General X, Survey Research Unit (1973-1996).

General Report on the Activities of the European Communities (1979-1995).

Official Journal of the European Communities, C-series (1989-1996).

Secondary Sources

Aldrich, John H. (1994): 'A Model of a Legislature with Two Parties and a Committee System', *Legislative Studies Quarterly* XIX:3, pp. 313-339.

Ameller, Michel (1964): *Les Questions: Instrument du Controle Parlementaire*, Montecitorio, Paris.

Andeweg, Rudy (1995): 'The Reshaping of National Party Systems', *West European Politics* 18:3, pp. 58-78.

Andeweg, Rudy B. (1996): Fractiocracy? Limits to the Ascendancy of the Parliamentary Party in the Netherlands, paper to the ECPR Oslo Joint Sessions of Workshops.

Arndt, Rudi (1992): 'The Political Groups in the European Parliament', in *The European Community in the Historical Context of its Parliament*. Proceedings of the 40th Anniversary Symposium, Strasbourg, pp. 65-68.

Arp, Henning A. (1992): The European Parliament in European Community Environmental Policy, *EUI Working Paper EPU* No. 92/13, EUI, Florence.

Attinà, Fulvio (1990): 'The voting behaviour of the European Parliament members and the problem of the Europarties', *European Journal of Political Research* 18:4, pp. 557-579.

Attinà, Fulvio (1992a): *Il sistema politico della Comunita Europea*, Giuffre, Milano.

Attinà, Fulvio (1992b): 'Parties, Party Systems and Democracy in the European Union', *The International Spectator* XXVII:3, pp. 67-86.

Attinà, Fulvio (1993): Parties and Party System in the EC Political System, paper to the ECPR Leiden Joint Sessions of Workshops.

Attinà, Fulvio (1994a): On Political Representation in the European Union: Party Politics, Electoral System, and Territorial Representation, paper to the ECPR Madrid Joint Sessions of Workshops.

Attinà, Fulvio (1994b): 'Political Parties, Federalism and the European Union', in *Federal Conceptions in EU Member States: Traditions and Perspectives*, edited by Franz Knipping, Nomos, Baden-Baden, pp. 284-299.

Attinà, Fulvio (1997): 'Party fragmentation and discontinuity in the European Union', in *Transnational Party Politics in the European Union*, edited by David S. Bell and Christopher Lord, Dartmouth, Aldershot (forthcoming).

Banzhaf, John III (1965): 'Weighted Voting Doesn't Work: A Mathematical Analysis', *Rutgers Law Review* 19, pp. 329-330.

Bardi, Luciano (1989): *Il parlamento della Comunita Europea. Legittimita e riforma*, Il Mulino, Bologna.

Bardi, Luciano (1992): 'Transnational Party Federations in the European Community', in *Party Organizations: A Data Handbook on Party Organizations in Western Democracies, 1960-90*, edited by Richard S. Katz and Peter Mair, SAGE, London, pp. 931-973.

Bardi, Luciano (1993): Transnational Party Federations, EP Party Groups, and the Building of a European Party System, paper to the ECPR Leiden Joint Sessions of Workshops.

Bardi, Luciano (1994): 'Transnational Party Federations, European Parliamentary Party Groups, and the Building of Europarties', in *How Parties Organize: Change and Adaptation in Party Organizations in Western Democracies*, edited by Richard S. Katz and Peter Mair, SAGE, London, pp. 357-372.

Bardi, Luciano (1996): 'Transnational Trends in European Parties and the 1994 European Elections of the European Parliament', *Party Politics* 2:1, pp. 99-113.

Baron, David, P. (1994): 'A Sequential Choice Theory Perspective on Legislative Organization', *Legislative Studies Quarterly* XIX:2, pp. 267-296.

Bay Brzinski, Joanne (1995): 'Political Group Cohesion in the European Parliament, 1989-1994', in *The State of the European Union, Vol. 3: Building a European Polity?*, edited by Carolyn Rhodes and Sonia Mazey, Lynne Rienner, Boulder, pp. 135-158.

Bell, David (1996): 'Western communist parties and the European Union', in *Political Parties and the European Union*, edited by John Gaffney, Routledge, London, pp. 220-234.

Bell, David S. and Lord, Christopher eds. (1997): *Transnational Party Politics in the European Union*, Dartmouth, Aldershot (forthcoming).

Bieber, Roland (1990): 'Democratic Control of European Foreign Policy', *European Journal of International Law* 1:1, pp. 148-173.

Bieber, Roland (1991): 'Democratization of the European Community through the European Parliament', *Aussenwirtschaft* 46:3, pp. 391-410.

Birch, A.H. (1971): *Representation*, Pall Mall, London.

Bogdanor, Vernon (1986): 'The Future of the European Community: Two Models of Democracy', *Government and Opposition* 21:2, pp. 161-176.

Bogdanor, Vernon ed. (1987): *The Blackwell Encyclopaedia of Political Institutions*, Blackwell, Oxford.

Bogdanor, Vernon (1989): 'Direct Elections, Representative Democracy and European Integration', *Electoral Studies* 8:3, pp. 205-216.

Bomberg, Elizabeth (1993): 'The German Greens and the European Community: Dilemmas of a Movement-Party', in *A Green Dimension for the European Community: Political Issues and Processes*, edited by David Judge, Frank Cass, London, pp. 160-185.

Boumans, Etienne and Norbart, Monica (1989): 'The European Parliament and Human Rights', *Netherlands Quarterly of Human Rights* 1/1989, pp. 36-56.

Bourguignon-Wittke, R. et al. (1985): 'Five Years of the Directly Elected European Parliament: Performance and Prospects', *Journal of Common Market Studies* XXIV:1, pp. 39-59.

Bowler, Shaun and Farrell, David M. (1992a): *MEPs, Voters and Interest Groups: Representation at the European Level*, Final Report to the Commission of the European Community, DG for Information, Communication, Culture.

Bowler, Shaun and Farrell, David M. (1992b): 'Profile: The Greens at the European Level', *Environmental Politics* 1:1, pp. 132-137.

Bowler, Shaun and Farrell, David M. (1993a): 'Legislator Shirking and Voter Monitoring: Impacts of European Parliament Electoral Systems upon Legislator-Voter Relationships', *Journal of Common Market Studies* XXXI:1, pp. 45-69.

Bowler, Shaun and Farrell, David M. (1993b): Parliamentary Norms of Behaviour: The Case of the European Parliament, *EPRU Paper* 4/93, University of Manchester, Manchester.

Bowler, Shaun and Farrell, David M. (1995): 'The Organizing of the European Parliament: Committees, Specialization and Co-ordination', *British Journal of Political Science* 25:2, pp. 219-243.

Bowler, Shaun, Farrell, David M., and Katz, Richard S. eds. (1997): *Party Cohesion, Party Discipline, and the Organization of Parliaments*, Ohio State University Press, Columbus (forthcoming).

Boyce, Brigitte (1993): 'The Democratic Deficit of the European Community', *Parliamentary Affairs* 46:4, pp. 458-477.

Boyce, Brigitte (1995): 'The June 1994 Elections and the Politics of the European Parliament', *Parliamentary Affairs* 48:1, pp. 141-156.

Bréchon, Pierre, Cautrès, Bruno, and Denni, Bernard (1995): 'L'évolution des attitudes à l'égard de l'Europe', in *Le Vote Des Douze: Les élections européennes de juin 1994*, edited by Pascal Perrineau and Colette Ysmal, Département d'études politiques du Figaro & Presses de sciences po, Paris, pp. 155-180.

Buck, Karl H. (1989): 'Europe: The "Greens" and the "Rainbow Group" in the European Parliament', in *New Politics in Western Europe: The Rise and Success of Green Parties and Alternative Lists*, edited by Ferdinand Müller-Rommel, Westview Press, Boulder, pp. 167-172.

Buffotot, Patrice (1994): 'The Security and Defence Policies of European Christian Democracy', in *Christian Democracy in Europe: A Comparative Perspective*, edited by David Hanley, Pinter, London, pp. 202-211.

Burgess, Michael (1993a): 'Federalism and Federation: A Reappraisal', in *Comparative Federalism and Federation: Competing traditions and future directions*, edited by Michael Burgess and Alain-G. Gagnon, Harvester Wheatsheaf, Hemel Hempstead, pp. 3-14.

Burgess, Michael (1993b): 'Federalism as Political Ideology: Interests, Benefits and Beneficiaries in Federalism and Federation', in *Comparative Federalism and*

Federation: Competing traditions and future directions, edited by Michael Burgess and Alain-G. Gagnon, Harvester Wheatsheaf, Hemel Hempstead, pp. 102-114.

Chapman, Ralph J.K. (1993): 'Structure, Process and the Federal Factor: Complexity and Entanglement in Federations', in *Comparative Federalism and Federation: Competing traditions and future directions*, edited by Michael Burgess and Alain-G. Gagnon, Harvester Wheatsheaf, Hemel Hempstead, pp. 69-93.

Chester, Norman and Bowring, Nona (1962): *Questions in Parliament*, Oxford University Press, Oxford.

Claeys, Paul-H. and Loeb-Mayer, Nicole (1979): 'Trans-European Party Groupings: Emergence of New and Alignment of Old Parties in the Light of the Direct Elections to the European Parliament', *Government and Opposition* 14:4, pp. 455-478.

Clausen, Aage R. and Holmberg, Sören (1977): 'Legislative Voting Analysis in Disciplined Multi-Party Systems: The Swedish Case', in *The History of Parliamentary Behaviour*, edited by William O. Aydelotte, Princeton University Press, Princeton, N.J., pp. 159-185.

Cohen, Lionel H. (1979): 'The Development of Question Time in the European Parliament: With Special Reference to the Role of British Members', *Common Market Law Review* 16:1, pp. 41-59.

Collie, Melissa P. (1984): 'Voting Behaviour in Legislatures', *Legislative Studies Quarterly* IX:1, pp. 3-50.

Cox, Gary W. and McCubbins, Mathew D. (1991): 'On the Decline of Party Voting In Congress', *Legislative Studies Quarterly* XVI:4, pp. 547-570.

Cox, Gary W. and McCubbins, Mathew D. (1993): *Legislative Leviathan: Party Government in the House*, University of California Press, Berkeley.

Crombez, Christophe (1996): 'Legislative Procedures in the European Community', *British Journal of Political Science* 26:2, pp. 199-228.

Curtice, John (1989): 'The 1989 European Election: Protest or Green Tide?', *Electoral Studies* 8:3, pp. 217-230.

Damgaard, Erik (1994): 'Parliamentary Questions and Control in Denmark', in *Parliamentary Control in the Nordic Countries: Forms of Questioning and Behavioural Trends*, edited by Matti Wiberg, The Finnish Political Science Association, Helsinki, pp. 44-76.

Damgaard, Erik (1995): 'How Parties Control Committee Members', in *Parliaments and Majority Rule in Western Europe*, edited by Herbert Döring, Campus and St. Martin's Press, Frankfurt and New York, pp. 308-325.

Dehousse, Renaud (1995): 'Constitutional Reform in the European Community: Are there Alternatives to the Majoritarian Avenue?', *West European Politics* 18:3, pp. 118-136.

Delwit, Pascal and De Waele, Jean-Michel (1995): 'Les élections européennes et l'évolution des groupes politiques au Parlement européen', in *Democratie et Construction Européenne*, edited by Mario Telò, editions de l'Université de Bruxelles, Brussels, pp. 277-291.

Elles, James (1990): 'The Foreign Policy Role of the European Parliament', *The Washington Quarterly* 13:4, pp. 69-78.

Elster, Jon (1986): 'The market and the forum: three varieties of political theory', in *Foundations of Social Choice Theory*, edited by Jon Elster and Aanund Hylland, Cambridge University Press, Cambridge, pp. 103-132.

Esaiasson, Peter and Holmberg, Sören (1996): *Elected by the People: Members of Parliament and Representative Democracy*, Dartmouth, Aldershot.

Ewing, Winifred (1989): 'The Political Groups in Parliament', in *Towards 1992: The European Parliament and the Single European Act*, edited by Allan Macartney, University of Edinburgh, Edinburgh, pp. 19-23.

Featherstone, Kevin (1986): 'Socialist Parties and European Integration: Variations on a Common Theme', in *The Future of Social Democracy: Problems and Prospects of Social Democratic Parties in Western Europe*, edited by William E. Paterson and Alastair H. Thomas, Clarendon Press, Oxford, pp. 242-260.

Featherstone, Kevin (1988): *Socialist Parties and European Integration: A Comparative History*, Manchester University Press, Manchester.

Fieschi, Catherine, Shields, James, and Woods, Roger (1996): 'Extreme right-wing parties and the European Union: France, Germany and Italy', in *Political Parties and the European Union*, edited by John Gaffney, Routledge, London, pp. 235-253.

Fitzmaurice, John (1975): *The Party Groups in the European Parliament*, Saxon House, Farnborough.

Fitzmaurice, John (1978): 'Direct Elections and the Future of the European Parliament', *West European Politics* 1:2, pp. 208-225.

Fowler, Linda L., Polhuis, Pieter L., and Paine, Scott C. (1983): 'Changing Patterns of Voting Strength in the European Parliament', *Comparative Politics* 15:2, pp. 159-175.

Franklin, Mark and Norton, Philip eds. (1993a): *Parliamentary Questions*, Clarendon Press, Oxford.

Franklin, Mark and Norton, Philip (1993b): 'Questions and Members', in *Parliamentary Questions*, edited by Mark Franklin and Philip Norton, Clarendon Press, Oxford, pp. 104-122.

Gaffney, John ed. (1996): *Political Parties and the European Union*, Routledge, London.

Gagnon, Alain-G. (1993): 'The Political uses of Federalism', in *Comparative Federalism and Federation: Competing traditions and future directions*, edited by Michael Burgess and Alain-G. Gagnon, Harvester Wheatsheaf, Hemel Hempstead, pp. 15-44.

Gallagher, Michael, Laver, Michael, and Mair, Peter (1992): *Representative Government in Western Europe*, McGraw-Hill, New York.

Garrett, Geoffrey and Tsebelis, George (1996): 'An institutional critique of intergovernmentalism', *International Organization* 50:2, pp. 269-299.

Gerbet, Pierre (1992): 'The Common Assembly of the European Coal and Steel Community', in *The European Community in the Historical Context of its Parliament*. Proceedings of the 40th Anniversary Symposium, Strasbourg, pp. 11-16.

Gilligan, Thomas W. and Krehbiel, Keith (1994): 'The Gains from Exchange Hypothesis of Legislative Organization', *Legislative Studies Quarterly* XIX:2, pp. 181-214.

Grabitz, Eberhard et al. (1988): *Direktwahl und Demokratisierung - Eine Funktionenbilanz des Europäischen Parlaments nach der ersten Wahlperiode*, Europa Union Verlag, Bonn.

Green, Pauline (1994): 'The challenge of the future: Parliament urged to play to its strengths', in *The Times Guide to the European Parliament 1994*, edited by Robert Morgan, Times Books, London, pp. 26-28.

Greven, Michael Th. (1995): 'Political institutions and the building of democracy: Some issues in recent German literature', *European Journal of Political Research* 27:3, pp. 463-475.

Haas, Ernst B. (1958): *The Uniting of Europe. Political, Social and Economical Forces 1950-1957*, Stevens & Sons, London.

Hagevi, Magnus (1996): Party Activity Among the Members of the Swedish Riksdag, paper to the ECPR Oslo Joint Sessions of Workshops.

Hagger, Mark and Wing, Martin (1979): 'Legislative Roles and Clientele Orientations in the European Parliament', *Legislative Studies Quarterly* IV:2, pp. 165-196.

Hanley, David (1994): 'The European People's Party: towards a new party form?', in *Christian Democracy in Europe: A Comparative Perspective*, edited by David Hanley, Pinter, London, pp. 185-201.

Hedetoft, Ulf (1994): 'The State of Sovereignty in Europe: Political Concept or Cultural Self-Image', in *National Cultures and European Integration: Exploratory Essays on Cultural Diversity and Common Policies*, edited by Staffan Zetterholm, Berg, Oxford, pp. 13-48.

Heidar, Knut and Koole, Ruud A. (1996): Approaches to the Study of Parliamentary Party Groups, paper to the ECPR Oslo Joint Sessions of Workshops.

Heidar, Knut and Koole, Ruud eds. (1997): *Behind Closed Doors: parliamentary party groups in European democracies*, Routledge (forthcoming).

Held, David (1995): 'Democracy and the New International Order', in *Cosmopolitan Democracy: An Agenda for a New World Order*, edited by Daniele Arhibugi and David Held, Polity Press, Cambridge, pp. 96-120.

Henig, Stanley and Pinder, John (1969): *European Political Parties*, George Allen & Unwin, London.

Herne, Kaisa and Nurmi, Hannu (1993): 'The Distribution of A Priori Voting Power in the EC Council of Ministers and the European Parliament', *Scandinavian Political Studies* 16:3, pp. 269-284.

Hill, Christopher (1994): 'The Capability-Expectations Gap, or Conceptualizing Europe's International Role', in *Economic and Political Integration in Europe: Internal Dynamics and Global Context*, edited by Simon Bulmer and Andrew Scott, Blackwell, Oxford., pp. 103-126.

Hix, Simon (1993): European Integration and Party Behaviour: party adaption to extra-system challenges, paper to the ECPR Leiden Joint Sessions of Workshops.

Hix, Simon (1994a): "Parties at the European Level" as an Alternative Source of Legitimacy: The Party Federations and the EU Socio-Economic Agenda, paper to the ECPR Madrid Joint Sessions.

Hix, Simon (1994b): 'The Study of the European Community: The Challenge to Comparative Politics', *West European Politics* 17:1, pp. 1-30.

Hix, Simon (1995): 'Parties at the European Level and the Legitimacy of EU Socio-Economic Policy', *Journal of Common Market Studies* 33:4, pp. 527-554.

Hix, Simon (1996): 'The transnational party federations', in *Political Parties and the European Union*, edited by John Gaffney, Routledge, London, pp. 308-331.

Hix, Simon and Lord, Christopher (1996): 'The Making of a President: The European Parliament and the Confirmation of Jacques Santer as President of the Commission', *Government and Opposition* 31:1, pp. 62-76.

Hofrichter, Jurgen and Klein, Michael (1993): *The European Parliament in the Eyes of the EC Citizens*, Report on behalf of the European Parliament, DG III, Information and Public Relations, July 1993, ZEUS, Universität Mannheim, mimeo.

Hosli, Madeleine O. (1995): 'The Balance Between Small and Large: Effects of a Double-Majority System on Voting Power in the European Union', *International Studies Quarterly* 39, pp. 351-370.

Hosli, Madeleine O. (1996): 'Coalitions and Power: Effects of Qualified Majority Voting in the Council of the European Union', *Journal of Common Market Studies* 34:2, pp. 255-273.

Hrbek, Rudolf (1976): 'Eine neue politische Infrastruktur? Zum Problem transnationaler Kooperation und Koalition politischer Parteien in der EG', in *Zusammenarbeit der Parteien in Westeuropa: Auf dem Weg zu einer neuen politischen Infrastruktur?*, Institut für Europäische Politik, Europa Union Verlag, Bonn, pp. 341-390.

Hrbek, Rudolf (1988): 'Transnational links: the ELD and Liberal Party Group in the European Parliament', in *Liberal Parties in Western Europe*, edited by Emil J. Kirchner, Cambridge University Press, Cambridge, pp. 455-469.

Hrbek, Rudolf, and Schweitzer, Carl-Christoph (1989): 'Die deutschen Europa-Parlamentarier", *Aus Politik und Zeitgeschichte* B3/89, pp. 3-18.

Hurwitz, Leon (1983): 'Partisan Ideology or National Interest? An Analysis of the Members of the European Parliament', in *The Harmonization of European Public Policy: Regional Responses to Transnational Challenges*, Greenwood Press, edited by Leon Hurwitz, Praeger, Westport, pp. 197-217.

Hurwitz, Leon (1987): *The European Community and the Management of International Cooperation*, Greenwood Press, Westport.

Ilonszki, Gabriella (1996): Parties and Parliamentary Parties in the Making: Hungary, 1989-1996, paper to the ECPR Oslo Joint Sessions of Workshops.

Ionescu, Ghita (1996): 'Conclusion', in *Parliaments and Parties: The European Parliament in the Political Life of Europe*, edited by Roger Morgan and Clare Tame, Macmillan, Basingstoke, pp. 343-367.

Jacobs, Francis, Corbett, Richard, and Shackleton, Michael (1992): *The European Parliament*, Second edition, Longman, Harlow.

Jacobs, Francis, Corbett, Richard, and Shackleton, Michael (1995): *The European Parliament*, Third edition, Cartermill, London.

Johansson, Karl Magnus (1993): Transnational Party Co-operation: The Case of the European People's Party, paper to the ECPR Leiden Joint Sessions of Workshops.

Johansson, Karl Magnus (1996): 'The Nature of Political Parties in The European Union', in *The Impact of European Integration: Political, Sociological, and Economic Changes*, edited by George A. Kourvetaris and Andreas Moschonas, Praeger, Westport, pp. 201-232.

Johansson, Karl Magnus (1997): 'Party Group Dynamics in the European Parliament', in *National Interest and Integrative Politics in Transnational Assemblies*, edited by Ernst Kuper and Uwe Jun, Frank Cass, London (forthcoming).

Johnson, Nevil (1961): 'Parliamentary Questions and the Conduct of Administration', *Public Administration* 39:2, pp. 131-148.

Judge, David (1974): 'Backbench Specialization - A Study in Parliamentary Questions', *Parliamentary Affairs* 27:2, pp. 171-186.

Judge, David (1993): ''Predestined to Save the Earth': The Environment Committee of the European Parliament', in *A Green Dimension for the European Community: Political Issues and Processes*, edited by David Judge, Frank Cass, London, pp. 186-212.

Judge, David and Earnshaw, David (1994): 'Weak European Parliament Influence? A Study of the Environment Committee of the European Parliament', *Government and Opposition* 29:2, pp. 262-276.

Katz, Richard S. (1996): Role Orientations and Representational Behavior in the European Parliament: First Findings from a Survey of Candidates in the 1994 European Election (ms).

Kerr, Henry H. Jr. (1973): 'Changing Attitudes through International Participation: European Parliamentarians and Integration', *International Organization* 27:1, pp. 45-83.

Kirchner, Emil J. (1984): *The European Parliament: Performance and Prospects*, Gower, Aldershot.

Kiser, Larry L. and Ostrom, Elinor (1982): 'The Three Worlds of Action: A Metatheoretical Synthesis of Institutional Approaches', in *Strategies of Political Inquiry*, edited by Elinor Ostrom, Sage, Beverly Hills, pp. 179-222.

Kopecký, Petr (1996): Limits of Whips and Watchdogs: Cohesion of Parliamentary Parties in the First Czech Parliament (1992-1996), paper to the ECPR Oslo Joint Sessions of Workshops.

Krehbiel, Keith (1991): *Information and Legislative Organization*, The University of Michigan Press, Ann Arbor.

Kuper, Ernst (1991): 'Transnationale Versammlung und nationales Parlament. Einige Überlegungen zu Funktion und Leistung des Parlamentarismus in den internationalen Beziehungen', *Zeitschrift für Parlamentsfragen* 22:4, pp. 620-638.

Kuper, Ernst (1995): *Transnationale Parteienbünde zwischen Partei- und Weltpolitik.* Peter Lang, Frankfurt am Main.

Kuper, Ernst and Jun, Uwe eds. (1997): *National Interest and Integrative Politics in Transnational Assemblies*, Frank Cass, London (forthcoming).

Laakso, Markku and Taagepera, Rein (1979): '"Effective' Number of Parties: A Measure with Application to West Europe', *Comparative Political Studies* 12:1, pp. 3-27.

Ladrech, Robert (1996): 'Political parties in the European Parliament', in *Political Parties and the European Union*, edited by John Gaffney, Routledge, London, pp. 291-307.

Ladrech, Robert and Brown-Pappamikail, Peter (1995): 'Towards a European Party System?', in *Democratie et Construction Européenne*, edited by Mario Telò, Editions de l'Université de Bruxelles, Brussels, pp. 267-275.

Lane, Jan E., Maeland, Reinert, and Berg, Sven (1996): 'Voting Power Under the EU Constitution', in *The European Union: How Democratic Is It?*, edited by Svein S. Andersen and Kjell A. Eliassen, SAGE, London, pp. 165-185.

Lanfranchi, Prisca and Lüthi, Ruth (1995): Cohesion of party groups and interparty conflict in the Swiss Parliament: Roll call voting in the National Council, paper to the ECPR Bordeaux Joint Sessions of Workshops.

Laursen, Finn (1994): 'The Not-So-Permissive Consensus: Thoughts on the Maastricht Treaty and the Future of European Integration', in *The Ratification of the Maastricht Treaty: Issues, Debates and Future Implications*, edited by Finn Laursen and Sophie Vanhoonacker, European Institute of Public Administration, Maastricht, pp. 295-317.

Lécureuil, Christophe (1996): 'Prospects for a European Party System after the 1994 European Elections', in *The 1994 Elections to the European Parliament*, edited by Juliet Lodge, Pinter, London, pp. 183-197.

Lodge, Juliet (1988): 'The European Parliament and Foreign Policy', in *Foreign Policy and Legislatures: An Analysis of Seven Parliaments*, edited by Manohar L. Sondhi, Abhinav Publications, New Delhi, pp. 113-133.

Lodge, Juliet (1992): 'Democratic Legitimacy and the EC: Crossing the Rubicon', in *The European Community in the Historical Context of its Parliament*. Proceedings of the 40th Anniversary Symposium, Strasbourg, pp. 43-59.

Lord, Christopher (1994): Party Groups in the European Parliament: Rethinking the role of Transnational Parties in the Democratization of the European Union, paper to the ECPR Madrid Joint Sessions of Workshops.

Lupia, Arthur and McCubbins, Mathew D. (1994): 'Who Controls? Information and the Structure of Legislative Decision Making', *Legislative Studies Quarterly* XIX:3, pp. 361-384.

Lynch, Peter (1994): Transnational Links Between Regionalist Parties, paper to the ECPR Madrid Joint Sessions of Workshops.

Maass, Arthur (1983): *Congress and the Common Good*, Basic Books, New York.

March, James G. and Olsen, Johan P. (1989): *Rediscovering Institutions: The Organizational Basis of Politics*, The Free Press, New York.

Mattson, Ingvar (1994): 'Parliamentary Questions in the Swedish Riksdag', in *Parliamentary Control in the Nordic Countries: Forms of Questioning and Behavioural Trends*, edited by Matti Wiberg, The Finnish Political Science Association, Helsinki, pp. 276-356.

Mattson, Ingvar and Strøm, Kaare (1995): 'Parliamentary Committees', in *Parliaments and Majority Rule in Western Europe*, edited by Herbert Döring, Campus and St. Martin's Press, Frankfurt and New York, pp. 249-307.

Mengelberg, Sabine (1994): 'The European Parliament and the Ratification of the Maastricht Treaty', in *The Ratification of the Maastricht Treaty: Issues, Debates and Future Implications*, edited by Finn Laursen and Sophie Vanhoonacker, European Institute of Public Administration, Maastricht, pp. 279-292.

Middlemas, Keith (1995): *Orchestrating Europe: The Informal Politics of European Union, 1973-1995*, Fontana Press, London.

Mikkelsen, Hans Christian (1994): 'Udviklingen i partisammenholdet', *Politica* 26:1, pp. 25-31.

Morgan, Robert ed. (1994): *The Times Guide to the European Parliament 1994*, Times Books, London.

Morgan, Roger and Tame, Clare eds. (1996): *Parliaments and Parties: The European Parliament in the Political Life of Europe*, Macmillan, Basingstoke.

Müller, Wolfgang C. and Steininger, Barbara (1996): Parliamentary Parties in Austria: Legal Status, resources, internal organization, and relations with party organization, paper to the ECPR Oslo Joint Sessions of Workshops.

Neunreither, Karlheinz (1990): 'The European Parliament: an emerging political role?', in *Europe's Global Links: The European Community and Inter-Regional Cooperation*, edited by Geoffrey Edwards and Elfriede Regelsberger, St.Martin's Press, New York, pp. 169-187.

Niedermayer, Oskar (1983): *Europäische Parteien? Zur grenzüberschreitenden Interaktion politischer Parteien im Rahmen der Europäischen Gemeinschaft*, Campus, Frankfurt.

Niedermayer, Oskar (1984): 'The Transnational Dimension of the Election', *Electoral Studies* 3:3, pp. 235-243.

Niedermayer, Oskar (1991): 'Public Opinion about the European Parliament', in *Eurobarometer: The Dynamics of European Public Opinion. Essays in Honour of Jacques-René Rabier*, edited by Karlheinz Reif and Ronald Inglehart, Macmillan, Basingstoke, pp. 27-44.

Niedermayer, Oskar and Sinnott, Richard (1995a): 'Democratic Legitimacy and the European Parliament', in *Public Opinion and Internationalized Governance*, edited by Oskar Niedermayer and Richard Sinnott, Oxford University Press, Oxford, pp. 277-308.

Niedermayer, Oskar and Sinnott, Richard eds. (1995b): *Public Opinion and Internationalized Governance*, Oxford University Press, Oxford.

Norton, Philip (1995): 'Conclusion: Addressing the Democratic Deficit', *The Journal of Legislative Studies* 1:3, pp. 177-193.

Nyholm, Pekka (1961): Suomen eduskuntaryhmien koheesio vuosien 1948-1951 vaalikaudella ja vuoden 1954 valtiopäivillä. *Bidrag till kännedom av Finlands natur och folk utgivna av Finska Vetenskaps-Societeten* H. 106. Helsinki.

Nyholm, Pekka (1972): Parliament, Government and Multi-Dimensional Party Relations in Finland, *Commentitationes Scientiarum Socialum*, 2, 1972, Societas Scientiarum Fennica, Helsinki.

Nyholm, Pekka and Hagfors, Carl (1968): Ryhmäyhtenäisyyden kehityksestä eduskunnassa 1930-1954, *Helsingin yliopisto, valtio-opin laitos, tutkimuksia* 14/1968. (mimeo)

Ollerenshaw, Steve (1993): The European Parliament: More Democracy or More Rhetoric? The European Parliament, the Single European Act and the Interinstitutional Agreement, *Occasional Papers in European Studies* 2, Centre for European Studies, University of Essex.

Ozbudun, Ergun (1970): Party Cohesion in Western Democracies: A Causal Analysis, *Sage Professional Papers in Comparative Politics*, Series 01, No. 001, Sage, Beverly Hills.

Palmer, Michael (1981): *The European Parliament: What it is, What it does, How it works*, Pergamon Press, Oxford.

Patterson, Samuel C. (1995): 'Legislative Institutions and Institutionalism in the United States', *The Journal of Legislative Studies* 1:4, pp. 10-29.

Pedersen, Mogens N. (1996): 'Euro-parties and European Parties: New Arenas, New Challenges and New Strategies', in *The European Union: How Democratic Is It?*, edited by Svein S. Andersen and Kjell A. Eliassen, SAGE, London, pp. 15-39.

Penders, Jean J.M. (1988): 'The European Parliament and European Political Cooperation', *Irish Studies in International Affairs* 2:4, pp. 41-48.

Peters, Torsten (1996a): Decision Making after the EU-Intergovernmental Conference, paper to the ECPR Oslo Joint Sessions of Workshops.

Peters, Torsten (1996b): Voting Power after the Enlargement and Options for Decision Making in the European Union (ms.).

Peterson, M.J. (1992): 'Transnational Activity, International Society and World Politics', *Millennium* 21:3, pp. 371-388.

Pflimlin, Pierre (1992): 'Comments', in *The European Community in the Historical Context of its Parliament*. Proceedings of the 40th Anniversary Symposium, Strasbourg, pp. 69-70.

Pitkin, Hanna (1967): *The Concept of Representation*, University of California Press, Berkeley.

Polsby, Nelson W. (1968): 'The Institutionalization of the U.S. House of Representatives', *American Political Science Review* LXII:1, pp. 144-168.

Pridham, Geoffrey (1986): 'European Elections, Political Parties and Trends of Internalization in Community Affairs', *Journal of Common Market Studies* XXIV:4, pp. 279-296.

Pridham, Geoffrey and Pridham, Pippa (1979a): *Towards Transnational Parties in the European Community*, Studies in European Politics 2, Policy Studies Institute, London.

Pridham, Geoffrey and Pridham, Pippa (1979b): 'Transnational Parties in the European Community I: The Party Groups in the European Parliament', in *Political Parties in the European Community*, edited by Stanley Henig, George Allen & Unwin, London, pp. 245-277.

Pridham, Geoffrey and Pridham, Pippa (1979c): 'Transnational Parties in the European Community II: The Development of European Party Federations', in *Political Parties in the European Community*, edited by Stanley Henig, George Allen & Unwin, London, pp. 278-298.

Pridham, Geoffrey and Pridham, Pippa (1981): *Transnational Party Co-operation and European Integration. The Process Towards Direct Elections*, George Allen & Unwin, London.

Quanjel, Marcel and Wolters, Menno (1992): 'Het Europees Parlement', in *Democratie en beleid in de Europese Gemeenschap*, edited by Menno Wolters, Samson H.D. Tjeenk Willink, Alphen aan den Rijn, pp. 67-86.

Quanjel, Marcel and Wolters, Menno (1993): Growing cohesion in the European Parliament, paper to the ECPR Leiden Joint Sessions of Workshops.

Rae, Douglas W. (1967): *The Political Consequences of Electoral Laws*, Yale UP, New Haven.

Rasch, Bjørn Erik (1994): 'Question Time in the Norwegian Storting - Theoretical and Empirical Considerations', in *Parliamentary Control in the Nordic Countries: Forms of Questioning and Behavioural Trends*, edited by Matti Wiberg, The Finnish Political Science Association, Helsinki, pp. 247-275.

Rasch, Bjørn Erik (1995): Party Discipline in Parliament: A Note on the Case of the Norwegian Storting, paper to the ECPR Bordeaux Joint Sessions of Workshops.

Rattinger, Hans (1982): 'Abstimmungsmacht, politische Distanzen und Abstimmungskoalitionen zwischen den Fraktionen im Europäischen Parlament', *Zeitschrift für Soziologie* 11:2, pp. 133-149.

Raunio, Tapio (1995): The Cohesion of and Distance Between Political Groups in the European Parliament: MEP Voting Behaviour, 1989-1994, paper to the ECPR Bordeaux Joint Sessions of Workshops.

Raunio, Tapio (1996a): 'Parliamentary Questions in the European Parliament: Representation, Information, and Control', *The Journal of Legislative Studies* 2:4, pp. 356-382.

Raunio, Tapio (1996b): *Party Group Behaviour in the European Parliament: An Analysis of Transnational Political Groups in the 1989-94 Parliament*, Acta Universitatis Tamperensis A:521, Tampere University Press, Vammala.

Raunio, Tapio (1996c): Towards A Better Understanding of EP Party Groups: Internal Organisation and Collective Action, paper to the ECPR Oslo Joint Sessions of Workshops.

Raunio, Tapio (1997a): 'The Challenge of Diversity: Party Cohesion in the European Parliament', in *Party Cohesion, Party Discipline, and the Organization of Parliaments*, edited by Shaun Bowler, David M. Farrell and Richard S. Katz, Ohio State University Press, Columbus (forthcoming).

Raunio, Tapio (1997b): 'Cleavages and Alignments in the European Parliament: MEP Voting Behaviour, 1989-1994', in *Transnational Party Politics in the European Union*, edited by David S. Bell and Christopher Lord, Dartmouth, Aldershot (forthcoming).

Raunio, Tapio (1997c): 'Parliamentary Questions and the Concept of Representation in the European Parliament', in *National Interest and Integrative Politics in Transnational Assemblies*, edited by Ernst Kuper and Uwe Jun, Frank Cass, London (forthcoming).

Rhodes, R.A.W. (1995): 'The Institutional Approach', in *Theory and Methods in Political Science*, edited by David Marsh and Gerry Stoker, Macmillan, Basingstoke, pp. 42-57.

Rice, S.A. (1928): *Quantitative Methods in Politics*, Knopf, New York.

Rohde, David W. (1994): 'Parties and Committees in the House: Member Motivations, Issues, and Institutional Arrangements', *Legislative Studies Quarterly* XIX:3, pp. 341-359.

Rüdig, Wolfgang (1996): 'Green parties and the European Union', in *Political Parties and the European Union*, edited by John Gaffney, Routledge, London, pp. 254-272.

Saalfeld, Thomas (1990): 'The West German Bundestag after 40 Years: The Role of Parliament in a 'Party Democracy'', *West European Politics* 13:3, pp. 68-89.

Saalfeld, Thomas (1995): 'Rational-Choice Theory in Legislative Studies: Models of Politics without Romanticism', *The Journal of Legislative Studies* 1:1, pp. 32-64.

Sabic, Zlatko (1994): Democratising International Organisations: The Role of International Parliamentary Organs, paper to the XVIth World Congress of the International Political Science Association, Berlin.

Sanders, David (1995): 'Behavioural Analysis', in *Theory and Methods in Political Science*, edited by David Marsh and Gerry Stoker, Macmillan, Basingstoke, pp. 58-75.

Sbragia, Alberta M. (1992): 'Thinking about the European Future: The Uses of Comparison', in *Euro-Politics: Institutions and Policymaking in the "New" European Community*, edited by Alberta M. Sbragia, The Brookings Institution, Washington, D.C., pp. 257-291.

Schmuck, Otto and Wessels, Wolfgang eds.(1989): *Das Europäische Parlament im dynamischen Integrationsprozeß: Auf der Suche nach einem zeitgemäßen Leitbild*, Europa Union Verlag, Bonn.

Schneider, Gerald (1995): 'The Limits of Self-Reform: Institution-Building in the European Union', *European Journal of International Relations* 1:1, pp. 59-86.

Scholl, Edward L. (1986): 'The Electoral System and Constituency-oriented Activity in the European Parliament', *International Studies Quarterly* 30:3, pp. 315-332.

Searing, Donald D. (1987): 'New Roles for Postwar British Politics: Ideologues, Generalists, Specialists, and the Progress of Professionalization in Parliament', *Comparative Politics* 19:4, pp. 431-452.

Searing, Donald D. (1991): 'Roles, Rules, and Rationality in the New Institutionalism', *American Political Science Review* 85:4, pp. 1239-1260.

Searing, Donald D. (1995): 'Backbench and Leadership Roles in the House of Commons', *Parliamentary Affairs* 48:3, pp. 418-437.

Seiler, D.-L. (1980): *Partis et familles politiques*, Presses Universitaires de France, Paris.

Shapley, Lloyd and Shubik, Martin (1954): 'A Method for Evaluating the Distribution of Power in a Committee System', *American Political Science Review* 48, pp. 787-792.

Shepsle, Kenneth A. (1989): 'Studying Institutions: Some Lessons from the Rational Choice Approach', *Journal of Theoretical Politics* 1:2, pp. 131-147.

Shepsle, Kenneth A. and Weingast, Barry R. (1984): 'When Do Rules of Procedure Matter?', *The Journal of Politics* 46:1, pp. 206-221.

Shepsle, Kenneth A. and Weingast, Barry R. (1994a): 'Editors' Introduction: Formal Models of Legislatures', *Legislative Studies Quarterly* XIX:2, pp. 145-147.

Shepsle, Kenneth A. and Weingast, Barry R. (1994b): 'Positive Theories of Congressional Institutions', *Legislative Studies Quarterly* XIX:2, pp. 149-179.

Shull, Steven A. and Vanderleeuw, James M. (1987): 'What do Key Votes Measure?', *Legislative Studies Quarterly* XII:4, pp. 573-582.

Slater, Martin (1982): 'Political Elites, Popular Indifference and Community Building', *Journal of Common Market Studies* 21:1, pp. 69-87.

Smith, Julie (1995): *Voice of the People: The European Parliament in the 1990s*, The Royal Institute of International Affairs, London.

Sørensen, Carsten Lehmann (1989): The Influence of the Directly Elected MEPs on EC Decision Making, paper to the ECPR Paris Joint Sessions of Workshops.

Sørensen, Carsten Lehmann et al. (1980): 'A European Security Policy? The Attitudes of Candidates for the European Parliament', *Scandinavian Political Studies* 3:4, pp. 347-371.

Sprokkereef, Annemarie (1993): The EC and the Fall of Yugoslavia: The Community's Decisionmaking Process in Times of Crisis, paper to the ECPR Leiden Joint Sessions of Workshops.

Stavridis, Stelios (1992): 'The Forgotten Question of the European Parliament's Current Lack of Legitimacy', *The Oxford International Review* III:2, pp. 27-29.

Steed, Michael (1985): 'The Constituency', in *Representatives of the People? Parliamentarians and Constituents in Western Democracies*, edited by Vernon Bogdanor, Gower, Aldershot, pp. 267-285.

Steed, Michael and Hearl, Derek (1985): *Party Families: An Examination of the Evidence gathered by Political Scientists on the Characteristics and Kinship Patterns of Liberal and related Parties in the European Communities*, Liberal Action Group, London.

Strøm, Kaare (1995): 'Parliamentary Government and Legislative Organisation', in *Parliaments and Majority Rule in Western Europe*, edited by Herbert Döring, Campus and St. Martin's Press, Frankfurt and New York, pp. 51-82.

Sweeney, Jane P. (1984): 'The Left in Europe's Parliament: The Problematic Effects of Integration Theory', *Comparative Politics* 16:2, pp. 171-190.

Telò, Mario ed. (1995): *Democratie et Construction Européenne*, Editions de l'Université de Bruxelles, Brussels.

Theato, Diemut R. and Graf, Rainer (1994): *Das Europäische Parlament und der Haushalt der Europäischen Gemeinschaft*, Nomos Verlagsgesellschaft, Baden-Baden.

Thiebault, Jean-Louis and Dolez, Bernard (1996): Parliamentary Parties in the French Fifth Republic, paper to the ECPR Oslo Joint Sessions of Workshops.

Thomas, Stafford T. (1992): 'Assessing MEP Influence on British EC Policy', *Government and Opposition* 27:1, pp. 3-18.

Tsebelis, George (1990): *Nested Games: Rational Choice in Comparative Politics*, University of California Press, Berkeley.

Vallance, Elizabeth and Davies, Elizabeth (1986): *Women of Europe: Women MEPs and equality policy*, Cambridge University Press, Cambridge.

Van Oudenhove, Guy (1965): *The Political Parties in the European Parliament: The First Ten Years (September 1952 - September 1962)*, A.W. Sijthoff, Leyden.

Van Schendelen, M.P.C.M. (1976): 'Information and Decision Making in the Dutch Parliament', *Legislative Studies Quarterly* I:2, pp. 231-250.

Viola, Donatella Maria (1994): Foreign Policy of the European Union: A Future Role for the European Parliament?, paper to the ECPR Madrid Joint Sessions of Workshops.

Viola, Donatella Maria (1996): European Parliament Party Groups and Decision-Making in Foreign Policy Issues within the European Union, paper to the ECPR Oslo Joint Sessions of Workshops.

Von Beyme, Klaus (1985): *Political Parties in Western Europe*, Gower, Aldershot.

Weiler, J.H.H. (1991): 'Problems of Legitimacy in Post 1992 Europe', *Aussenwirtschaft* 46:3, pp. 411-437.

Weiler, J.H.H., Haltern, Ulrich R., and Mayer, Franz C. (1995): 'European Democracy and Its Critique', *West European Politics* 18:3, pp. 4-39.

Wendt, Alexander (1994): 'Collective Identity Formation and the International State', *American Political Science Review* 88:2, pp. 384-396.

Wenturis, Nikolaus (1996): 'Greece', in *Parliaments and Parties: The European Parliament in the Political Life of Europe*, edited by Roger Morgan and Clare Tame, Macmillan, Basingstoke, pp. 283-303.

Wessels, Wolfgang (1992): 'The Development of the European Parliament after Direct Elections', in *The European Community in the Historical Context of its Parliament.* Proceedings of the 40th Anniversary Symposium, Strasbourg, pp. 39-41.

Westlake, Martin (1990): The Origin and Development of the Question Time Procedure in the European Parliament, *EUI Working Paper EPU* No. 90/4, Florence.

Westlake, Martin (1994a): *Britain's Emerging Euro-Elite? The British in the Directly-Elected European Parliament, 1979-1992*, Dartmouth, Aldershot.

Westlake, Martin (1994b): *The Commission and the Parliament: Partners and Rivals in the European Policy-making Process*, Butterworths, London.

Westlake, Martin (1994c): *A Modern Guide to the European Parliament*, Pinter, London.

Wiberg, Matti (1991a): *Analysis and Politics*, Studies on Political Science No 11, Department of Political Science, University of Turku, Turku.

Wiberg, Matti (1991b): 'Nice Timing! - Electoral Cycles of Parliamentary Questioning in the Finnish Parliament 1945-1987', in *The Political Life of Institutions: Scripta in honorem professoris Jaakko Nousiainen sexagesimum annum complentis*, edited by Matti Wiberg, The Finnish Political Science Association, Helsinki, pp. 189-203.

Wiberg, Matti ed. (1994a): *Parliamentary Control in the Nordic Countries: Forms of Questioning and Behavioural Trends*, The Finnish Political Science Association, Helsinki.

Wiberg, Matti (1994b): 'To Keep the Government on Its Toes: Behavioural Trends of Parliamentary Questioning in Finland 1945-1990', in *Parliamentary Control in the Nordic Countries: Forms of Questioning and Behavioural Trends*, edited by Matti Wiberg, The Finnish Political Science Association, Helsinki, pp. 103-200.

Wiberg, Matti (1995): 'Parliamentary Questioning: Control by Communication?', in *Parliaments and Majority Rule in Western Europe*, edited by Herbert Döring, Campus and St. Martin's Press, Frankfurt and New York, pp. 179-222.

Wiberg, Matti and Koura, Antti (1994): 'The Logic of Parliamentary Questioning', in *Parliamentary Control in the Nordic Countries: Forms of Questioning and Behavioural Trends*, edited by Matti Wiberg, The Finnish Political Science Association, Helsinki, pp. 19-43.

Wiberg, Matti and Raunio, Tapio (1997): 'Controlling Voting Outcomes: Voting Power in the European Parliament, 1979-1995', in *National Interest and Integrative Politics in Transnational Assemblies*, edited by Ernst Kuper and Uwe Jun, Frank Cass, London (forthcoming).

Wilcox, Clyde and Clausen, Aage (1991): 'The Dimensionality of Roll-Call Voting Reconsidered', *Legislative Studies Quarterly* XVI:3, pp. 393-406.

Williams, Mark (1995): 'The European Parliament: Political Groups, Minority Rights and the "Rationalisation" of Parliamentary Organisation. A Research Note', in *Parliaments and Majority Rule in Western Europe*, edited by Herbert Döring, Campus & St. Martins Press, Frankfurt and New York, pp. 391-404.

Wolters, Menno (1982): European Interspaces: a roll call analysis of European Parliament divisions since the direct elections, paper to the ECPR Århus Joint Sessions of Workshops.

Wolters, Menno (1988): Parties in the European Parliament: European or national public policy?, paper to the ECPR Rimini Joint Sessions of Workshops.

Wood, Alan ed. (1989): *The Times Guide to the European Parliament 1989*, Times Books, London.

Zellentin, Gerda (1967): 'Form and function of the opposition in the European Communities', *Government and Opposition* 2:3, pp. 416-435.

Zetterholm, Staffan (1994): 'Why is Cultural Diversity a Political Problem? A Discussion of Cultural Barriers to Political Integration', in *National Cultures and European Integration: Exploratory Essays on Cultural Diversity and Common Policies*, edited by Staffan Zetterholm, Berg, Oxford, pp. 65-82.